The Global Child Poverty Challenge

CW00551806

Praise for this book

'This book makes a compelling case that a "child-sensitive" approach is both morally right and practically feasible for ending extreme poverty and achieving sustainable development goals.'

Kul Chandra Gautam was formerly Assistant Secretary-General of the United Nations, and Deputy Executive Director of UNICEF

Practical Action Publishing has done it again, this time by producing an up-to-date briefing on what works – or doesn't – for reducing child poverty. About half of the world's poor are children, with higher rates of poverty among children than among adults in both developing and better off countries. Richard Morgan and supporters have reviewed a list of actions at the top of today's thinking about what can be done, with professional assessments in everyday language of the lessons for mobilizing more action in the future. Most useful and an important read for all concerned.'

Professor Sir Richard Jolly, Institute of Development Studies, Sussex

'The book is a breakthrough in terms of building knowledge on child poverty in Africa on at least three counts: it gives prominence to an issue that is otherwise one of gross research neglect in Africa; it provides an authoritative benchmark for future efforts that aims to take stock of progress made in tackling child poverty; and third, it makes an historical departure from the usual doom and gloom depiction to a discussion of what has worked and what can be done better.'

Théophane Nikyèma, Executive Director, The African Child Policy Forum (ACPF)

'The pathway to poverty reduction begins through collective action, allowing children to acquire foundational skills, develop their confidence as change-makers, build a solid asset base and secure future livelihoods as full economic citizens. CYFI believes that both this publication, and the Global Coalition to End Child Poverty, provides timely inspiration to policy makers and practitioners working to tackle child poverty through practical interventions and far reaching systems change under the 2030 Agenda for Sustainable Development.'

Jeroo Billimoria, Founder and Managing Director of Child and Youth Finance International (CYFI)

The Global Child Poverty Challenge
In search of solutions

Edited by Richard Morgan

PRACTICAL ACTION
Publishing

Practical Action Publishing Ltd
The Schumacher Centre,
Bourton on Dunsmore, Rugby,
Warwickshire, CV23 9QZ, UK
www.practicalactionpublishing.org

ISBN 978-1-85339-966-4 Hardback
ISBN 978-1-85339-967-1 Paperback
ISBN 978-1-78044-966-1 Library Ebook
ISBN 978-1-78044-967-8 Ebook

Citation: Morgan, R. (ed.) (2016) *The Global Child Poverty Challenge: In search of solutions*, Rugby, UK: Practical Action Publishing, <http://dx.doi.org/ 10.3362/ 9781780449661>

Since 1974, Practical Action Publishing has published and disseminated books and information in support of international development work throughout the world. Practical Action Publishing is a trading name of Practical Action Publishing Ltd (Company Reg. No. 1159018), the wholly owned publishing company of Practical Action. Practical Action Publishing trades only in support of its parent charity objectives and any profits are covenanted back to Practical Action (Charity Reg. No. 247257, Group VAT Registration No. 880 9924 76).

The views and opinions in this publication are those of the author and do not represent those of Practical Action Publishing Ltd or its parent charity Practical Action. Reasonable efforts have been made to publish reliable data and information, but the authors and publisher cannot assume responsibility for the validity of all materials or for the consequences of their use.

Typeset by Allzone Digital Services Limited
Printed by Short Run Press, UK

Contents

About the Editor

Richard Morgan has worked in international development for almost forty years, focusing on policy and practical issues of poverty reduction in the developing world. Until recently the head of policy for UNICEF, he now leads a global initiative to combat child poverty with Save the Children. He is also the co-convenor of the new Coalition to End Child Poverty. Richard trained as an economist and worked initially in southern Africa, with roles ranging from small enterprise promotion to food security and rural development. Since the mid-1980s, he has focused on questions of policy and programme design for children. His wide-ranging interests and experience span social protection, inclusive basic services, livelihood strategies and how child rights principles can be used to deliver progress for the poorest children.

CHAPTER 1
Addressing child poverty: an overview

Richard Morgan

Abstract

This chapter introduces the case for development policy to treat the reduction of child poverty as an urgent and central issue, based on the still-pervasive nature of the problem and the extensive deprivations and socio-economic losses associated with it. Summaries are provided of the contributions to this book, which present findings and experience from a range of policies and interventions intended to benefit the poorest children in different societies while increasing their capacities and opportunities. An argument is made for adopting 'child-sensitive' approaches to policies and designs for economic strengthening programmes, in ways that recognize the vulnerabilities, voices, and agency of children in poverty themselves.

Keywords: child poverty, inequality, developing countries, child labour, child refugees

ACROSS ALL REGIONS, CHILD POVERTY has long been an unduly neglected issue in national policy. Its implications for economic development have been underestimated and its impacts on societies, future prosperity, and for disadvantaged children themselves have been poorly understood.

Within an apparently renewed global push towards poverty reduction goals, the persistence of poverty among children needs to be addressed as a distinct and urgent priority. Children are by far the most vulnerable to poverty's damaging effects, while harms suffered by poor children, such as stunting in early childhood and learning deprivation, are hard to recover from in later years. Such deprivations have major costs not only for the young people affected but also for their whole societies, and poverty's effects are powerfully transmitted to the next generation.

The elimination of extreme poverty among children cannot be safely left to the forces of economic growth alone. Particularly in quite unequal societies, rising average incomes may not translate powerfully into gains for the poorest children, while improvements in basic services, if they occur, may fail to reach the most deprived. Specific, strongly targeted interventions for the poorest families and children are needed to ensure that girls and boys and young people around the world are able to fulfil their potential, including as future entrepreneurs and wealth creators.

<http://dx.doi.org/ 10.3362/9781780448879.001

Of the roughly 1 billion people currently living in extreme income poverty, *almost half are children*: while in low-income countries, some 52 per cent of under-12s live in income poverty, compared with 42 per cent of people over this age (Olinto et al., 2013). Rates of poverty are significantly higher among children compared with adults in many rich world countries too (UNICEF, 2012). Such patterns will continue unless there is a concerted focus on child poverty in its own right.

Low family economic status is associated with poor outcomes and major deprivations in young lives. Children born in the lowest household wealth quintile in developing countries are over twice as likely to die before the age of five years as their counterparts in the top quintile, while the prevalence of malnutrition among young children is about 2.5 times higher in the poorest families in developing countries compared with the richest (UNICEF, 2010).

The physical stunting of children is not only a poverty trap for them as individuals: it also represents a fundamental squandering of human potential. It often leads to long-term damage – through poorer school performance, lower work capacity, and diminished productivity in adulthood. Girls who suffer under-nutrition are more likely to see their own children afflicted by it – one of the key ways in which poverty is transmitted between generations.

Across all regions, as illustrated by the World Inequality Database on Education, educational access and learning achievement among girls and boys from income-poor and socially marginalized families are often dramatically lower. Children from poor families, even in wealthy societies, speak forcefully of the shame, humiliation, and exclusion they may suffer at school, as well as of wider stigma in society (Save the Children, 2016).

Children in one part of the United Kingdom are quoted in the Save the Children report, saying that: 'Folks look down on them (children who are poor). They don't have the things everyone else has like trainers, a nice school bag, a school bag with a name. Names are important.'

An eight-year-old girl in India relates:

> The boys from the other community always call us names, call us dirty. Even if we bathe … the other children call us dirty and say we smell … if we ever complain to the teachers, they warn us that if we tell anyone they will cut our names from the school.

Harmful child labour, early and forced marriage, and other forms of exploitation such as child prostitution and trafficking are also closely related to poverty in many parts of the world. Social pressures within the poorest families and communities for girls to marry at an early age are often intense. Vulnerability to many forms of exploitation has intensified with the increase in child refugees, unaccompanied children, and displacement affecting children in several regions.

A Bangladeshi girl, the youngest of three child brides, was married at 15: 'We were very poor – sometimes we would eat every two or three days. Even though [my parents] really wanted all three of their daughters to study it wasn't possible, so they got me married'.

And a 12-year-old Syrian refugee in Jordan explained why he worked and did not go to school: 'I feel responsible for my family. I feel like I am still a child, and would like to go back to school, but my only option is to work hard to put food on the table for my family' (Save the Children, 2016).

With often low education and skill levels, limited resources and inadequate social networks, Income-poor and socially marginalized young people face major challenges in obtaining secure livelihoods or safe employment because of their low education and skill levels, limited resources and inadequate social networks. Adolescents entering the world of work without having completed secondary or vocational education may have few prospects beyond day-labour in the informal sector. They are often exposed to dangerous, poorly paid, and exploitative conditions. They need to develop a wide range of competencies that empower them to navigate economic and social risks; to overcome current and accumulated deprivations; and to seize scarce economic opportunities. These competencies may need to encompass not only technical and vocational knowledge, but also basic literacy and numeracy, financial awareness, life skills, social networks, and self-esteem.

In this context, an important consideration for economic strengthening and microenterprise programme design is that of the potential impacts of interventions for children's rights, capability development, and wellbeing – both in the immediate and longer term. This encompasses not only the conventional measures of 'benefit' but also the necessity to guard against unintended negative effects and possibly irreversible harms. The concept of *child sensitivity* is one which can guide programme designers and policy-makers to more systematically consider such impacts, based on contextually relevant risk assessment and monitoring. Economic interventions of various kinds can make use of child-related indicators to help maximize benefits for child capabilities and avoid harms. Programmes can and should also be improved by listening to the voices of children and young people themselves.

This book is primarily concerned with the question of how best to intervene in support of children born into and growing up in poverty – including in support of their families, when they have them. It asks how children in poor families and settings can better be supported to make successful transitions into good livelihoods and decent work as young adults. The contributors in the chapters that follow address a range of experiences that help to illustrate what effective, child-sensitive approaches may look like; while also exploring options and potential solutions for expanding young people's access to enterprise and economic opportunities in poorer societies.

In the following chapter, ground-breaking longitudinal studies of child cohorts in four countries undertaken by the *Young Lives* initiative, for which four survey rounds have now been completed, are reported by *Paul Dornan* and *Kirrily Pells*. The most recent findings give strong indications of the negative impacts of poverty and inequalities on children's physical growth and development paths; and point to policies and interventions that can mitigate the harms they suffer and help build a stronger basis for success in adolescence through education, nutrition, and transitions to work.

In an international review of NGO-associated randomized control trials, *Cali Mortenson Ellis* and *Josh Chaffin* review evidence from several categories of micro-economic interventions aimed at strengthening poor families and in some cases targeted directly to adolescents themselves, in terms both of benefits and harmful impacts for children. Their review identifies a range of positive impacts associated with interventions such as social cash transfers, training, and microcredit – but also evidence of adverse effects (on, for example, school attendance and hours of child work) relating to both the design and nature of some types of intervention. *Nicola Hypher* and *Katherine Richards* look in more depth at experience, particularly in Africa and South Asia, with one major category of intervention – social protection measures, including cash transfers – with a view to building design and implementation features that can strengthen investments for children in poverty through child-sensitive approaches. Their review suggests practical considerations through which sensitivity to the rights and vulnerabilities of both girls and boys can be built directly into the design, implementation, and monitoring of social protection programmes. Meanwhile, in a 'Taking Stock' piece, *Stephen Devereux's* pair of archetypal development professionals debate the different sides of a major policy issue in social protection – the concept of 'graduation' – and discuss whether this is an appropriate approach from a children's and child rights perspective.

With a more specific focus on children's learning, *Munshi Sulaiman* considers country-specific evidence from programme interventions to improve livelihoods among ultra-poor households in Bangladesh supported by BRAC, a major NGO. The findings from this review caution against an automatic assumption that educational indicators for girls and boys will necessarily be improved and child labour time decline as family incomes rise.

The failures of societies to protect children against harm, including those involved in economic activity, are dramatized around the world by the testimonies of girls and boys themselves. The experiences they recount are a stark reminder of the suffering that may ensue in cases and places where children's rights are not respected and remain neglected.

One Syrian child quoted by Save the Children recounts:

> When the man selling the diesel gives it to his customer, I stand next to him and soak up the diesel that has fallen to the ground with a sponge. I hate the diesel market and the clothes that I wear there; all of it makes me sick. One day some red spots appeared on my body and when I went to the doctor he said it was because of the diesel ...

While another Syrian child relates:

> Once we arrive at the field, we are given huge bags that we attach to our waist. We then start harvesting potatoes. We have to be really fast and we shouldn't leave any potatoes behind or else we get beaten with a plastic hose ... I collect about 30 bags of potatoes each day and my

back hurts a lot. When we come back to the tent I immediately go to sleep ...

Against a backdrop of the still-widespread incidence of harmful forms of child labour, *Patricia Richter* and *Sophie de Coninck* put forward a framework and options for the responsible design of different types of programmes directed at the underlying causes of child labour. They report on the varied impact of several sets of interventions on child work and schooling, as found by ILO research, and point to the need for greater awareness of and capacity to address child labour issues within financial institutions themselves. Meanwhile, in a qualitative and in-depth account of microfinance project activities in Egypt, *Richard Carothers* identifies positive measures and methods used by microfinance providers to improve the protection and conditions of children who contribute to family enterprise, while reducing their exposure to risks and harm. A notable and innovative feature of this approach, in line with the Convention on the Rights of the Child, is the use of techniques which enable the views of working children themselves to be taken into account.

The phenomenon of independent migration among children is often and necessarily viewed through a lens of concern for the risks to child protection rights which may be involved, including trafficking. *Shahin Yaqub*'s cross-regional literature review focuses on an alternative or at least complementary approach. This is based on an understanding that migration may offer solutions to poor development opportunities at home, presenting migrant children as, in many cases, risk-informed agents in search of income and assets for a better future, as well as safer living environments.

Karen Moore's review of efforts to promote economic opportunities for young people in Africa, including those supported by the MasterCard Foundation, emphasizes the importance of combining broad-based enterprise-oriented training with access to business opportunities and financial services. Her findings further emphasize the need to recognize the roles that informal and mixed livelihood strategies, including in agriculture, continue to play. Meanwhile, *Rani Deshpande* reports evidence from the testing in Ghana and three other countries of a specific youth-oriented intervention in which considerable hope has been placed – the promotion of financial savings. The promising but mixed findings from the *YouthSave* initiative suggest that the impact of well-designed savings programme initiatives among older girls and boys may be heightened by complementary measures to involve parents, provide financial education, and strengthen psychosocial, health-related, or educational support.

With this body of evidence in mind, and with growing confidence that practical, child-centred solutions can be found, the last word in this overview goes to Paul Dornan, of the *Young Lives* study. He summed up the challenge we face in a contribution to the work of the Global Coalition to End Child Poverty, a new grouping of agencies which aims to promote action by decision-makers across nations:

> There is a clear imperative for action to eradicate child poverty. To tackle child poverty is to invest to fulfil human potential. It is to promote child

rights and to address the wider needs of fast changing societies. It is to intervene to prevent the intergenerational disadvantages which cost societies dearly (P. Dornan, personal communication).

References

Olinto, P., Beegle, K., Sobrado, S. and Uematsu, H. (2013) *The State of the Poor: Where Are The Poor, Where Is Extreme Poverty Harder to End, and What Is the Current Profile of the World's Poor?* Washington, DC: World Bank.

Save the Children (2016) *Child Poverty: What Drives It and What It Means to Children across the World*, London: Save the Children.

UNICEF (2010) *Progress for Children: Achieving the MDGs with Equity*, New York: UNICEF.

UNICEF (2012) *Measuring Child Poverty: New League Tables of Child Poverty in the World's Rich Countries*, Florence: Innocenti Research Centre.

World Inequality Database on Education [online], UNESCO <www.education-inequalities.org/> [accessed 15 April 2014].

About the author

Richard Morgan is Director of the Child Poverty Global Initiative, Save the Children.

CHAPTER 2

Building strong foundations for later livelihoods by addressing child poverty: evidence from Young Lives

Paul Dornan and Kirrily Pells

Abstract

Improving children's life chances is central to development in low- and middle-income countries. Half the population of sub-Saharan Africa are aged 18 or younger, and young people comprise nearly half of all people living in extreme poverty worldwide. Poverty undermines not only children's rights to life, survival, and development, as enshrined in the UN Convention on the Rights of the Child, but also the skills and capabilities that fast-changing economies need for future growth. By extension, given poverty is a key mechanism shaping later chances, eradicating it is key to improving equality of opportunity. This article presents longitudinal analysis on inequities in children's development trajectories, drawing on data from the Young Lives cohort study. Young Lives is following the lives of 12,000 children growing up in Ethiopia, India, Peru, and Vietnam. The article's central questions are to understand how, why, and when inequalities become established through childhood. We explore how children and young people's trajectories diverge over time; and we provide preliminary findings on education, nutrition, and youth transitions to higher education, work, and marriage and parenthood, from the latest survey round. We find that the poorest children, those in rural areas and/or from marginalized social groups, are consistently being 'left behind' in terms of nutritional status, learning, and opportunities to continue in education. We conclude by considering how policy interventions at different stages of the early life-course can mitigate the development of such inequalities.

Keywords: child poverty, inequality, livelihoods, education, youth

> For any job they require you to have finished secondary school, and I think that to be a driver, or whatever, you need to have finished your secondary schooling … [If I left school] I wouldn't be able to keep myself in the future. With studies I can be something (Susan, 16-year-old girl, Lima, Peru).

> If one can learn and study hard, they will always have a good job at the end that can change their family's life (Fatuma, 15-year-old girl, Addis Ababa, Ethiopia).

<http://dx.doi.org/ 10.3362/9781780448879.002>

Education is a major driving force for human development. It opens doors to the job market, combats inequality, improves maternal health, reduces child mortality, fosters solidarity, and promotes environmental stewardship. Education empowers people with the knowledge, skills and values they need to build a better world (Ban Ki-moon, 2012).

WE BEGIN WITH THREE QUOTATIONS: two from girls growing up thousands of miles apart on very different continents, and a third from the UN Secretary-General. All three quotations convey a remarkably similar message regarding the social and economic power of education. Yet, as we will argue in this article, despite increased access to schooling accompanied by raised aspirations and expectations, many barriers persist in turning this transformative potential into decent livelihoods. Drawing on analysis from the Young Lives longitudinal study of childhood poverty, this article examines how poverty and inequalities develop through the early life-course in order to identify priority intervention points by which stronger foundations for later opportunities can be built.

Rapidly changing societies are shaping the opportunities of children like Susan and Fatuma. Between 1990 and 2012 under-5 child mortality halved and stunting reduced from two-fifths to one-quarter of young children (UN, 2014). In low-income countries average primary school enrolment increased from 59 per cent in 1999 to 82 per cent in 2011, with children now expected to experience about three more years of education at the end of this period than at the beginning (UNESCO, 2014: Tables 10 and 4). While this progress is very positive, such average gains mask substantial, and often growing, inequalities between children within countries, with the poorest children still most likely to die, to be malnourished, or to be out-of-school (UNGA, 2014). If the Millennium Development Goals centred on child survival and building basic services, the challenge facing the Sustainable Development Goals is surely to address wide inequalities within countries, which will otherwise hold back overall gains.

National economic indicators tell a similar story. Globally extreme poverty fell by half from 1990 (UN, 2014), influenced particularly by economic growth in China (Olinto et al., 2013: Figure 5). While there remain problems of fragile and conflict-affected countries where governance and development challenges remain acute (Collier, 2008), a second phenomenon of countries getting richer while much of the population remains extremely poor is increasingly clear (Sumner, 2012). Such uneven development is reflected by geographic differences, by region or urban/rural differences. For example, most extreme poverty is concentrated in rural areas (Olinto et al., 2013: Figure 7) and children in rural areas face higher deprivation than in urban areas (Gordon et al., 2003). Inequalities between individuals and communities in accessing opportunities exist, either because they are actively excluded or lack the necessary skills or human capital (Boyden and Dercon, 2012) or because vulnerability undermines opportunities to participate (Malik, 2014). The challenge for such countries, with the growing fiscal space which economic growth affords, is how to use social policies to share the overall gains in society more equitably.

To explore this central question of the relationship between societal inequalities and inequalities between groups, this article discusses how inequalities develop over the early life-course, drawing on evidence from the Young Lives longitudinal study. Young Lives has collected survey and qualitative data on children born in 1994/5 (1,000 per country) and in 2000/01 (2,000 per country) in four countries: Ethiopia, India (in the former state of Andhra Pradesh, which was divided into Andhra Pradesh and Telangana in June 2014), Peru, and Vietnam. We find that inequalities appear very early in life, shaped by household circumstances and typically continue to widen during middle childhood, with the school playing a pivotal role. During adolescence children's development is shaped both by these early disadvantages and by new pressures, particularly to work or marry, which further entrench inequalities. We conclude by presenting a life-course model for how policy can support children's healthy development, so improving life chances and social mobility in adulthood.

Child poverty and social mobility

The case to eradicate child poverty rests centrally on the recognition that societies have a particular responsibility to children embodied by the nearly universal ratification of the United Nations (1989) Convention on the Rights of the Child. Poverty violates children's fundamental rights to life, survival, and development in the present, and given the critically sensitive nature of childhood for the formation of human capacities, deprivation has severe and lasting impacts (Grantham-McGregor et al., 2007). Since poverty in childhood can affect healthy development and learning, the risk is that today's poor children will become tomorrow's poor parents (Bird, 2007). Addressing child poverty is therefore foundational to addressing the persistence of wider poverty.

With these harmful effects in mind, it is therefore particularly concerning that children typically face a higher risk of poverty than other age groups. Both monetary and multidimensional measures of poverty identify children as facing a higher risk of being poor than other age groups (Olinto et al., 2013; Vaz, 2014). The extent of over-representation of children living in poverty according to monetary measures varies depending on assumptions made of the relative need of households of different sizes and compositions but this relationship is maintained across a number of accepted approaches (Batana et al., 2013). The reasons for this over-representation include that poorer societies often have more children and that households with children tend to be both larger and to have more members who are not economically active (Batana et al., 2013; Vaz, 2014). Such evidence of the extra costs of dependent children to households often provides the justification for the importance of child grants as an anti-poverty measure in high-income countries (Bradshaw and Finch, 2002).

As has already been argued, there are substantial expectations among young people and their families that investments in education and schooling will bring life-changing results. In many countries, policy changes around education reflect a dramatic generational shift. For example in Ethiopia in 1999, 37 per cent of children were enrolled, rising to 87 per cent by 2011 (UNESCO, 2014). Increases in enrolment have been pro-poor, reaching previously excluded groups. Among the Young Lives children at age 12, between three-quarters (Ethiopia) and nine-tenths (Peru) aspired to education beyond compulsory formal schooling (Dornan and Pells, 2014). Children do not wish to follow in their parents' footsteps and work in agriculture (Morrow, 2013) and often express the desire to migrate in order to access decent and secure livelihoods (Crivello, 2011).

While education is often assumed to be critical to social mobility (as reflected in the opening quotation from the UN Secretary-General), improving opportunities for poorer children requires a more radical approach than more time in school alone. First, enrolment in schools may have increased but this does not automatically equate to higher learning levels, with UNESCO (2014) identifying a 'global crisis in learning' of poor quality education and low learning levels. Second, despite increased enrolment, 57 million children are still missing out on primary school, particularly children affected by conflict, with disabilities, or living in rural areas or slums (UNESCO, 2014: 55). Third, even when children attend school, education does not automatically act as a social leveller and it may widen gaps and segregate groups within education systems (Lewin, 2011; Woodhead et al., 2013b; Cueto et al., 2014). Fourth, studies from high-income countries highlight the association not only between economic mobility and education, but also between higher generational economic mobility and lower economic inequality (Blanden et al., 2005; Wilkinson and Pickett, 2009; Chetty et al., 2014). Studies encompassing low-income countries link intergenerational transmission with: factors beyond the household (culture, exclusion, conflict etc.); household experiences of shocks, including health; ownership of productive assets (each likely to vary geographically within countries); and child-level factors such as early care and nutrition alongside schooling (Bird, 2007; Krishna, 2007). Fifth, greater education and skills (summarized in the rather bloodless term 'human capital', used here because of its prominence within policy debates) in the absence of jobs and livelihoods will not enable transformation of lives, and job creation is a broader agenda than increasing skill levels alone (World Bank, 2012). While schooling for poor children offers a key opportunity to improve children's life chances, for it to deliver on that promise also requires a broader approach to reduce poverty and exclusion, and to create opportunities for newly skilled young people.

What does cohort evidence suggest for how inequalities in human capital develop?

This section examines how broader environmental and institutional factors, such as household poverty, school systems, social norms, and labour markets opportunities, shape children's physical, cognitive, and psychosocial development leading to diverging trajectories between groups of children. Children's development is shaped by complex interactions between individual characteristics and biology, with children's experiences, actions, and interactions, as well as by broader environmental factors, including poverty and social norms (Rogoff, 2003; Walker et al., 2007; Sameroff, 2009; Engle et al., 2011; Boyden and Dercon, 2012).

Under-nutrition results in lost development potential

Inequalities between children are already established during infancy with children's early development closely linked to household circumstances. It has been estimated that '200 million children under 5 years fail to reach their potential in cognitive development because of poverty, poor health and nutrition, and deficient care' (Grantham-McGregor et al., 2007: 60). Under-nutrition is one of the principal transmission routes of inequalities by threatening children's healthy development and well-being. UNICEF (2013) attributes a third of under-five child deaths to under-nutrition. For those children who survive, under-nutrition has widespread lasting detriments to their development and trajectories.

Analysis uses stunting as a proxy indicator for chronic under-nutrition; stunting is a common experience in many countries (with stunting defined as –2 standard deviations below the World Health Organization's (2006) growth norms). Stunting rates varied considerably among Young Lives children at age 12 – 30 per cent in Andhra Pradesh, 29 per cent in Ethiopia, 21 per cent in Peru, and 20 per cent in Vietnam – but the rates of stunting affecting the poorest third of children were much higher. Poor children face between 1.7 times (Ethiopia) and 3.1 times (Peru) the risk of being stunted in infancy than less-poor children. Across the four countries children living in rural areas and those with low levels of parental education were also much more likely to be stunted. Figure 1, using the example of Peru, summarizes the emergence of marked differences in stunting levels across age points by age 12.

Stunted growth is associated with impaired cognitive and psychosocial development (Woodhead et al., 2013a). For example, children who were stunted in infancy showed lower levels of cognitive ability at age five, and those stunted at eight had lower reading, writing, and mathematical skills by age 12 (Helmers and Patnam, 2011). Being stunted by age eight was associated with lower self-efficacy, self-esteem, and educational aspirations among children at age 12 (Dercon and Sánchez, 2013). Stunting reduces human capital and amplifies the intergenerational transmission of inequalities.

While it is powerfully argued that under-nutrition in the first 1,000 days after conception leads to irreversible consequences, there is also increasing recognition of some change after the critical infancy period (Alderman and

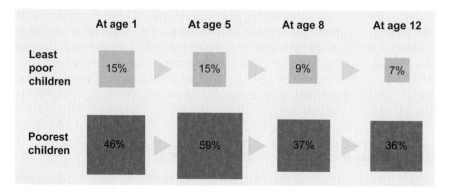

Figure 2.1 Parallel lives: stunting trajectories of children in Peru
Source: Dornan and Pells (2014: 7)

Walker, 2014). Cross-country analysis of Young Lives children identifies change after the infancy period, with both recovery and faltering in height gain trajectories (Lundeen et al., 2013). Changes in height gain trajectories were linked with material conditions and community factors (Schott et al., 2013). Such change post-infancy does not take away from the importance of the critical early period, but shows the need to protect early gains from faltering. In addition, if policy can affect the chances of recovery this may also have wider benefits for children's development; relative gain in children's height between 1 and 8 years was associated with better cognitive test results (Crookston et al., 2013). But since higher socio-economic position is a factor associated with a greater chance of recovering, this also suggests that disparities between children are likely to widen with age.

The critical importance of the very earliest period of life is a reminder that prevention remains a more just and cost-effective strategy than later remediation. However, this evidence of later change shows both that efforts are needed to protect good nutrition and growth (to prevent faltering), and that remedial programmes may have the potential to support recovery later in childhood with wider gains for learning.

School can reinforce or mitigate inequalities during middle childhood

As with children's physical development, systematic differences in the average learning levels of groups of children are established early in life, and are associated with key household characteristics. Learning gaps develop before school enrolment and are then associated with later performance; this shows the need to intervene before children start school to secure better later learning (Singh, 2014; Woodhead et al., 2013a). Household characteristics are also associated with different opportunities to learn, with systematically different experiences of pre-school services (Woodhead et al., 2009).

Once children are in school, the school environment has the potential to mitigate or to compound previous disadvantage. The school is a key intermediary institution, given both its centrality to children's lives and the fact that enrolment is now almost universal among Young Lives children; 95 per cent (Ethiopia), 97 per cent (Andhra Pradesh), 98 per cent (Vietnam), and 99 per cent (Peru) of children at the age of 12 are reported as enrolled in school. However, across each country, there is a consistent difference in learning levels, with children in rural areas, or with low maternal education, poorer children, and those from minority or marginalized ethnic and caste groups the most likely to score poorly in tests of literacy, vocabulary, and numeracy. At age 12 in Ethiopia, where 35 per cent of children have a reading problem, poor children were 1.6 times more likely to experience difficulties than average, while the least-poor children were half as likely to experience these problems. At this age boys and girls scored similarly, with differences emerging later (see next section).

While differences between groups of children exist even before children enter school, during middle childhood the school itself becomes a key determinant of how much progress children make in their learning (Rolleston and James, 2011). Across the Young Lives countries there are different patterns of learning gain, with a higher gain observed in primary schools in Vietnam than in Peru, Andhra Pradesh, and Ethiopia (Singh, 2014). Within countries there are also differences in the degree to which school systems are equitable: in Andhra Pradesh the growing private-school system is linked with worsening socio-economic and gender equity (Woodhead et al., 2013b), while in Vietnam the school system seems to narrow gaps between ethnic-minority and ethnic-majority children during primary school (Rolleston et al., 2013). Such evidence reinforces the need to go beyond a focus on access only and towards learning, but it also highlights the need to understand education improvement challenges within the national context, particularly since across contexts it is always the most marginalized children who are left behind.

Adolescence: a pivotal decade for intergenerational transmission of inequalities

We have so far seen how inequalities experienced early in life result in diverging trajectories in children's nutritional status, school enrolment, and learning. Across each of these indicators the poorest children, those in rural areas and from marginalized social groups, and those in families with the lowest education levels tend to do least well. Such outcomes at age 12 are precisely the roots of some of the disadvantages apparent for the older cohort at age 19. Despite young people's high aspirations for education and work, the reality for many young people is very different. While formal education remains central for many young people, there are transitions beyond school, economic transitions towards livelihoods, and preparation for social transitions into partnership and parenthood. Many of these transitions are shaped by new inequalities, in particular wider social norms and expectations of the later roles young people will play, with 'social reputations' becoming increasingly important while social as well as physical risk exerts an influence on choices (Pells and Woodhead, 2014).

Enrolment rates peak during middle childhood and decline during adolescence, particularly for the poorest children after the age of 15. Figure 2 shows how across the four countries the gap in enrolment between children from the poorest and least-poor households widens during adolescence, as poorer children typically leave school earlier, ranging from a difference of 23 percentage points in Ethiopia to 34 percentage points in Vietnam at the age of 19. As children grow up, other pressures compete with schooling, such as the need to work to support the household, especially for more disadvantaged groups – and so the opportunity costs of studying increase (Pells and Woodhead, 2014).

Though instructive, high enrolment rates can actually mask slow progression through school. In Andhra Pradesh, of the 49 per cent of 19-year-olds still enrolled, one in five of these still had not completed secondary school. In Ethiopia, there are high rates of retention (59 per cent of young people still report studying at age 19), but many of these young people had been delayed in their grade progression through school. By the age of 19, young people who had enrolled on time (age 7) and then progressed by one school grade each year would have reached grade 12. However, one in five young people had not passed grade 8 by the age of 19, and a further third had not passed grade 10

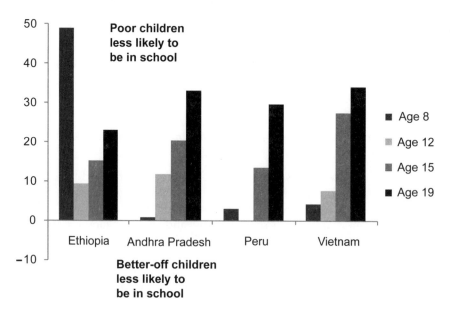

Figure 2.2 Growing socio-economic enrolment gaps by age (% point)
Source: Dornan and Pells (2014: 12)

by that point. Two in five young people are in more advanced levels of study (vocational, pre-university, and university), with one in ten of those enrolled at 19 reporting being at university.

In addition, many young people combine studying with paid work, as illustrated by Figure 3 for Andhra Pradesh and Vietnam. Young people from the poorest households are most likely to be working, whereas young people from the least poor households are most likely to be studying. Across the countries, around 1 in 20 young men and between one in ten and one in four young women report not being in either education or work. The rates for young women are highest, because many are looking after young children.

By the age of 19, 37 per cent of girls in Andhra Pradesh, 25 per cent in Peru, 19 per cent in Vietnam, and 13 per cent in Ethiopia had married or cohabited. Early marriage is strongly associated with adolescent pregnancy and poorer girls and those living in rural areas are more likely to have married and had babies. For example, 28 per cent of girls from the poorest third of households had given birth by age 19 in Vietnam compared with 5 per cent from the least poor households. Early marriage and childbearing are not only a risk to the individual, but constitute costs for wider society through lost social and economic contributions, as well as the intergenerational transmission of poverty (Bird, 2007; UNDESA, 2013).

Social norms are reinforced by poverty as early marriage is often seen by communities as 'protective' of girls by ensuring that they are provided for in adulthood (Boyden et al., 2013). Seeking to abolish such practices without

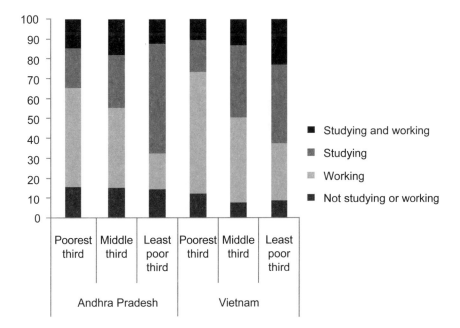

Figure 2.3 Study and work status at age 19, Andhra Pradesh and Vietnam

fully addressing the underlying issues of risk reduces the chances of success. Delaying family formation is an important strategy to improve young women's access to livelihoods but effective responses to delay marriage and fertility policy need to address the underlying economic vulnerabilities which contribute to the persistence of early marriage.

The availability of employment opportunities also shapes young people's decision-making over staying in education and training or seeking wage employment. Despite the high aspirations for education, young people are uncertain whether skilled jobs will be available in the future and so believe learning manual skills is important (Morrow, 2013). A young man in Andhra Pradesh explained:

> As it is, we are not sure of getting employment after completion of education ... We have to take up studies and work simultaneously during holidays. If we do these two things at a time, maybe we will be able to do some work to survive in case we don't get a job ... If we depend totally on education alone we will not be able to do any work in case we don't get a job (Rolleston and James, 2011).

Young people have very different employment opportunities depending on where they live. In Ethiopia, young people in rural areas were nearly five times more likely to be working in agriculture than their urban counterparts at age 19. In urban areas young people were nearly three times more likely to be employed in non-agriculture (Woldehanna and Pankhurst, 2014).

Adolescence is increasingly recognized both as a 'pivotal decade when poverty and inequity often pass to the next generation' and as another window of opportunity for improving life chances (UNICEF, 2011: 3; Diers, 2013). As skills gained through formal schooling become increasingly valued within labour markets in many countries, barriers to progression through education and training present a waste of potential talent. Overcoming the differences that determine which social groups are most likely to progress to the highest levels of formal education and training also provides a strategy for improving equality of opportunity.

Conclusion: Life-course approaches to tacking child poverty

In understanding the impacts that child poverty has on individuals, we have argued both that this is a factor of uneven ongoing economic and social development, and that it is possible to observe the ways in which, over the early life-course, inequalities between groups in societies mount up. We have further identified that some children – often girls, marginalized ethnic groups, and children with disabilities – experience particular disadvantage and discrimination. We conclude by identifying implications for policy aiming to mitigate the development of such inequalities. We close with four key points: societal and community, household, child level, and life-course.

First, it makes little sense to abstract the life-course from the contexts, often expressed geographically, in which children are growing up. Children growing up in agricultural areas, for example, are likely to have greater pressures to work which may conflict with schooling. To abstract individual lives from the social circumstances which shape the life-course risks individualizing reasons individuals remain poor. Broad-based economic and social development which widens opportunities is important to create an enabling environment for other policies to operate more effectively.

Second, child poverty needs to be understood in the wider context of households. It is the household which will modify the impact of poverty on children, typically protecting children but sometimes discriminating between children, for example between girls and boys. Helping parents and households, is a key strategy to help parents help children. Household social protection and health insurance policies are important means to protect and promote livelihood security.

Third, across countries child poverty is higher than poverty experienced by other groups, highlighting the basic truth that dependent children bring additional costs to households. The International Labour Organization (ILO) estimates that Western Europe invests 2.2 per cent of gross domestic product (GDP) through family benefits, compared with 0.2 per cent in sub-Saharan Africa (ILO, 2014). Narrowing the coverage gap of family benefits is an important strategy to support children's development. In recent years consensus has grown over the importance of social pensions in reducing poverty in old age; the time has come for a similar approach to cash transfers for children.

Finally, what can be done for those children who are growing up in poverty? This article has taken a life-course perspective to examine how inequalities between groups of children develop. We conclude with three priorities for policy. Firstly, during early childhood preventative social policy implies a need to focus on early circumstances, both material health and early childhood. As we have shown there are often inequities in who has access to early childhood services, and so prioritizing the extension of early childhood services to reach the poorest children provides an important foundation for later life. Secondly, in middle childhood high enrolment rates provide an opportunity for policy interventions, but school can actually widen inequities. Improving school outcomes requires a greater understanding of where learning gains are being made, and maximizing these for the poorest children. Overcoming background disadvantage within schools requires systems to be more flexible to the needs of different children; poor children may need to work, disabled children often face access and learning barriers, and the language of tuition may disadvantage ethnic minority groups. Thirdly, during adolescence children's experiences widen beyond the family and future expectations of young people increase. While early aspirations are universally high, expectations are likely to be different by socio-economic status, given the different resources and pressures on families. Supporting poorer young people to remain in school and training for longer, by reducing the 'push out' from school and the 'pull out' of poverty provide strategies to even up the impact of education and training for social mobility.

References

Alderman, H. and Walker, S. (2014) *Enhancing Resilience to Nutritional Shocks* [online], 2020 Conference Brief 17, Washington, DC: International Food Policy Research Institute (IFPRI) <http://ebrary.ifpri.org/cdm/ref/collection/ p15738coll2/id/128139> [accessed 22 January 2015].

Ban Ki-moon (2012) 'An initiative of the Secretary-General' [online], Global Education First Initiative <www.globaleducationfirst.org/289.htm> [accessed 23 January 2015].

Batana, Y., Bussolo, M. and Cockburn, J. (2013) 'Global extreme poverty rates for children, adults and the elderly', *Economics Letters* 120: 405–7 <http:// dx.doi.org/10.1016/j.econlet. 2013.05.006>.

Bird, K. (2007) *The Intergenerational Transmission of Poverty: An Overview*, ODI Working Paper 286/CPRC Working Paper 99, London: Overseas Development Institute.

Blanden, J., Gregg, P. and Machin, S. (2005) *Intergenerational Mobility in Europe and North America: A Report Supported by the Sutton Trust*, London: Centre for Economic Performance.

Boyden, J. and Dercon, S. (2012) *Child Development and Economic Development: Lessons and Future Challenges*, Oxford: Young Lives.

Boyden, J., Pankhurst, A. and Tafere, Y. (2013) *Harmful Traditional Practices and Child Protection: Contested Understandings and Practices of Female Child Marriage and Circumcision*, Working Paper 93, Oxford: Young Lives.

Bradshaw, J. and Finch, N. (2002) *A Comparison of Child Benefit Packages in 22 Countries*, Department for Work and Pensions Research Report No. 174, London: Corporate Document Services.

Chetty, R., Hendren, N., Kline, P. and Saez, E. (2014) *Where is the Land of Opportunity? The Geography of Intergenerational Mobility in the United States*, Working Paper 19844, Cambridge, MA: National Bureau of Economic Research.

Collier, P. (2008) *The Bottom Billion*, Oxford: Oxford University Press.

Crivello, G. (2011) '"Becoming somebody": youth transitions through education and migration in Peru', *Journal of Youth Studies* 14: 395–411 <http://dx.doi. org/10.1080/13676261.2010. 538043>.

Crookston, B., Schott, W., Cueto, S., Dearden, K., Engle, P., Georgiadis, A., Lundeen, E., Penny, M., Stein, A. and Behrman, J. (2013) 'Post-infancy growth, schooling, and cognitive achievement: young lives', *American Journal of Clinical Nutrition*, [online version September 2013] <http://dx.doi.org/ 10.3945/ajcn.113.067561>.

Cueto, S., Guerrero, G., Leon, J., Zapata, M. and Freire, S. (2014) 'The relationship between socioeconomic status at age one, opportunities to learn and achievement in mathematics in fourth grade in Peru', *Oxford Review of Education* 40: 50–72 <http://dx.doi.org/10.1080/03054985.2013. 873525>.

Dercon, S. and Sánchez, A. (2013) 'Height in mid childhood and psychosocial competencies in late childhood: evidence from four developing countries',

Economics & Human Biology 11: 426–32 <http://dx.doi.org/10.1016/j. ehb.2013.04.001>.

Diers, J. (2013) 'Why the world needs to get serious about adolescents: a view from UNICEF', *Journal of Research on Adolescence* 23: 214–22 <http://dx.doi. org/10.1111/jora.12042>.

Dornan, P. and Pells, K. (2014) *From Infancy to Adolescence: Preliminary Findings from Round 4 of Young Lives*, Oxford: Young Lives.

Engle, P., Fernald, L., Alderman, H., Behrman, J.R., O'Gara, C., Yousafzai, A., Cabral de Mello, M., Hidrobo, M., Ulkuer, N., Ertem, I., Iltus, S. and the Global Child Development Steering Group (2011) 'Strategies for reducing inequalities and improving developmental outcomes for young children in low-income and middle-income countries', *The Lancet* 378: 1339–53 <http://dx.doi.org/10.1016/S0140-6736(11)60889-1>.

Gordon, D., Nandy, S., Pantazis, C., Pemberton, S. and Townsend, P. (2003) *Child Poverty in the Developing World*, Bristol: Policy Press.

Grantham-McGregor, S., Cheung, Y., Cueto, S., Glewwe, P., Richter, L. and Strupp, B. (2007) 'Developmental potential in the first 5 years for children in developing countries', *The Lancet* 369: 60–70 <http://dx.doi.org/10.1016/ S0140-6736(07)60032-4>.

Helmers, C. and Patnam, M. (2011) 'The formation and evolution of childhood skill acquisition: evidence from India', *Journal of Development Economics* 95: 252–66 <http://dx.doi.org/10.1016/j.jdeveco.2010.03.001>.

International Labour Organization (ILO) (2014) *World Social Protection Report 2014/15: Building Economic Recovery, Inclusive Development and Social Justice*, Geneva: International Labour Organization.

Krishna, A. (2007) 'For reducing poverty faster: target reasons before people', *World Development* 35: 1947–60 <http://dx.doi.org/10.1016/j. worlddev.2006.12.003>.

Lewin, K. (2011) *Making Rights Realities: Researching Educational Access, Transitions and Equity*, Brighton, UK: CREATE, University of Sussex.

Lundeen, E., Behrman, J.R., Crookston, B., Dearden, K., Engle, P., Georgiadis, A., Penny, M. and Stein, A. (2013) 'Growth faltering and recovery in children aged 1–8 years in four low- and middle-income countries: Young Lives', *Public Health Nutrition* 7: 2131–7 <http://dx.doi.org/10.1017/ S1368980013003017>.

Malik, K. (ed.) (2014) *Safeguarding Human Progress: Reducing Vulnerabilities, Building Resilience*, New York: UNDP.

Morrow, V. (2013) 'Whose values? Young people's aspirations and experiences of schooling in Andhra Pradesh', *Children and Society* 27: 258–69 <http:// dx.doi.org/10.1111/chso.12036>.

Olinto, P., Beegle, K., Sobrado, C. and Uematsu, H. (2013) *The State of the Poor: Where Are The Poor, Where Is Extreme Poverty Harder to End, and What Is the Current Profile of the World's Poor?* Washington, DC: World Bank.

Pells, K. and Woodhead, M. (2014) *Changing Children's Lives: Risks and Opportunities*, Oxford: Young Lives.

Rogoff, B. (2003) *The Cultural Nature of Human Development*, Oxford: Oxford University Press.

Rolleston, C. and James, Z. (2011) *The Role of Schooling in Skill Development: Evidence from Young Lives in Ethiopia, India, Peru and Vietnam*, Background paper prepared for the Education for All Global Monitoring Report 2012, Paris: UNESCO.

Rolleston, C., James, Z., Pasquier-Dumer, L., Tran, T. and Le, T.D. (2013) *Making Progress: Report of the Young Lives School Survey in Vietnam*, Working Paper 100, Oxford: Young Lives.

Sameroff, A. (ed.) (2009) *The Transactional Model of Development: How Children and Contexts Shape Each Other*, Washington, DC: American Psychological Association.

Schott, W., Crookston, B., Lundeen, E., Stein, A., Behrman, J. and the Young Lives Determinants and Consequences of Child Growth Project Team (2013) 'Periods of child growth up to age 8 years in Ethiopia, India, Peru and Vietnam: key distal household and community factors', *Social Science & Medicine* 97: 278–87 <http://dx.doi.org/10.1016/j.socscimed.2013.05.016>.

Singh, A. (2014) *Emergence and Evolution of Learning Gaps across Countries: Panel Evidence from Ethiopia, India, Peru and Vietnam*, Working Paper 124, Oxford: Young Lives.

Sumner, A. (2012) *Where Will the World's Poor Live? An Update on Global Poverty and the New Bottom Billion*, Working Paper 305, Washington, DC: Center for Global Development.

United Nations (1989) *Convention on the Rights of the Child*, General Assembly Resolution 44/25, 20 November 1989, New York: United Nations.

United Nations (2014) *The Millennium Development Goals Report*, New York: United Nations.

United Nations Department of Economic and Social Affairs (UNDESA), Population Division (2013) *Adolescent Fertility since the International Conference on Population and Development (ICPD) in Cairo*, New York: United Nations.

UNESCO (2014*) Teaching and Learning: Achieving Quality for All, EFA Global Monitoring Report 2013/4*, Paris: UNESCO.

UN General Assembly (2014) *Status of the Convention on the Rights of the Child, Report of the Secretary-General*, New York: United Nations.

UNICEF (2011) *The State of the World's Children 2011: Adolescence: An Age of Opportunity*, New York: UNICEF.

UNICEF (2013) *Improving Child Nutrition: The Achievable Imperative for Global Progress*, New York: UNICEF.

Vaz, A. (2014) *Are Children Among the Poorest?* Oxford: OPHI.

Walker, S., Wachs, T., Meeks Gardner, J., Lozoff, B., Wasserman, G., Pollitt, E., Carter, J. and the International Child Development Steering Group (2007) 'Child development: risk factors for adverse outcomes in developing countries', *The Lancet* 369: 145–57 <http://dx.doi.org/10.1016/S0140-6736(07)60076-2>.

Wilkinson, R. and Pickett, K. (2009) *The Spirit Level*, London: Penguin.

Woldehanna, T. and Pankhurst, A. (2014) *Youth and Development: Round 4 Preliminary Findings*, Addis Ababa, Ethiopia: Young Lives.

Woodhead, M., Ames, P., Vennam, U., Abebe, W. and Streuli, N. (2009) *Equity and Quality? Challenges for Early Childhood and Primary Education in Ethiopia, India and Peru*, Bernard van Leer Foundation Working Paper 55, The Hague: Bernard van Leer Foundation.

Woodhead, M., Dornan, P. and Murray, H. (2013a) *What Inequality Means for Children: Evidence from Young Lives*, Oxford: Young Lives.

Woodhead, M., Frost, M. and James, Z. (2013b) 'Does growth in private schooling contribute to Education for All? Evidence from a longitudinal, two cohort study in Andhra Pradesh, India', *International Journal of Educational Research* 33: 65–73 <http://dx.doi.org/10.1016/j.ijedudev.2012.02.005>.

World Bank (2012) *Jobs: World Development Report 2013*, Washington, DC: World Bank.

World Health Organization (2006) *WHO Child Growth Standards: Length/height-for-age, weight-for-age, weight-for-length, weight-for-height and body mass index-for-age: Methods and Development* [pdf], Geneva: World Health Organization <www.who.int/childgrowth/standards/Technical_report.pdf?ua=1> [accessed 29 April 2015].

About the authors

Paul Dornan (paul.dornan@qeh.ox.ac.uk) is Senior Policy Officer.

Kirrily Pells (kirrily.pells@qeh.ox.ac.uk) is Policy Officer at Oxford Department of International Development, University of Oxford, UK. We would like to acknowledge the involvement of Young Lives participants on whose experience this analysis is based. Young Lives is an international study of childhood poverty, following the lives of 12,000 children in four countries over 15 years (www.younglives.org.uk). Young Lives is core-funded from 2001 to 2017 by UK aid from the UK Department for International Development (DFID) and co-funded by Irish Aid from 2014 to 2015. The views expressed are those of the authors. They are not necessarily those of, or endorsed by, Young Lives, the University of Oxford, DFID, or other funders.

CHAPTER 3

Evaluations of outcomes for children and youth from NGO-supported microeconomic interventions: a research synthesis

C.M. Ellis and Josh Chaffin

Abstract

Economic strengthening (ES) approaches are increasingly applied in resource-poor environments, including in humanitarian crisis settings, in order to achieve a wide variety of socio-economic goals. At the same time, randomized control trial (RCT) methodology has become more prevalent in evaluations of ES and other microeconomic interventions. This review is a systematic research synthesis of randomized impact evaluations of NGO-implemented interventions in low-income countries that work to build income and/or economic assets either of the caregiver, the household, or the individual child, adolescent, or youth, where the evaluation looked at any child-level or youth-level outcomes. The papers evaluate interventions that work to build household or individual income and/or assets, such as conditional and unconditional cash and asset transfers, savings, and training. We find a wide variety of direct and indirect interventions that can potentially affect children. Most of the statistically significant findings from these studies are good for children across a range of outcome measures; however among the studies included here, there is no discernible pattern of any particular intervention category (skills training, savings, etc.) being more effective than any other at achieving better outcomes for children. In many outcome categories, researchers could find no short-term impact on children from ES programming at all. Unintended negative effects for children were found in over 20 per cent of the studies in our document set. By focusing on RCT evaluations of non-governmental programmes, we provide information about the highest quality evaluations of interventions that may be feasible to implement for programmers interested in this topic.

Keywords: microfinance, children, evaluation

ECONOMIC STRENGTHENING (ES) APPROACHES are increasingly applied in resource-poor environments, including in humanitarian crisis settings, in order to achieve a wide variety of socio-economic goals. Programmes are often implemented by actors in child protection, health, nutrition, and other sectors, on the assumption that greater household wealth can lead to better outcomes in their category of focus.

http://dx.doi.org/10.3362/9781780448879.003

Until recently the impacts of ES on children's welfare were rarely evaluated, but external research has now begun to look more closely at impacts for children, and this review is our second attempt at compiling the results so far (Chaffin, 2011). The 2011 study found emerging evidence of the potential positive and negative impacts ES approaches have on girls and boys. However, the review also concluded that the evidence base at that time was still limited. This review looked at effects on children both from interventions engaging caregivers as direct beneficiaries and those engaging children and youth themselves with ES programmes.

To follow up, the current review is a research synthesis of randomized impact evaluations of NGO-implemented interventions in low-income countries that work to build income and/or economic assets either of the caregiver, the household, or the individual child, adolescent, or youth, where the evaluation looked at any child-level or youth-level outcomes. Forty-six published or publicly available randomized control trial (RCT) studies were selected for inclusion. The papers evaluate conditional or unconditional cash transfer programmes (12 and 12 papers, respectively), vocational skills training (7), group and individual savings schemes (4 and 7 papers, respectively), microcredit loans (7), and non-cash asset transfers (6), or some combination of these and other non-economic interventions.

We aimed to include only ES approaches that could be implemented within the budget and time constraints of NGOs, making this research particularly useful to programmers. However, for comprehensive literature reviews of the findings on the interventions included here see research such as Barrientos et al. (2014), a systematic literature review of social transfers on child protection outcomes in the developing world, or Arnold et al. (2011), which focuses specifically on cash transfers, explaining in policy-friendly language the differential effects of such programmes depending on their objective, design, and implementation. The RCT focus of this study aims to complement this work.

Why RCTs?

We limited this study only to those reports which utilized an RCT methodology, strictly defined as an intervention with at least one treatment group and one control group, where the selection of membership in each group is *completely at random*. RCTs provide the most effective set of tools to understand the *causation* of mechanisms underlying observed outcomes in real-world settings. As Dean Karlan and Nathanael Goldberg argued on these pages in 2009:

> RCTs – where they are feasible and practical – are the best method for measuring impact because they allow us to estimate what would have happened without the intervention under study. Measuring the counter-factual – what would have happened – is essential for establishing causality. Without it, we have no way of knowing whether changes in participants' lives are caused by the programme, by outside factors or, most problematic, by unmeasured characteristics of the participants themselves.

While this study looks at the reported effects of RCTs only, future research could consider the inclusion of quasi-experimental designs that may be less certain about causation, but could provide additional useful information about the effects of these interventions.

Methods

Depending on the field, the term *research synthesis* can be used interchangeably with terms such as *meta-analysis* or *systematic review*. Cooper et al. (2009: 6) define research synthesis as an 'attempt to integrate empirical research for the purpose of creating generalizations. Implicit in this definition is the notion that seeking generalizations also involves seeking the limits of generalizations'. For this research, we do not include the statistical analysis of findings (specifically, effect sizes) found in many meta-analytic studies, but we did conduct most of the same procedures for data collection.

We conducted a search for published or publicly available studies in English, without regard to field, from 1990 to 2014, that utilized experimental methods to evaluate the economic components of programmes implemented in resource poor environments in the developing world. While the direct beneficiaries of programmes are often adult caregivers, the review focused on reports looking at outcomes for children and youth ages 0–18, both within and outside of household care.

We utilized eight of the largest academic databases for peer-reviewed publications, where our search contained the words: ((randomi*) AND ((child*) OR (youth)) AND ((health) OR (educat*) OR (develop*) OR (skill) OR (cash) OR (micro*) OR (protect*) OR (nutrit*))). The first two search terms capture the type of study (randomized) and population of interest (children), while the remaining terms are outcome-based from the UN Convention on the Rights of the Child (UNCRC). We also systematically searched for non-peer-reviewed research on the websites of large NGOs, funders of development research, and development-focused academic organizations, and included relevant studies from a previous report on this theme (Chaffin, 2011), and six relevant studies from the CPC network evaluation repository.

After screening all results to exclude quasi-experimental or non-experimental designs, evaluations of government programmes, and non-ES programming, we developed a coding protocol for the studies that accounted for setting, participants, methodology, treatment, dependent variables, effect direction, and statistical significance of each child-focused outcome of interest.

To facilitate analysis, we first grouped studies by intervention, then by child protection and child well-being outcomes, which were categorized into the following groups:

- school enrolment;
- school performance;
- school completion/graduation (progress);

- labour force participation;
- household spending on children;
- health clinic visits;
- nutrition/food;
- psychological health;
- gender-based violence;
- illness/disease;
- height/weight;
- sexual and reproductive health, incl. marriage/pregnancy;
- general health.

The largest number of studies by far (11) took place in Uganda, followed by Malawi (4) and India (2). While some studies had just one or a few child outcomes as part of a larger study, others focused all of their outcome measures on children. Figure 1 shows the distribution of interventions and outcomes of interest among the RCT studies reviewed here.

Results

Figure 2 shows the distribution of statistically significant findings by treatment. All figures in this section refer to outcome measures, not individual studies, as none of the studies reported on only one outcome of interest.

What this figure shows is, for example, that non-cash asset transfer interventions had more findings with regards to child well-being outcomes that were not statistically significant than those that were. This does not

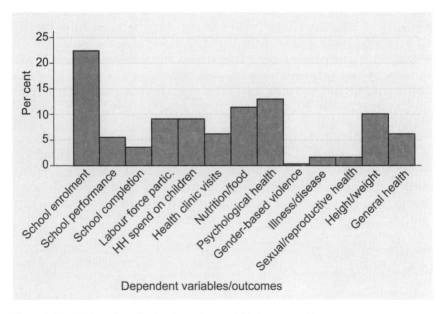

Figure 1 Distribution of studies by dependent variable/outcome of interest

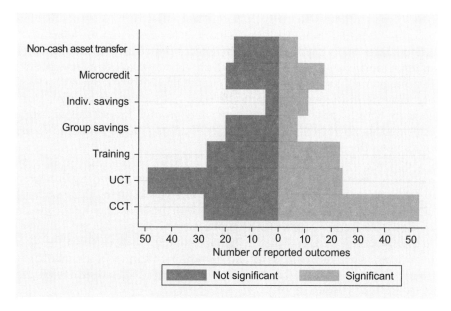

Figure 2 Statistically significant findings by treatment

mean that the outcomes were negative, rather that there was 'zero effect' of the intervention, across a range of outcomes. On the other hand, there is more certainty about the findings from conditional cash transfer (CCT) interventions, a finding that dovetails with the large observational literature. Only three of the studies (Aker et al., 2011; Crépon et al., 2015; Tarozzi et al., 2015) found no statistically significant impacts on children at all.

Studies of ES programmes engaging caregivers

Microcredit

Although one of the most common ES approaches, the question of microcredit impact in general is one of intense controversy and little firm evidence. Sometimes credit is the principal intervention of a programme, and in other cases it is but one strategy among others including savings, agricultural support, and noneconomic interventions. Microcredit loans played a role in 14 evaluations in the adults-as-beneficiaries category of our document set.

Compared to other outcome measures, there are a larger number of statistically significant findings of the effects of microcredit on nutrition and food outcomes of children. All of these findings were good for children, with no negative outcomes. For all of the other outcomes which were measured with this intervention, the majority of the findings showed no effect, as indicated by outcomes which are not statistically significant.

Food and nutrition outcomes for children were part of the studies of MkNelly and Watson (2003), Das et al. (2013) and Bandiera et al. (2013), each evaluating microcredit as part of a larger package of interventions. MkNelly and Watson found a statistically significant positive effect on nutrition outcomes for children under 3 in Ghana, but not in Bolivia. Bandiera et al. found a statistically significant positive effect on food security measured for children in Bangladesh. In Bangladesh, Das et al.'s evaluation of BRACs CFPR-TUP programme focused primarily on non-child outcomes, but did include one measure of women's input into decision-making around giving milk to children, with a statistically significant and positive result. This is strong evidence that microcredit programmes with training can be helpful to young children on the dimension of food security.

Augsburg et al. (2015) analysed the impact of microcredit on poverty reduction, child and teenage labour supply, and education among borrowers in Bosnia and Herzegovina, and found the intervention had the unintended negative consequence of a substantial increase in the labour supply of children aged 16–19, together with a reduction in their school attendance.

Banerjee et al. (2014) looked at group lending for caregivers through a microfinance institution in India and found no difference in the number of hours worked by children 5 to 15 years old, although they did see a reduction in teenage girls' labour supply.

In Mongolia, Attanasio et al.'s (2015) evaluation of a group loan intervention for poor women found a statistically significant negative effect of the microcredit intervention on work hours (a 'good' outcome) for adolescents, but no effect for other age groups.

There were no statistically significant findings for reductions in child labour supply in Tarozzi et al. (2015) in Ethiopia or Crépon et al. (2015) in Morocco, and there were no statistically significant findings for school enrolment in the microcredit-only interventions evaluated by Tarozzi et al. (2015), Crépon et al. (2015), Attanasio et al. (2015), or Banerjee et al. (2014).

Savings

Savings programmes are delivered by many different types of providers including informal financial service providers (rotating savings and credit associations, accumulating savings and credit associations, etc.), and in many different iterations. Both group and individual savings interventions were included in our review.

There were no statistically significant findings of the effect of group savings on height/weight or school enrolment in the two included Village Savings and Loans Association (VSLA) studies (Annan et al., 2013 and Brunie et al., 2014). At the same time, all of the effects of group savings on household spending for children were statistically significant and positive, except one from Annan et al. (2013) on spending on child health, discussed in more detail below.

Overall, there were mixed findings of statistical significance for children's psychological health and labour force participation. The lack of statistically significant findings for these and school enrolment indicates that adult group savings may not be the best vehicle for programmers seeking to influence these outcomes. However, the statistically significant findings for household spending on children are encouraging.

For individual savings interventions, pooled among all age groups receiving the intervention directly, the studies included are Han et al. (2013), Karlan and Linden (2014), and Fred Ssewamala's studies, reviewed in more detail in the section on youth as direct ES recipients. Here, the effects on psychological health outcomes and general health outcomes were only statistically significant, and only positive. There was more certainty than zero effects for positive outcomes on sexual and reproductive health, as well. But results for labour force participation, school performance, and school enrolment were mixed, primarily driven by Karlan and Linden's insignificant results for an intervention of child savings accounts without a parent outreach component.

Cash and non-cash asset transfers

In development contexts, cash transfer programmes have been implemented at great scale, and are often made conditional upon households making investments in children. Increasingly cash transfers are delivered without such conditions, in what is known as an unconditional cash transfer (UCT). As noted above, this review excluded studies of large-scale government-implemented cash programmes, as this topic is already well researched, and focused solely on community-level small scale cash interventions that NGOs could feasibly deliver.

CCT studies

Figure 3 shows the distribution of statistically significant and not significant findings of CCTs by outcome of interest. Because CCTs are often, but not

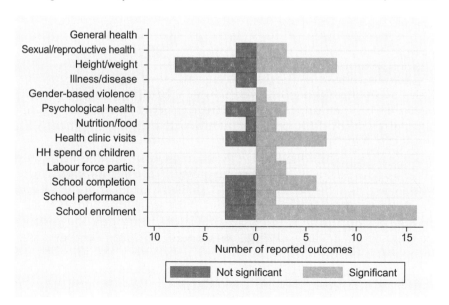

Figure 3 Statistically significant findings for conditional cash transfers

exclusively, conditional on school enrolment, it is not surprising that so many significant effects are found along this measure. However, there is also an interesting pattern of effects for other outcomes.

Evaluations of programmes where the cash transfer was conditional on schooling included Benhassine et al. (2013) in Morocco, Macours et al. (2008) in Nicaragua, Robertson et al. (2013) in Zimbabwe, and Baird et al. (2011b) in Malawi. Mo et al. (2013) was the only study analysing outcomes in China, an important location due to the large number of children living in poverty. Evans et al. (2014) evaluated a pilot CCT programme in Tanzania that devolved responsibility for beneficiary targeting and payment administration to the community level, in contrast to most national-level CCT programmes. Akresh et al. (2013) carried out a randomized evaluation in Burkina Faso comparing the effects of CCTs and UCTs on school enrolment, focusing on 'marginal,' lower ability, or disfavoured children (girls and younger children).

Barrera-Osorio et al. (2011) evaluated the relative efficacy of different CCT programme designs, of particular interest to programmers. They found the most support for programmes where cash was postponed until tertiary enrolment, but also found important negative effects of programme design discussed below.

UCT studies

Many of the studies compared CCTs to UCTs and/or non-cash asset transfer options. Figure 4 shows a different pattern of statistically significant findings

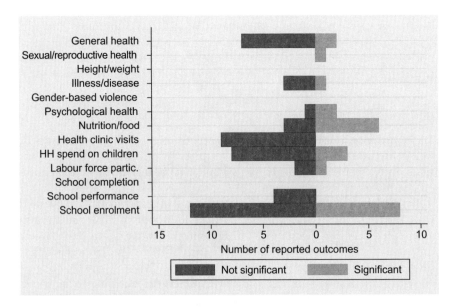

Figure 4 Statistically significant findings for unconditional cash transfers

for UCTs when compared to CCTs. Nutrition and food is the only outcome measure where there are more statistically significant findings than not. On most other measures, there were more findings that were not statistically significant, and there were no significant findings at all for health clinic visits or school performance. This may be because there was such a variety of intervention types among the UCT studies.

In an evaluation of male and female microenterprise owners in Sri Lanka, de Mel et al. (2009) studied the effect of randomly allocated cash grants, while in Uganda, Fiala (2014) compared the effects of grants versus loans, with or without training, to male and female microenterprise owners and Blattman et al. (2014) evaluated a programme for impoverished war-displaced Ugandan households, focusing on women seeking to start up small non-farm businesses.

In Burkina Faso, Akresh et al. (2012) conducted a randomized evaluation of CCTs versus UCTs, examining the outcomes of routine preventative health services depending on which parent received which intervention.

Jenny Aker (2013a, b) evaluated the relative effects of cash versus non-cash vouchers in an internally displaced persons (IDP) camp in Democratic Republic of Congo; and in Ecuador, Hidrobo et al. (2012) compared the effects of unconditional cash versus food vouchers on a variety of child nutrition indicators.

Finally, two studies focused on delivery mechanisms for UCTs. Haushofer and Shapiro (2013) evaluated the effects of the GiveDirectly UCT, which implements funding through the mobile money system M-Pesa in Kenya. Aker et al. (2011) examined the difference in delivery mechanisms for a cash transfer programme in Niger, looking specifically at a mobile phone delivery mechanism.

Few of these studies were primarily interested in children's outcomes, which were reported out of a large set of dependent variables of primary interest to the researchers. Nonetheless, the presence of both statistically significant and not significant outcomes for children indicates that UCTs are an intervention that deserves further study that focuses on child welfare outcomes.

Non-cash asset transfer studies

Many of the non-cash asset transfer interventions showed no effect on child well-being outcomes, except for two findings for nutrition. There were no statistically significant findings for psychological health, household spending on children or school enrolment.

Banerjee et al. (2011) evaluated a programme of direct transfer of livestock with training, and found no effects on child labour or children skipping meals. Hoddinott et al. (2014), in a randomized evaluation in Niger, found that direct food transfers were better than cash transfers for a number of child nutritional outcomes.

With these results and with only two studies, the outcomes of non-cash asset transfer interventions are less certain for child-focused outcomes than other interventions reviewed here.

Studies of ES programmes engaging children directly

Many older children have the ability, the desire, and the need to engage in economic activities. In the country contexts considered in the research, the majority of older adolescents may already be economically active. After conflict and especially in high HIV prevalence contexts, there may be a large number of adolescent household heads, orphans, and other vulnerable children who will need to learn skills to make a living and to manage their money. Thus, older children are sometimes engaged directly in training and other ES activities. In the category of programmes engaging children directly, our document set includes only individual savings, job training, and cash transfers.

Savings and financial education

As with most of the approaches considered in this paper, savings schemes are often delivered in a package of non-economic services, such as career planning and financial education.

Individual savings featured in five of the child-focused programmes considered in our document set. Our review found multiple statistically significant interventions of savings programmes engaging with youth directly, all of which were positive for children. The significant effects of child individual savings on general health, psychological health, and school enrolment should provide confidence to programmers seeking to implement these types of interventions. Even in sexual and reproductive health, much more is known than not known, and again, all of the significant results are positive.

Karlan and Linden (2014) measured the programme's effects on test scores, school attendance, and child labour indicators. They found that parental engagement with a flexible child savings account resulted in more spending on basic educational supplies, helping student outcomes.

In Ghana, Berry et al. (2014) evaluated a financial literacy training programme, complemented by school savings clubs and child empowerment training. They were surprised to find that pre-adolescent students in the group receiving the child empowerment training were *more* likely to be working while in school than those in the savings-only group, a surprising negative result.

The research of Fred M. Ssewamala and his colleagues with AIDS-orphaned adolescents in Uganda (Ssewamala et al., 2008, 2009, 2010a, b, 2012; Han et al. 2013; Nabunya et al. 2014) utilizes 'Child Development Accounts (CDA)', where youth were responsible for depositing money into a matched savings account, for later use to pay for educational expenses or microenterprise development. They measured not only school enrolment, but also sexual and reproductive health, and a variety of psychological indicators, finding largely statistically significant effects across the board.

The statistically significant results from this RCT research into the effects of savings for children directly is strong evidence for the effectiveness of these programmes on child-focused outcomes of interest.

Job training

Many ES interventions, especially for youth, revolve around job skills or self-employment training. This review found three RCTs that met the inclusion criteria evaluating a job training scheme targeting youth.

For adolescents and youth only, more is known than not known (more significant findings than not significant findings) about the effects of training programmes on sexual and reproductive health – and in the studies reviewed here, all of the statistically significant reported effects of training are positive.

Rotheram-Borus et al. (2012) evaluated a Ugandan pilot programme entitled 'Street Smart' which consisted of HIV prevention training plus immediate vocational training for adolescent youth living in slum conditions. They found significant effects of the programme for youth employment, as well as most of their outcomes of interest, ranging from sexual risk behaviours to delinquency, but the lack of information about the long-term results of these training interventions indicates the need for further research in this area.

While girl-focused programmes are increasing in number and have been evaluated with other methodologies, only one of the child-targeted ES programmes that have been evaluated as an RCT aims to promote the rights of adolescent girls explicitly.

Bandiera et al. (2012) evaluated BRAC's Empowerment and Livelihood for Adolescents (ELA) programme, which provides life skills training to adolescent girls from community-based 'adolescent development clubs' instead of schools, and encourages establishment of small-scale entrepreneurial endeavours. Evaluated 2–3 years after implementation, this study took a generally positive view of the programme, and found statistically significant results for the programme's effect on HIV and pregnancy awareness, and the development of entrepreneurial skills. They did not find any significant effects of the programme on wage employment income and hours, or the likelihood of suffering from an STD.

Cash transfers to adolescents

We found four studies where cash transfers were given directly to orphaned adolescents, some of whom were household heads. Sarah Baird and her colleagues at the Development Research Group of the World Bank have carried out a number of high-quality RCT evaluations of cash transfers to adolescents in Malawi. Baird et al. (2010) evaluated the Zomba Cash Transfer Programme, which involved a CCT (conditional on school attendance) of approximately US$10 per month, paid directly to schoolgirls and recent dropouts. They found statistically significant effects for school attendance, marriage, and measures of sexual activity. Similarly, Baird et al. (2012), published in *The Lancet*, found that the intervention had a statistically significant effect on sexual activity and HIV/HSV2 (herpes simplex virus 2) prevalence, but no significant effects found for ever married, currently pregnant, sexual debut, or unprotected sex.

Baird et al. (2011a, b) directly compared CCTs and UCTs to a control group, in part testing the effect of a programme where the adolescents themselves receive the payments directly. The authors were focused on the difference between the effects of UCTs and CCTs for school enrolment, test scores (English, maths, cognitive), and marriage/pregnancy only. They found unsurprisingly significant effect of the CCT (and the surprisingly significant effect of the UCT) on school enrolment. More importantly, this comparison illustrates the differences between CCT and UCT on secondary outcomes: UCT has no effect on performance, and CCT has no effect on sexual and reproductive health. These studies also found surprising negative effects, discussed below.

Negative outcomes

In resource-poor environments, children themselves are often active participants in operating microenterprises (CIDA, 2007), and since most ES interventions work to shore up or establish new microenterprises, ES interventions have the potential to inadvertently cause harm to children. For example, changes in time-use patterns for caregivers and children themselves can reduce the time a child spends under caregiver supervision, can increase the time that children spend caring for their younger siblings, and can increase the time children spend working vs. going to school.

Statistically significant unintended negative effects for children were found associated with the ES interventions in nine studies, over 20 per cent of the studies in our document set.

Evans et al. (2014) found that participation in a CCT programme was associated with fewer health centre visits for very young children and with children being less likely to receive needed medication. The authors find this conclusion 'difficult to interpret' (Evans et al., 2014: 98).

Augsburg et al. (2015) found that a business loan intervention for borrowers who were previously denied credit had the negative consequence of a substantial increase in the labour supply of children aged 16–19, together with a reduction in their school attendance. Similarly, de Mel et al. (2009) found reduced household expenditure on education may have resulted from an unconditional cash transfer to low-capital microenterprise owners.

In their study of an intervention package that included skills training, cash grants, business supervision, and encouragement to form support groups, Blattman et al. (2014) found a reduction in the proportion of household children under 18 in school.

Baird et al. (2011b) found that conditional cash transfers given to the parents of schoolgirls in Malawi shifted at least part of the burden of household support over to teens. As a result, they showed statistically significant negative effects on multiple measures of mental health, at least during the treatment process. This effect was not observed when the funds were given to the adolescent directly.

Annan et al. (2013) found that VSLA and VSLA paired with family-based discussion groups were both associated with decreased spending on child health. In Ghana, Berry et al. (2014) found that a child empowerment training intervention that supplemented school savings clubs and financial literacy training resulted in more labour force participation among children, when compared to a programme without the empowerment component.

Negative effects can also spill over to non-beneficiary children. Barrera-Osorio et al. (2011) found that restricting CCT programme eligibility to certain ages (instead of randomizing by entire households) caused a reallocation of resources within families such that eligible children who were not randomly selected attended school less often if one of their siblings received the intervention.

Baird et al. (2011a) found negative spillover effects of their cash transfer intervention on measures of psychological distress for eligible girls who were randomized into the control group, an important ethical consideration in RCT evaluations. Baird et al. (2011a) were able to explicitly measure the effect of the programme on these eligible-but-not-selected girls. They found statistically significant negative mental health effects on control group girls who were *not* in the same household as the treated group girls, but no effect on control group girls, who *were* part of the same household. This effect was only observed during the evaluation, indicating a temporary negative effect of the programme.

Discussion

These trials encompass a wide range of interventions and outcomes of interest. The number of possible permutations of programme components and outcomes is enormous, and rating the relative efficacy of different ES approaches in generating positive impacts for children was beyond the scope of what we could accomplish in the present study. Instead, we have collected the most reliable information on the effect of individual programme components on specific outcomes of interest.

Among the studies included here, there is no discernible pattern of any particular intervention category (skills training, savings, etc.) being more effective than any other at achieving better outcomes for children. As Figure 5 shows, the large majority of statistically significant findings in the studies reviewed did have positive effects on some outcomes for children; in fact, all but three found at least one significant positive impact on children. In other words, all of the classes of interventions considered here are potentially beneficial, and each could be a viable programming option depending on the specific interests and capabilities of the implementing agency.

However, in many outcome categories, researchers could find no short-term impact on children from ES programming at all. This confirms the need for

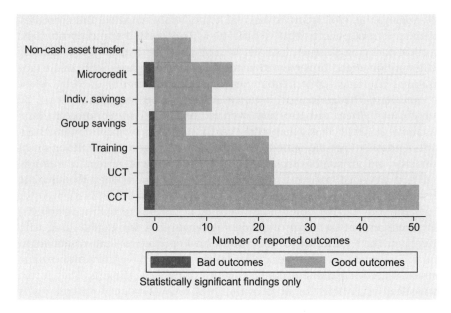

Figure 5 Positive effects of statistically significant interventions

programmers to specifically measure ES impacts on children and not assume that changes in household income or assets will have positive impacts on all children in a household, or on all the dimensions of child well-being that implementers want to influence.

Some of these results, such as the generally positive effects of CCTs, complement existing research from observational data. But the findings from rigorous RCT evaluations should give these findings even more weight for programmers and policymakers. Furthermore, the studies illustrate how individuals and families respond to CCTs beyond the direct carrot-and-stick approach of the programme conditions, finding positive and statistically significant indirect effects on teen sexual activity (Baird et al., 2010, 2012), psychological distress (Baird et al., 2011b), and child nutrition (Macours et al., 2008; Mo et al., 2013). Such findings show that programmers can amplify the effects of single interventions, potentially benefiting children in multiple ways.

The implications of negative effects on children

In the RCT context, negative findings can be considered particularly significant, as the strict standards of an RCT reduce uncertainty about causality, particularly when complemented by qualitative research.

There are different causes of negative outcomes, some of which are more apparent than others. In the study of Augsburg et al. (2015), for example, microcredit loans to the parents of adolescents had the unsurprising effect of causing the adolescents to help with the family business, and spend less time in school. Such a negative outcome is built in to the intervention, and policies carrying out such interventions need to consider how to counteract this specific effect. However, other negative outcomes were unrelated to the nature of the intervention, but rather *how* it was delivered.

Recalling the review of negative effects, some researchers found an observable pattern of harms that occurred when individual children within a family are targeted, as opposed to entire households or entire communities. While most studies did not address this issue, two addressed spillover effects directly, and may be of special interest to programmers. Barrera-Osorio et al. (2011) found that targeting certain ages of children and not others resulted in intra-household resource reallocation towards the children who received the intervention. On the other hand, Baird et al. (2011a) found that providing the intervention to certain individual girls within a family had a *beneficial* effect on their untreated siblings, but a *harmful* effect on other girls in the community who were not selected. Clearly, this is a topic that requires more research, but a cautious approach to implementing these policies would suggest interventions that occur at the group level as much as possible.

Conclusion and directions for future research

With the relative newness of RCTs in the literature on child well-being, much more needs to be done to synthesize the results and connect findings to empirical research based on observational data and systematically make these public for comprehensive reviews. Specifically, the data on treatment, control, and conditions should be made public through a system such as the US National Institutes of Health Clinical Trials Database.

But for all their strengths, and given the lack of a clear 'winner' among ES programme approaches in improving children's outcomes, this review shows that we cannot rely on RCTs alone to understand what kinds of ES programmes work for children. Investments are needed in more mixed-method approaches that can help us understand the 'whys' and 'hows', including explanatory qualitative research after endline to get in-depth perceptions of observed effects.

Further, since the effects on children might not be expected to accrue for perhaps years after the end of an ES intervention, there is an obvious need for longitudinal studies in this area. Research should also prioritize comparative costing, to establish programme cost-per-person and cost-per-effect-size, in order to understand the economic price of any observed differences between study groups.

Turning to individual outcomes of interest, this review finds that very few studies looked at changes in children's exposure to violence, in its many forms, and only one study happened to include an indicator on children's exposure to gender-based violence. The global community of child protection agencies and donors would be particularly interested to know which ES interventions might hold promise in helping to reduce child–family separation, which was not an outcome of interest included in any of the studies we found.

Finally, this review exposes an urgent need for agencies and evaluators to more systematically include children's outcomes in their standard indicators for ES programme evaluation. Some of these studies included dozens of outcome measures, but may have included only one or two child-level indicators. With greater attention to ES effects on children, evaluation research can contribute to protecting children and breaking the intergenerational cycle of poverty.

References

Aker, J.C. (2013) *Examining Differences in the Effectiveness and Impacts of Vouchers and Unconditional Cash Transfers*, Technical Report, New York: UNICEF and London: Concern Worldwide.

Aker, J.C., Boumnijel, R., McClelland, A. and Tierney, N. (2011) *Zap It to Me: The Short-Term Impacts of a Mobile Cash Transfer Program*, Working Paper 268, Washington, DC: Center for Global Development.

Akresh, R., de Walque, D. and Kazianga, H. (2012) *Alternative Cash Transfer Delivery Mechanisms: Impacts on Routine Preventative Health*, Working Paper Series 17785, Cambridge, MA: National Bureau of Economic Research.

Akresh, R., de Walque, D. and Kazianga, H. (2013) *Cash Transfers and child Schooling: Evidence from a Randomized Evaluation of the Role of Conditionality*, Policy Research Working Paper 6340, Washington, DC: World Bank.

Annan, J., Bundervoet, T., Seban, J. and Costigan, J. (2013) *Final Evaluation: 'Urwaruka Rushasha' (New Generation): A Randomized Impact Evaluation of Village Savings and Loans Associations and Family-Based Interventions in Burundi*, Technical report, New York: International Rescue Committee and Washington, DC: USAID.

Arnold, C., Conway, T. and Greenslade, M. (2011) *Cash Transfers: Literature Review*, Technical Report, London: UK Department for International Development.

Attanasio, O., Augsburg, B., De Haas, R., Fitzsimons, E. and Harmgart, H. (2015) 'The impacts of microfinance: evidence from joint-liability lending in Mongolia', *American Economic Journal: Applied Economics* 7(1): 90–122 <http://dx.doi.org/10.1257/app.20130489>.

Augsburg, B., Haas, R. D., Harmgart, H. and Meghir, C. (2015) 'The impacts of microcredit: evidence from Bosnia and Herzegovina', *American Economic Journal: Applied Economics* 7(1): 183–203 <http://dx.doi.org/10.1257/app.20130272>.

Baird, S., Chirwa, E., McIntosh, C. and Özler, B. (2010) 'The short-term impacts of a schooling conditional cash transfer program on the sexual behavior of young women', *Health Economics* 19(S1): 55–68 <http://dx.doi.org/10.1002/hec.1569>.

Baird, S., de Hoop, J. and Özler, B. (2011a) *Income Shocks and Adolescent Mental Health*, Policy Research Working Paper 5644, Washington, DC: World Bank.

Baird, S., McIntosh, C. and Özler, B. (2011b) 'Cash or condition? Evidence from a cash transfer experiment', *The Quarterly Journal of Economics* 126(4): 1709–53 <http://dx.doi.org/10.1093/qje/qjr032>.

Baird, S.J., Garfein, R.S., McIntosh, C.T. and Özler, B. (2012) 'Effect of a cash transfer programme for schooling on prevalence of HIV and herpes simplex type 2 in Malawi: a cluster randomised trial', *The Lancet* 379(9823): 1320–9 <http://dx.doi.org/10.1016/S0140-6736(11)61709-1>.

Bandiera, O., Buehren, N., Burgess, R., Goldstein, M., Gulesci, S., Rasul, I. and Sulaiman, M. (2012) 'Empowering adolescent girls: evidence from a randomized control trial in Uganda', unpublished working paper.

Bandiera, O., Burgess, R., Das, N., Gulesci, S., Rasul, I. and Sulaiman, M. (2013) *Can Basic Entrepreneurship Transform the Economic Lives of the Poor?* Cambridge, MA: Abdul Latif Jameel Poverty Action Lab.

Banerjee, A., Duflo, E., Chattopadhyay, R. and Shapiro, J. (2011) *Targeting the Hard-Core Poor: An Impact Assessment*, Cambridge, MA: Abdul Latif Jameel Poverty Action Lab.

Banerjee, A., Duflo, E., Glennerster, R. and Kinnan, C. (2014) *The Miracle of Microfinance: Evidence from a Randomized Evaluation*, Technical Report, Cambridge, MA: Abdul Latif Jameel Poverty Action Lab.

Barrera-Osorio, F., Bertrand, M., Linden, L. and Perez-Calle, F. (2011) 'Improving the design of conditional transfer programs: evidence from a randomized education experiment in Colombia', *American Economic Journal: Applied Economics* 3(2): 167–95 <http://dx.doi.org/10.1257/app.3.2.167>.

Barrientos, A., Byrne, J., Peña, P. and Villa, J.M. (2014) 'Social transfers and child protection in the south', *Children and Youth Services Review* 47(P2): 105–12 <http://dx.doi.org/10.1016/j.childyouth.2014.07.011>.

Benhassine, N., Devoto, F., Duflo, E., Dupas, P. and Pouliquen, V. (2013) *Turning a Shove into a Nudge? A 'Labeled Cash Transfer' for Education*, Working Paper Series 19227, Cambridge, MA: National Bureau of Economic Research.

Berry, J., Karlan, D. and Pradhan, M. (2014) 'The impact of financial education for youth in Ghana', unpublished working paper, Cambridge, MA: Abdul Latif Jameel Poverty Action Lab.

Blattman, C., Green, E. P., Jamison, J. and Annan, J. (2014) 'Employing and empowering marginalized women: a randomized trial of microenterprise assistance', unpublished working paper.

Brunie, A., Fumagalli, L., Martin, T., Field, S. and Rutherford, D. (2014) 'Can village savings and loan groups be a potential tool in the malnutrition fight? Mixed method findings from Mozambique', *Children and Youth Services Review* 47(P2): 113–20 <http://dx.doi.org/10.1016/j.childyouth.2014.07.010>.

Canadian International Development Agency (CIDA) (2007) *Impacts of Microfinance Initiatives on Children*, Technical Report, Gatineau, Quebec: Canadian International Development Agency.

Chaffin, J. (2011) *The Impacts of Economic Strengthening Programs on Children: A Review of the Evidence*, Technical Report, New York: Child Protection in Crisis (CPC) Livelihoods and Economic Strengthening Task Force.

Cooper, H., Hedges, L.V. and Valentine, J.C. (eds) (2009) *The Handbook of Research Synthesis and Meta-Analysis*, 2nd edn, New York: Russell Sage Foundation.

Crépon, B., Devoto, F., Duflo, E. and Parienté, W. (2015) 'Estimating the impact of microcredit on those who take it up: evidence from a randomized experiment in Morocco', *American Economic Journal: Applied Economics* 7(1): 123–50 <http://dx.doi.org/10.1257/app.20130535>.

Das, N., Yasmin, R., Ara, J., Kamruzzaman, M., Davis, P., Behrman, J.A., Roy, S. and Quisumbing, A.R. (2013) *How Do Intrahousehold Dynamics Change*

When Assets Are Transferred to Women? Evidence from BRAC's Challenging the Frontiers of Poverty Reduction – Targeting the Ultra Poor Program in Bangladesh, IFPRI Discussion Paper 01317, Washington, DC: International Food Policy Research Institute.

de Mel, S., McKenzie, D. and Woodruff C. (2009) 'Are women more credit constrained? Experimental evidence on gender and microenterprise returns', *American Economic Journal: Applied Economics* 1(3): 1–32.

Evans, D.K., Hausladen, S., Kosec, K. and Reese, N. (2014) *Community-Based Conditional Cash Transfers in Tanzania: Results from a Randomized Trial*, Technical Report, Washington, DC: World Bank.

Fiala, N. (2014) 'Stimulating microenterprise growth: results from a loans, grants and training experiment in Uganda', unpublished working paper.

Han, C.-K., Ssewamala, F. M. and Wang, J. S.-H. (2013) 'Family economic empowerment and mental health among AIDS-affected children living in AIDS-impacted communities: evidence from a randomised evaluation in southwestern Uganda', *Journal of Epidemiology & Community Health* 67(3): 225–30 <http://dx.doi.org/10.1136/jech-2012-201601>.

Haushofer, J. and Shapiro, J. (2013) 'Policy brief: impacts of unconditional cash transfers', unpublished working paper.

Hidrobo, M., Hoddinott, J., Peterman, A., Margolies, A. and Moreira, V. (2012) *Cash, Food, or Vouchers? Evidence from a Randomized Experiment in Northern Ecuador*, Discussion Paper 01234, Washington, DC: International Food Policy Research Institute (IFPRI).

Hoddinott, J., Sandström, S. and Upton, J. (2014) *The Impact of Cash and Food Transfers: Evidence from a Randomized Intervention in Niger*, Discussion Paper 01341, Washington, DC: International Food Policy Research Institute (IFPRI).

Karlan, D. and Linden, L.L. (2014) *Loose Knots: Strong versus Weak Commitments to Save for Education in Uganda*, Cambridge, MA: Abdul Latif Jameel Poverty Action Lab.

Macours, K., Schady, N. and Vakis, R. (2008) *Cash Transfers, Behavioral Changes, and Cognitive Development in Early Childhood*, Policy Research Working Paper Series 4759, Washington, DC: World Bank.

MkNelly, B. and Watson, A. (2003) *Credit with Education Impact Review No. 3: Children's Nutritional Status*, Davis, CA: Freedom from Hunger.

Mo, D., Zhang, L., Yi, H., Luo, R., Rozelle, S. and Brinton, C. (2013) 'School dropouts and conditional cash transfers: evidence from a randomised controlled trial in rural China's junior high schools', *The Journal of Development Studies* 49(2): 190–207 <http://dx.doi.org/10.1080/00220388. 2012.724166>.

Nabunya, P., Ssewamala, F.M. and Ilic, V. (2014) Reprint of 'Family economic strengthening and parenting stress among caregivers of AIDS-orphaned children: results from a cluster randomized clinical trial in Uganda', *Children and Youth Services Review* 47(P2): 182–6 <http://dx.doi.org/10.1016/ j.childyouth.2014.07.018>.

Robertson, L., Mushati, P., Eaton, J.W., Dumba, L., Mavise, G., Makoni, J., Schumacher, C., Crea, T., Monasch, R., Sherr, L., Garnett, G.P., Nyamukapa, C. and Gregson, S. (2013) 'Effects of unconditional and conditional cash transfers on child health and development in Zimbabwe: a cluster-randomised trial', *The Lancet* 381: 1283–92 <http://dx.doi.org/10.1016/S0140-6736(12)62168-0>.

Rotheram-Borus, M.J., Lightfoot, M., Kasirye, R. and Desmond, K. (2012) 'Vocational training with HIV prevention for Ugandan youth. *AIDS Behavior* 16(5): 1133–7 <http://dx.doi.org/10.1007/s10461-011-0007-y>.

Ssewamala, F.M., Alicea, S., Bannon, Jr W.M. and Ismayilova, L. (2008) 'A novel economic intervention to reduce HIV risks among school-going AIDS orphans in rural Uganda', *Journal of Adolescent Health* 42: 102–4 <http://dx.doi.org/10.1016/j.jadohealth.2007.08.011>.

Ssewamala, F.M., Han, C.-K. and Neilands, T.B. (2009) 'Asset ownership and health and mental health functioning among AIDS-orphaned adolescents: findings from a randomized clinical trial in rural Uganda', *Social Science & Medicine* 69(2): 191–8 <http://dx.doi.org/10.1016/j.socscimed.2009.05.019>.

Ssewamala, F.M., Han, C.-K., Neilands, T.B., Ismayilova, L. and Sperber, E. (2010a) 'Effect of economic assets on sexual risk-taking intentions among orphaned adolescents in Uganda', *American Journal of Public Health* 100(3): 483–8 <http://dx.doi.org/10.2105/AJPH.2008.158840>.

Ssewamala, F.M., Ismayilova, L., McKay, M., Sperber, E., Bannon, W. and Alicea, S. (2010b) 'Gender and the effects of an economic empowerment program on attitudes toward sexual risk-taking among AIDS-orphaned adolescent youth in Uganda', *Journal of Adolescent Health* 46(4): 372–8 <http://dx.doi.org/10.1016/j.jadohealth.2009.08.010>.

Ssewamala, F.M., Neilands, T.B., Waldfogel, J. and Ismayilova, L. (2012) 'The impact of a comprehensive microfinance intervention on depression levels of AIDS-orphaned children in Uganda', *Journal of Adolescent Health* 50(4): 346–52 <http://dx.doi.org/10.1016/j.jadohealth.2011.08.008>.

Tarozzi, A., Desai, J. and Johnson, K. (2015) 'The impacts of microcredit: evidence from Ethiopia', *American Economic Journal: Applied Economics* 7(1): 54–89 <http://dx.doi.org/10.1257/app.20130475>.

About the authors

Cali Mortenson Ellis (cmortens@umich.edu) is a PhD Candidate, Public Policy and Political Science, at the University of Michigan, USA.

Josh Chaffin is a Senior Program Officer, Livelihoods and Child Protection, at the Women's Refugee Commission and Coordinator of the Task Force on Economic Strengthening and Child Protection, Child Protection in Crisis Learning Network, USA.

CHAPTER 4

Lessons from practice in child-sensitive social protection

Nicola Hypher and Katherine Richards

Abstract

Reducing child poverty has the potential to improve incomes and health for both present and future generations and, thereby, break the inter generational transmission of poverty that affects lives and livelihoods. For several decades evidence has shown the considerable impact of social protection programmes on human development outcomes for children. However, the impact varies across countries and depends critically on context, including availability of other services, as well as design and implementation of programmes. To maximize the impact on children it is essential to take a child-lens to the design and implementation of social protection systems, which comprise programmes to address risks across the life-cycle. This article will outline how child-sensitive social protection programmes impact on children and assess the extent and coverage in developing countries. The article will then outline principles of child-sensitive social protection and key aspects to improve impact on children, using examples from a number of social protection programmes globally. Lastly, the article will outline lessons on what works for children in social protection and will provide policy recommendations for policymakers and other actors, including civil society, that support social protection systems.

Keywords: social protection, children, child poverty

CHILDREN ARE MORE LIKELY to be poor and make up a disproportionate number of the total poor: 600 million children account for 47 per cent of the world's extreme poor (UNICEF, 2014; Jones and Sumner, 2011). Child poverty has devastating and long-term effects by distorting children's physical, cognitive, and social development, which limits future life chances (UNICEF, 2014). Children in poor households are more likely to receive poor healthcare, inadequate nutrition (see Box 1), achieve lower educational attainment, and, consequently, lower levels of attainment on the labour market; all of which are aggravated by crises. They are likely to grow up into poor adults. In Indonesia, a child born into the poorest 40 per cent of households in 2012 was nearly three times more likely to die than a child in the richest 10 per cent (Save the Children, 2015c). Therefore, investment in children and tackling child poverty is critical in securing human and child rights and contributes to social and economic gains from improved nutrition, education, and health.

http://dx.doi.org/10.3362/9781780448879.004

Box 1 Nutrition, poverty and inequality

Maternal and child malnutrition is the cause of 45 per cent of preventable child deaths and leads to irreversible, lifelong consequences for a child's physical and cognitive development. The effects of malnutrition on physical stature, cognitive development, and the ability to do physical work can lock children into poverty and entrench inequality.

Improving maternal and child nutrition is complex and requires contributions from many sectors. To achieve optimum nutrition children require access to: appropriate, affordable, diverse, and nutrient-rich food; appropriate maternal and child care practices; and adequate health services and a healthy environment including safe water, sanitation, and good hygiene (UNICEF, 2013). The right nutrition during the critical first 1,000 days, between a woman's pregnancy and her child's second birthday, can have a profound impact on a child's ability to grow, learn, and rise out of poverty. It can also shape a society's long-term health, stability, and prosperity (1,000 days partnership, 2014).

Poverty aggravates three types of vulnerability: physical, dependence-related, and institutional (Roelen and Sabates-Wheeler, 2012). Physical or biological vulnerability is related to children's immature immune systems and under-development. Evidence shows that malnutrition, lack of healthcare, and low levels of education during infancy and childhood have long-lasting, detrimental consequences for individual children and society as a whole. Secondly, children are dependent on adults and distribution of resources for their well-being and should not be economic agents in their own right. Some of the most vulnerable and marginalized groups of children live outside family structures and are self-reliant. Lastly, institutionalized disadvantage leads to voicelessness and entrenched inequalities based on wealth, gender, disability, ethnicity, religion, and age. Children living in poverty are often culturally disadvantaged, thereby reinforcing and perpetuating an already weakened socio-cultural position. Children are also affected by inequalities based on gender as women bear the greatest responsibility for children's care and protection so are affected by women's unequal access to livelihoods and resources in the household. Interventions to tackle child poverty should, therefore, cater for the practical and strategic needs of children, their carers, and community. Practical needs are those resulting from the concrete conditions they experience at a given stage in life, including long-term needs that children face as they develop into adulthood. Strategic needs are those related to limited autonomy and relative invisibility (Roelen and Sabates-Wheeler, 2012).

Social protection is the set of public actions that address poverty, vulnerability, and exclusion as well as provide the means to cope with life's major risks throughout the life-cycle (DFID et al., 2009). It plays a key role in reducing poverty and inequality as well as advancing human development outcomes and improving productivity (ILO 2014). Social protection policies are recognized as critical to realizing child rights, ensuring their well-being, and breaking the vicious cycle of poverty and vulnerability to help all children realize their full potential (ILO 2014). There is now a vast body of evidence that social protection programmes, when designed and delivered well, can effectively increase the nutritional, health, and educational status of children and reduce the risk of abuse, exploitation, and neglect across the life-cycle. Such interventions bring long-term benefits, not only for the individual but also for national economic and social development (DFID et al., 2009).

Maximizing the impact social protection has on child poverty requires a combination of the following:

- Advocacy to ensure all social protection programmes adhere to principles of child sensitivity, as many programmes reach and benefit children without explicitly targeting them.
- Introducing child-focused programmes, where relevant, that directly address child poverty, within an overall life-cycle approach, for example child grants and maternity grants.
- Wider policy reforms to address the causes of poverty, improve the quantity and quality of health, education and other basic services, and promote social equity and inclusion.

This article draws on recent evidence to outline how to strengthen the impact of social protection on children. The following section will outline the child sensitivity of existing social protection and provides evidence on the impact on child outcomes. We then draw on this evidence and specific programme examples to delineate the various components of child-sensitive programmes that should be considered in design, implementation, and evaluation.

The state of child-sensitive social protection

Only 27 per cent of the global working-age population and their families have access to comprehensive social security systems (ILO, 2014). Nearly half of all people over pensionable age do not receive a pension and for many that do, pension levels are inadequate. Coverage and spending levels are particularly low in countries that have greater need for social protection, as evidenced by high poverty and malnutrition as well as inadequate health and education (ILO, 2014). In particular, existing social protection policies do not sufficiently address the needs of children and families (ILO, 2014). In large parts of Africa and Asia, non-contributory programmes are not yet well-developed to cover substantial numbers of children and families; many programmes are at the pilot stage with limited geographic coverage. In addition, many programmes that address children's needs are not enshrined in legislation underpinned by financial sustainability and institutional capacity (ILO, 2014).

Specific child and family benefit programmes, including a non-contributory component, rooted in legislation, exist in 76 countries, covering only small sections of the population. In 107 countries no programmes anchored in legislation or only employment-related programmes exist. Levels of investment are lower in lower income countries and underpin low levels of coverage; on average governments allocate 0.4 per cent of GDP to child and family benefits ranging from 2.2 per cent in Western Europe to 0.2 per cent in Africa and Asia and the Pacific. Globally maternity protection provides effective coverage of 28 per cent of women in employment. An increasing number of countries are using non-contributory maternity cash benefits to improve income security and access to maternal and child healthcare for pregnant women and new mothers; however significant gaps remain. In many low- and middle-income countries, only a small minority of children and families receive child benefits and specific programmes tend to be focused on selected categories of disadvantaged children.

In addition, social protection programmes in low-income and many middle-income countries experience challenges of lack of funding, low coverage, poor coordination, and fragmentation of programmes. Overall, social protection programmes have lacked domestic commitment and funding. Many programmes are donor-funded and have not succeeded in leveraging government buy-in, despite providing evidence of success, because of insufficient focus on the political drivers and constraints of social protection policies (IDS et al., 2010). Many programmes originated from a concern about vulnerable populations, often in the context of food insecurity and HIV/AIDS. As a result, they have tended to narrowly target specific groups, such as orphans, ultra-poor, and labour-constrained households, that are overseen by different ministries with limited coordination. In Bangladesh, there are 95 programmes that are run out of different ministries for different purposes and target groups (Save the Children, 2014). These are currently being consolidated into a few major programmes.

In middle-income countries, flagship social transfer programmes (for example in Brazil, Mexico, South Africa, India, and China) now reach large sections of the population. For Brazil, Bolsa Familia reaches 11.3 million families and the Child Support Grant programme reached 10.8 million children in 2012, which represents more than half of all children under the age of 18 (ILO, 2014). In recent years social protection policies have been actively promoted in low-income countries in recognition of their role in reducing chronic poverty and vulnerability and in contributing to attainment of economic and social development objectives. Many countries have been introducing and expanding programmes, such as those in Table 1; Ethiopia's Productive Safety Net Programme is one of the largest programmes and reaches 8 million food-insecure people (Arnold et al., 2011). Countries are also increasingly developing national strategies for social protection and are moving towards a systems approach. Kenya has introduced five programmes that target orphans and vulnerable children, the elderly, people living with disabilities, poor households in four counties in the north and in urban areas, which by 2010 covered almost 14 per cent of the population (Republic of Kenya Ministry of State for Planning, 2012). Ethiopia, Myanmar, and Bangladesh, among others, are developing national social protection strategies to improve coordination and guide scale-up

Table 1 Selected social protection programmes

Programme	Objective	Target group	Coverage
Ethiopia – Productive Safety Net Programme	To smooth consumption, protect assets, create community assets	Chronic food insecure households	1.5 million households (8 million people)
Ghana – Livelihoods Empowerment Against Poverty Programme	Increase long-term human capital development	Extremely poor households	70,000 households (2013)
Kenya – Cash Transfer for Orphans and Vulnerable Children	To encourage fostering and retention of children and to promote their human capital development	Ultra-poor families living with orphans and vulnerable children	130,000 households (260,000 children) (2011)
Malawi – Social Cash Transfer Programme	To reduce poverty, hunger, and starvation, and improve school enrolment and attendance and health and nutrition of children	Ultra-poor and labour-constrained households	36,000 households (2013)
South Africa – Child Support Grant	To provide for the child's basic needs	Poor children (under the age of 18)	10.8 million children (2012)
Zambia – Social Cash Transfer Programme (including Child Grant Programme and Multiple Category Cash Transfer)	Reduce extreme poverty and intergenerational transfer of poverty	Multiple targeting criteria	145,000 households

Source: AIR (2013), Devereux et al. (2006), Arnold et al. (2011), From Protection to Production (2014), Kenya CT-OVC Evaluation Team (2012), ILO (2014), Miller et al. (2010)

of coverage of social protection programmes. National governments have committed to developing national Social Protection Floors (ILO, 2014) to guide the implementation of comprehensive social protection systems that include income security for children, the elderly, and those of active age who are unable to earn sufficient income as well as essential healthcare, including maternity care.

There has been consistent evidence of the impact of social cash transfers across a range of child outcomes. Social cash transfers have demonstrated strong evidence in increasing access to education by alleviating direct and indirect financial barriers, especially for secondary school enrolment. Kenya's Cash Transfers for Orphans and Vulnerable Children (CT-OVC) led to an 8 percentage point increase in secondary school enrolment (Kenya CT-OVC Evaluation Team 2012). Evidence also suggests improvements in several other education-related indicators, such as repetition and school attendance. In South Africa, early receipt of the Child Support Grant increased grade completion and attainment and reduced likelihood that adolescents will work outside of the home, with particularly strong impacts for girls (DSD et al., 2012). In Malawi, beneficiaries of the Social Cash Transfer Programme were more likely to attend school and had more money spent on education compared with comparison households. The programme was found to have increased children's role in household chores and farming but reduced participation in other income-generating activities (Miller et al., 2010). In Bangladesh, with the Female Secondary School Assistance Programme, the secondary school certificate pass rate for girls increased from 39 per cent to nearly 63 per cent over seven years (Chaudhury, 2008).

Social cash transfer programmes have also had positive impacts on health indicators. In Malawi's Social Cash Transfer Programme (SCTP), 81 per cent of beneficiary children experienced improved health compared with 15 per cent in comparison households (Yablonski and O'Donnell, 2009). In Bangladesh, Challenging the Frontiers of Poverty Reduction (CFPR) was found to have strong health impacts, including increased use of modern contraceptive measures and immunization coverage as well as use of antenatal care (Arnold et al., 2011; Davies, 2009). Although the impact of social cash transfer programmes on child anthropometric measures has been less clear across programmes, often explained by short-term programmes striving to impact long-term indicators (such as stunting), some impressive successes can be cited. The Child Support Grant (CSG) in South Africa bolstered childhood nutrition, evidenced by stunting among programme recipients (DSD et al., 2012). Achievements in wasting are also notable: the Child Grant Programme (CGP) in Zambia significantly improved wasting among children aged three to five years and increased infant and young child feeding by 22 per cent (AIR, 2013).

Substantial evidence of positive impacts also exists from other household-level programmes leading to improved child outcomes. For example, in Ethiopia 39 per cent of Productive Safety Net Programme (PSNP) beneficiary households enrolled their children in school and 50 per cent of beneficiaries kept their children in school for longer compared with times when cash or food was short; in both cases around 80 per cent of households credited the PSNP with these impacts (Devereux et al., 2006). South Africa's pension increased height for age for girls compared with non-eligible households (Yablonski and O'Donnell, 2009). Social cash transfer programmes have consistently led to increased food expenditure, consumption, and dietary diversity; for example, Ghana's Livelihood Empowerment Against Poverty (LEAP) led to improved food intake and beneficiaries were able to eat more diverse and nutritious foods. Social cash transfer programmes impact on productive activities of both beneficiary and non-beneficiary households in the communities where they are implemented, including increases in agricultural activities and increased participation in non-farm enterprises (FAO, 2014). This will increase the overall income within the household and could potentially positively impact on children.

Key aspects of child-sensitive social protection systems

Although the evidence shows positive impacts for children from social protection, the magnitude and types of impact depend on design, implementation, and evaluation of the programme (Davis and Handa, 2014; DFID et al., 2009). Child-sensitive social protection aims to maximize opportunities and development outcomes for children by considering different dimensions of child well-being. It focuses on addressing the inherent social disadvantages, risks, and vulnerabilities children may be born into, as well as those acquired later in childhood due to external shocks (DFID et al., 2009). This section uses evidence from programmes to develop recommendations for aspects to consider in the design and implementation of social protection systems and programmes.

A set of principles has been developed by agencies, bilateral donors, and international NGOs that should be considered in the design, implementation, and evaluation of child-sensitive systems (DFID et al., 2009):

- Mitigate the effects of shocks, exclusion, and poverty on families, recognizing they need support to ensure equal opportunity.
- Avoid adverse impacts on children, and reduce or mitigate social and economic risks that directly affect children's lives.
- Consider the age- and gender-specific risks and vulnerabilities of children throughout the life-cycle.
- Make special provision to reach children who are particularly vulnerable and excluded, including children without parental care and those who are marginalized within their families or communities due to gender, disability, ethnicity, HIV & AIDS, or other factors.
- Consider the mechanisms and intra-household dynamics that may affect how children are reached, with particular attention paid to the balance of power between men and women within the household and broader community.
- Intervene as early as possible where children are at risk, in order to prevent irreversible impairment or harm.
- Include the voices and opinions of children, their caregivers, and youth in the understanding and design of social protection systems and programmes.

Integrated social protection system to address multiple vulnerabilities for children

As demonstrated above, existing social protection is fragmented, consisting of separate, poorly integrated programmes. This undermines the ability of social protection to provide comprehensive coverage to address multiple and overlapping vulnerabilities, especially for children across the life-cycle. Therefore, child-sensitive social protection requires the development of an integrated social protection system, consisting of interconnected policies and programmes and linkages to other services (UNICEF and World Bank, 2013).

Children experience different risks as they age and a life-cycle-based approach seeks to address the specific economic and social vulnerabilities. This should be informed by robust analysis of child poverty and vulnerability and should encompass institutional frameworks and mechanisms to facilitate integration, monitoring and evaluation as well as participation and accountability. Figure 1 shows the various social protection programmes that address key stages in the life-cycle.

Robust analysis of the risks and vulnerabilities faced by children at different points in their life and the factors that underlie their vulnerability is an essential foundation to developing an appropriate child-sensitive social protection system and in determining the appropriate interventions. This is a different approach to identifying 'vulnerable groups' (such as children living on the street), which characterizes many social protection programmes, as the broader population may share the sources of vulnerability. Analysis should be conducted during the development of social protection systems as well as on an ongoing basis to assess the child sensitivity of programmes, and to identify any gaps that prevent access for certain groups, such as children and marginalized groups. Save the Children recently conducted an analysis of the causal pathways of malnutrition to inform design of social protection (see Box 2).

The social protection system should be defined and delineated in a comprehensive strategy that is aligned with national vision. It also requires institutional arrangements for implementation and oversight, strong

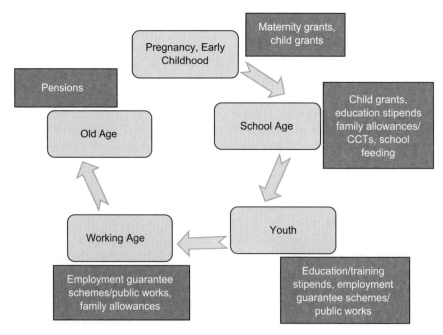

Figure 1 Social protection across the life-cycle

Box 2 Child-sensitive social protection in Bangladesh: improving impacts on nutrition by identifying the causal pathways

To tackle malnutrition, integrated child-sensitive social protection programmes in Bangladesh should address priority focus areas for outcomes and across all three nutrition pathways, according to robust analysis.

Specifically, caring practices for women and children is a critical pathway in Bangladesh. Child marriage, early pregnancy, and stunting at birth are critical points for malnutrition across the life-cycle and major concerns in Bangladesh. Empowering women and targeting adolescent girls through nutrition-sensitive social protection in Bangladesh must be a priority.

The development of social protection across the life-cycle, with effective communication on nutrition behaviour change, and a greater focus on adolescent girls, empowering women, and the 1,000-day window of opportunity between a woman's pregnancy and her child's second birthday, will help shape healthier and more prosperous futures for everyone in Bangladesh. For policy-makers and design implementers internationally, nutrition-sensitive social protection requires strong analysis, a focus on long-term gains, and integrated programmes that consider a number of the nutrition pathways.

Source: Save the Children (2015b)

---

governance, and sufficient resources to be able to develop and sustain comprehensive social protection. Social welfare and children's ministries tend to be weaker ministries and, therefore, these may need to be strengthened in order to ensure effective social protection programmes with sufficient coverage (IDS et al., 2010). This will also improve the extent to which policies are responding to the practical as well as strategic needs of children. Integrated administrative systems, such as a single registry, can improve the overall effectiveness of programmes and enhance impacts for children by promoting links between programmes and with other social services by ensuring that children receive a comprehensive package of social protection and services based on need and entitlements. Several countries, including Lesotho, Ghana, and Kenya, are developing single registries to improve overall effectiveness, which would therefore benefit children.

Child-sensitive social protection requires an effective monitoring and evaluation system that assesses the impacts of the programmes on different dimensions of child well-being, disaggregated by age and sex. Child-focused social accountability includes activities such as participatory planning and budgeting, accountability in implementation, and oversight to hold public officials and service providers accountable, through dialogue, for their commitments to children. This can also contribute to addressing voicelessness of children in social protection policies; thereby, tackling strategic needs as well as practical needs of children.

Coordination and linkages with social services

Given the multiple risks and deprivations that children face throughout their lives, ensuring that recipients of social protection also have access to a range of appropriate, quality services is a cornerstone of child-sensitive social protection. However, many social protection programmes do not effectively link to and promote access to social services. Linkages to promote access to social services include messaging, behavioural change communication and conditionalities, as well as referrals and case management. Ghana's LEAP programme (see Box 3) has established several mechanisms and an integrated approach to promote cross-sectoral coordination and linkages, including increased access to health.

There are several examples of programme design to improve awareness and change behaviour in relation to child outcomes. Evidence finds strong impacts from unconditional cash transfers and conditional cash transfer programmes, whereby the recipient has to meet certain conditions (such as a minimum level of school attendance) to receive the transfer. Given that the beneficiaries are likely to be poor or very poor, the use of conditions that are sanctioned may itself be controversial (ILO, 2014). The Kenya CT-OVC increased secondary enrolment and the magnitude of impact compares favourably with similar conditional programmes elsewhere (Kenya CT-OVC Evaluation Team, 2012). Similarly in South Africa, unconditional cash transfers have been used to improve nutrition, schooling, and care (DSD et al., 2012). There has been positive evidence of the impact of messaging, for example effective information and education campaigns, on child outcomes (Freeland, 2013). In Nigeria, the Child Development Grant Programme, which is targeted to pregnant women and mothers with children under the age of two, is accompanied by community-based nutrition activities focused on infant and young child feeding to improve impact on nutrition in recognition of the complex multiple underlying determinants of nutrition and the role of cultural beliefs and behaviour. Challenging the Frontiers of Poverty (CFPR) programme in Bangladesh and Juntos programme in Peru include activities to raise awareness around gender-based violence and promoting access to civic documentation (Jones and Holmes, 2010).

Lastly, cross-sectoral linkages can be enhanced through an effective case management system that ensures that all children receive an integrated package of appropriate care and support (Roelen and Sabates-Wheeler, 2012).

Box 3 Ghana's LEAP programme and cross-sectoral linkages

The LEAP programme in Ghana includes key design components to promote a cross-sec-toral and integrated approach. Overall coordination is overseen by the Department of Social Welfare while the participation of relevant line ministries – such as Education, Health, Labour, and others – is facilitated through an inter-ministerial committee. The Ministries of Employment and Social Welfare, Health and Education collaborate to facilitate link-ages with complementary services such as automatic enrolment in the National Health Insurance scheme for LEAP beneficiaries and participation in education fee waivers and uniform bursary programmes (UNICEF, 2012). The explicit links to the National Health Insurance Scheme led to a 20 percentage point increase in access to health insurance (Davis and Handa, 2014).

For example, social protection can become more sensitive to child protection issues by including aspects to provide support to families and identify and respond to children at risk. Social protection can promote a system of referrals to other social services and child protection systems through a cadre of social workers and community-based mechanisms. Social cash transfer programmes can also help in increasing birth registration. For example, the Kenya CT-OVC led to a 12 per cent increase in children with birth certificates and the Lesotho CGP was associated with an increase in birth registration of 37 per cent among beneficiary households, due to an unenforced requirement to have a birth certificate within six months of registering for the programme (Pellerano et al., 2014).

Coverage, targeting, and access

Coverage, targeting criteria, and mechanisms need to be in line with programme objectives and take into account the causes of multiple deprivations of poverty (Sabates-Wheeler et al., 2009). Therefore, it is recommended to use broad targeting criteria, for example based on age, rather than targeting based on poverty. Social protection is particularly useful for nutrition when targeted at the 1,000 days, helping maximize this unique window of opportunity to shape healthier and more prosperous futures. An initial age limit, focusing on the most vulnerable parts of the life-cycle may be required allowing gradual expansion as financing allows. Alternatively, income and poverty measures that exclude richer households may be more effective in low-income contexts than mechanisms to identify the poorest households.

As stated above, social protection programmes, especially in low-income countries, are characterized by low coverage and comprise narrow criteria for specific vulnerable groups such as the ultra-poor and labour-constrained households. This has been found to exclude other groups that may also be vulnerable (see Box 4) and has been associated with stigma. Several programmes in the sub-Saharan African region target orphans and vulnerable children or labour-constrained households; for example the Social Cash Transfer Programmes in Malawi and Zambia, which have a tendency to reach relatively older children and therefore fewer pre-school-age children. The CSG in South Africa was initially targeted to school-aged children but has been extended to include younger and older children over time following effective civil society advocacy on the limitations of the more restrictive age criteria (Save the Children, 2011).

Women are often the primary recipients of social cash transfer programmes, especially where the programme is child focused. Evidence from the pension in South Africa provides positive evidence on the impact of this on child outcomes: where pensions were received by women there was impact on the anthropometric status (weight for height and height for age) of children, especially for girls, that was not found with male beneficiaries (Duflo, 2003). Aside from making women the primary recipients, few programmes have

---

Box 4 Improving child sensitivity of social protection in Kenya

Kenya's social protection programmes have demonstrated significant impacts on children and children have been key beneficiaries of a range of programmes. However, recent analysis commissioned by UNICEF and Save the Children (Ayliffe, 2013; AIHD and Save the Children, 2015) have found some gaps in the ability of the programmes to have sustained impacts on the life-course of children and have provided some recommendations on how child sensitivity can be enhanced. The social protection system in Kenya comprises five programmes: the CT-OVC (Cash Transfer for Orphans and Vulnerable Children), Hunger Safety Net Programme (HSNP), Social Pension, Disability Grants, and Urban Food Subsidy Programme. The National Social Protection Policy in Kenya stipulates that children of poor and vulnerable households will enjoy income security through family and child transfers aimed at improving access to nutrition, education, and healthcare. The Government of Kenya is currently reforming the five programmes into the National Safety Net Programme that will be accompanied by expansion of coverage and improved effectiveness.

The programmes have many positive aspects in relation to impact on children as children are the primary beneficiaries of the social protection system. Overall, women are the primary recipients and have substantial control over how funds are spent, therefore potentially improving the positive impact on children. The CT-OVC targets households with orphans and vulnerable children. Although reforms of the National Safety Net Programme do not explicitly address child issues, the increased coverage and improved effectiveness will benefit children. With the planned scale-up, 13 per cent of poor households with children will benefit from the programme by 2016/17. However besides orphans, other groups of vulnerable children are neglected, especially younger children and children with moderate disabilities who are less likely to be covered than if the transfers were randomly allocated.

---

prioritized transforming intra-household relations, allocation of resources, and decision-making, which would translate into positive impacts on child well-being (Jones and Holmes, 2010).

Access to social protection is also an important consideration to ensure programmes are child sensitive. Access refers to whether eligible beneficiaries are able to enrol in programmes and receive their benefits. Vulnerable children and their carers are more likely than the general population to experience challenges in accessing programmes due to geographic and social marginalization, lower levels of education, cultural constraints, and poverty. This is aggravated for children not in conventional households, such as children without appropriate care or children on the move. Special consideration needs to be given to the particular barriers that vulnerable children and their carers face in accessing programmes and in ensuring that these children are able to access programmes. Given that women are often the primary recipients of transfers, issues that affect women's access to programmes is also important. Accountability mechanisms ensure that the right benefit gets to the right person at the right time. Where there are specific highly vulnerable or marginalized groups that do not access social protection programmes, it is recommended to address the barriers that affect their access rather than to create specific programmes that may lead to further fragmentation, increase costs, and create challenges around coordination.

In order to ensure access to all eligible beneficiaries, there needs to be an effective communication strategy on the objectives or the programme as well as eligibility criteria, benefit levels, and operational information. This should take into account challenges with illiteracy and other barriers related to social marginalization and should include informal communication channels that are more likely to be accessed by vulnerable children and their carers. In addition, programme design and implementation should take into account barriers to accessing programmes related to targeting and registration, such as minimizing the need for official documentation to prove age or citizenship (see Box 5) or including measures to ensure that all eligible beneficiaries are able to access these documents (such as through support for birth registration). Ensuring a gender balance in village or programme committees may promote the inclusion of children, women, and other excluded groups.

Programme design should also tackle barriers to accessing payments that may be due to education, time constraints, money, and mobility. For example, efforts should be made to reduce the cost of accessing transfers, in terms of both opportunity cost and transport. As women are often the main recipients of social cash transfers, the design should take into account any restrictions on women's movement and other demands on their time such as childcare and other unpaid work. In many cases, electronic payment systems have been found to reduce barriers to accessing payments as they can be accessed at any time. However, lack of familiarity with technology and low levels of literacy may pose challenges for some groups in accessing

---

Box 5 Reducing the barriers to accessing the Child Support Grant in South Africa

Evaluations of the Child Support Grant in South Africa found that receipt of the grant varies by age group, with take-up highest for children seven to ten years old, while infants and youth in newly eligible age groups have relatively low take-up rates.

There are many reasons behind eligible households not accessing the grant. Firstly, there is confusion around the eligibility criteria, with households perceiving the income threshold for the means test as lower than it is and incorrectly believing that any employment rules out eligibility. The criteria have been changed in recent years and the means test has become substantially more inclusive. This confusion reflects complexity around the means test and challenges in disseminating programme information to those that are often disconnected from reliable information sources. Eligible caregivers also often do not apply for the Child Support Grant due to problems with documents; in 2008, one in four poor eligible caregivers who did not apply cited problems with documents as the main reason; it was also the main reason for delays in application. Other challenges included that the application process was too time-consuming or costly, a general lack of awareness of the process, or the process was too complicated.

Analysis has found that there have been improvements in grant access over the past 15 years. This has included a reduction in the number of documents required, more effective communication about registration procedures, technological improvements, and reduction in the cost of accessing the grant due to improvements in financial inclusion mechanisms.

Source: DSD et al. (2012)

the payments; therefore measures should be accompanied by training to ensure that beneficiaries are able to use the payment mechanism. Paypoints should be located in close proximity to beneficiaries to reduce distances and therefore cost in accessing payments.

Grievance mechanisms within individual programmes can help to ensure that beneficiaries are able to access the benefits to which they are entitled and ensure that an effective, accessible mechanism is in place to receive and respond to complaints. The grievance mechanism and how it operates should be effectively communicated to beneficiaries and should include several channels so that it caters for all members of the community regardless of their literacy level, location, or status.

Adequacy and effectiveness

Social protection programmes need to ensure that transfer levels are adequate to address children's needs, including in accessing social services and a nutritious diet, as well as providing sufficient duration of benefits. Save the Children has developed a tool that calculates the cost of a nutritious diet and can be used to inform transfer size, alongside other factors (Save the Children, 2015a). Children's needs and the costs of meeting them should also be taken into account in consumption or income-related thresholds for graduation so as not to undermine investment in children and disadvantage households with children (Roelen, 2014). The CSG in South Africa provides evidence of the impact of duration of transfer and early impact as children who were enrolled at birth completed significantly more grades of schooling than children, especially girls, who were enrolled at age six and achieved higher scores on assessments (DSD et al., 2012).

Several programmes have resulted in unintended consequences on a range of child outcomes. For example, public works programmes have been shown to have an impact on child labour. Ethiopia's PSNP and India's National Rural Employment Guarantee Scheme (NREGS) were associated with increases in child labour, either through children participating in public work activities or substituting for their parents who participate in public works in other labour activities (such as agricultural work or within the household). The programmes recognized these challenges and have made attempts to tackle the increase in child labour by prohibiting children from participating in public works and gaining community acceptance on reducing child labour. Programmes have also been found to reinforce male and female traditional roles through making women the main recipients of programmes and the fact that they need to comply with conditionalities. Challenging the Frontiers of Poverty Reduction in Bangladesh recognized in the design that women's participation in the programme could exacerbate household tensions and sensitized male members of the household to the benefits of women's participation (Jones and Holmes, 2010).

Conclusion

Social protection has demonstrated considerable positive impacts on child poverty and human development outcomes. However, currently social protection provides insufficient coverage of children and inadequate consideration of children's needs. This is demonstrated by low coverage, especially in areas where child poverty and related indicators are highest, and a lack of coordinated and effective mechanisms that address children's issues. This paper has drawn on lessons from social protection mechanisms to provide practical recommendations for how social protection can address children's practical and strategic needs which can be summarized as follows.

1. Overall coverage of social protection is low, especially in countries with high levels of poverty and malnutrition and unequal access to education and health. Although impacts on children depend critically on design of programmes and intra-household allocation of resources, there is evidence of children benefiting from various social protection programmes that can be further strengthened. *An increase in investment and coverage of social protection is essential and will be beneficial for children.*

2. Social protection programmes do not sufficiently address the needs of children and families. Therefore, as part of an increase in coverage of social protection and based on a life-cycle approach, *particular efforts need to be taken in expanding coverage of children and in addressing children's needs within a social protection system.*

3. Children experience different risks and vulnerabilities as they age and these should be addressed through an integrated social protection system. *Robust analysis into the multiple risks and vulnerabilities is an essential foundation to an appropriate, child-sensitive social protection system.*

4. A social protection system that builds synergies across and within programmes can improve overall operational effectiveness as well as impact on children. *An integrated, systems approach should inform programming, including the development of a single registry to improve linkages with services.*

5. Child-focused social accountability can ensure that social protection programmes address the practical needs of children and strengthen the extent to which they address institutional disadvantage and address strategic needs. *Efforts should be made to strengthen child-focused accountability, especially in building the extent to which civil society organizations are able to hold public officials to account.*

6. Social protection programmes should link to other services to enhance access and child outcomes. *Case management, referrals, and support to access services (such as distribution of health cards) promote access to social services. In addition, messaging alongside social protection programmes can improve child outcomes.*

7. Multiple dimensions of poverty underlie child outcomes. *Therefore, it is necessary to use broad targeting criteria rather than targeting based on poverty or income.*

8. Vulnerable children and their carers are more likely than the general population to experience challenges in accessing social protection due to geographic and social marginalization, lower levels of education, cultural

constraints, and poverty. *Efforts should be taken to minimize barriers to access and to support access of groups that face particular constraints.*

9. Children have a particular set of needs and vulnerabilities that should be addressed in programme design. *Therefore, transfer sizes should take into account costs of accessing social services and a nutritious diet and the programme should be of a sufficient duration to address children's needs.*

10. Social cash transfer programmes can have negative impacts on child outcomes, such as encouraging child labour. *These unintended outcomes should be monitored and addressed through programme design.*

References

1,000 Days Partnership (2014) 'About 1,000 days' [online] <www.thousanddays.org/about/> [accessed 14 January 2015].

African Institute for Health and Development (AIHD) and Save the Children (2015) *A Qualitative Study on the Impact of Social Cash Transfer Programmes on the Life-course of Children*, Nairobi: Save the Children.

American Institutes for Research (AIR) (2013) *Zambia's Child Grant Program: 24-Month Impact Report* [online], AIR <www.air.org/resource/zambia%E2%80%99s-child-grant-program-24-month-impact-report> [accessed 29 April 2015].

Arnold, C., Conway, T. and Greenslade, M. (2011) *Cash Transfers Evidence Paper*, Policy Division, London: DFID.

Ayliffe, T. (2013) *Review of Child and Gender Sensitivity of National Social Assistance System in Kenya*, report for UNICEF Kenya, Nairobi: UNICEF Kenya.

Chaudhury, N. (2008) *Income Transfers and Female Schooling: The Impact of the Female School Stipend Programme on Public School Enrolments in Punjab*, Washington, DC: World Bank.

Davies, M. (2009) *DFID Social Transfers Evaluation Summary Report*, London: Department for International Development.

Davis, B. and Handa, S. (2014) *The Broad Range of Cash Transfer Impacts in Sub-Saharan Africa: Consumption, Human Capital and Productive Activity*, The Transfer Project Research Brief, FAO, Save the Children, UNICEF, University of North Carolina.

Devereux, S., Sabates-Wheeler, R., Tefera, M. and Taye, H. (2006) *Ethiopia's Productive Safety Net Programme: Trends in PSNP Transfers within Targeted Households* [pdf] IDS/INDAK <www.ids.ac.uk/download.cfm?objectid=F99718AB-5056-8171-7B9BD2F2382F1345> [accessed 29 April 2015].

DFID, HelpAge International, Hope & Homes for Children, Institute of Development Studies, International Labour Organization, Overseas Development Institute, Save the Children UK, UNDP, UNICEF and the World Bank (2009) *Advancing Child-Sensitive Social Protection* [pdf] joint statement <www.savethechildren.org.uk/sites/default/files/docs/Advancing_Child_Sensitive_Social_Protection_1.pdf> [accessed 29 April 2015].

DSD, SASSA and UNICEF (2012) *The South African Child Support Grant Impact Assessment: Evidence from a Survey of Children, Adolescents and their Households*, Pretoria: UNICEF South Africa.

Duflo, E. (2003) 'Grandmothers and granddaughters: old age pension and intra-household allocation in South Africa', *World Bank Economic Review* 17(1): 1–25.

FAO (2014) *The Economic Impacts of Cash Transfer Programmes in Sub-Saharan Africa* [pdf], From Protection to Production Policy Brief <www.fao.org/3/a-i4194e.pdf> [accessed 29 April 2015].

Freeland, N. (2013) *Mis-labelled Cash Transfers* [pdf], Pathways Perspectives on social policy in international development <www.developmentpathways.co.uk/downloads/perspectives/mislabelledcashtransfersfinal.pdf> [accessed 29 April 2015].

From Protection to Production (2014) *The Broad Range of Impacts of the LEAP Programme in Ghana*, Policy Brief, Rome: FAO.

IDS, ODI, UEA-DEV and RHVP (2010) *Social Protection in Africa: Where Next?* [pdf] <https://www.ids.ac.uk/files/dmfile/SocialProtectioninAfricaWhereNext.pdf> [accessed 29 April 2015].

International Labour Organization (ILO) (2014) *World Social Protection Report 2014–15*, Geneva: ILO.

Jones, N. and Holmes, R. (2010) *Gender, Politics and Social Protection: Why Social Protection is 'Gender Blind'*, ODI Briefing Paper, London: Overseas Development Institute.

Jones, N. and Sumner, A. (2011) *Child Poverty, Evidence and Policy: Mainstreaming Children in International Development*, Bristol: Policy Press.

Kenya CT-OVC Evaluation Team (2012) 'The impact of Kenya's cash transfer for orphans and vulnerable children on human capital', *Journal of Development Effectiveness* 4(1): 38–49.

Miller, C., Tsoka, M. and Reichert, K. (2010) 'Impacts on children of cash transfers in Malawi', in S. Handa, S. Devereux and D. Webb (eds), *Social Protection for Africa's Children*, pp. 96–116, London: Routledge Press.

Pellerano, L., Moratti, M., Jakobsen, M., Bajgar, M. and Barca, V. (2014) 'Lesotho Child Grants Programme Impact Evaluation', Follow-up Report [online], Oxford, UK: Oxford Policy Management Limited (OPM) <www.opml.co.uk/projects/lesotho-child-grants-programme-cgp-impact-evaluation> [accessed 29 April 2015].

Republic of Kenya Ministry of State for Planning (2012) *Kenya Social Protection Sector Review*, Nairobi, Kenya: Ministry of State for Planning, National Development and Vision 2030.

Roelen, K. (2014) 'Children: the key to sustainable graduation', presentation at the *Graduation and Social Protection Conference, Kigali, 6 May 2014* [pdf] <www.ids.ac.uk/files/dmfile/4.2.Roelen2014-Childrenthekeytosustainable graduationpptv205-may-14.pdf> [accessed 29 April 2015].

Roelen, K. and Sabates-Wheeler, R. (2012) 'A child-sensitive approach to social protection: serving practical and strategic needs', *Journal of Poverty and Social Justice* 20(3): 291–306 <http://dx.doi.org/10.1332/175982712X657118>.

Sabates-Wheeler, R., Devereux, S. and Hodges, A. (2009) 'Child poverty: designing child-sensitive policies', *id21 highlights*, special edition [pdf] <http://r4d.dfid.gov.uk/PDF/Outputs/IDS/highlights-child_poverty.pdf> [accessed 29 April 2015].

Save the Children (2011) *A Focus on Child Protection within Social Protection Systems: Transforming Children's Lives*, Stockholm: Save the Children.

Save the Children (2014) *Position Paper – Social Protection in Bangladesh: Priorities for Reducing Child Poverty*. Dhaka: Save the Children International Bangladesh.

Save the Children (2015a) 'About Cost of Diet' [online], Household Economy Approach <www.heawebsite.org/about-cod> [accessed 25 March 2015].

Save the Children (2015b) *Malnutrition in Bangladesh: Harnessing Social Protection for the Most Vulnerable*, London: Save the Children.

Save the Children (2015c) *The Lottery of Birth: Giving All Children an Equal Chance to Survive*, London: Save the Children.

UNICEF (2012) *Social Protection Strategic Framework*, New York: UNICEF.

UNICEF (2013) *Improving Child Nutrition: The Achievable Imperative for Global Progress*, New York: UNICEF.

UNICEF (2014) *Child Poverty in the Post-2015 Agenda* [pdf], UNICEF Issue Brief June 2014 <www.unicef.org/socialpolicy/files/Issue_Brief_Child_Poverty_in_the_post-2015_Agenda_June_2014_Final.pdf> [accessed 13 March 2015].

UNICEF and World Bank (2013) *Common Ground: UNICEF and World Bank Approaches to Building Social Protection Systems*, New York: UNICEF; Washington, DC: World Bank.

Yablonski, J. and O'Donnell, M. (2009) *Lasting Benefits: The Role of Cash Transfers in Tackling Child Mortality*, London: Save the Children.

About the authors

Nicola Hypher (n.hypher@savethechildren.org.uk) is Senior Social Protection Adviser, Save the Children, London.

Katherine Richards (k.richards@savethechildren.org.uk) is Nutrition and Inclusive Growth Policy and Advocacy Adviser, Save the Children, London

CHAPTER 5

Are graduation or rights-based programmes better for getting children out of poverty?

Stephen Devereux

Abstract

Governments such as Bangladesh are offering graduation programmes that provide transfers to extremely poor people for a fixed period in order to 'graduate' them out of poverty. Rights-based approaches emphasize a right to social protection that is not time-bound or conditional on certain behaviours. Stephen Devereux puts forward a hypothetical exchange between two NGO workers, 'The Graduator' and 'Mr Right', who are talking about life, the universe – and graduation.

Keywords: rights-based approaches, graduation programmes, social protection, cash transfers, livelihood approaches

G: Look, we all want to get children out of poverty, don't we? So graduation model programmes are the new big thing for doing this.

R: *Really? How do they work?*

G: Quite simple, actually. You find the poorest households in the village, you give them some livelihood support and special attention for a couple of years – and they graduate out of poverty!

R: *Just like that? They are no longer poor?*

G: Okay, they are still poor. But they are moderately poor. They are no longer extremely poor.

R: *So what does graduation actually mean? Graduating out of one definition of poverty into another definition of poverty?*

G: You are too cynical. It means graduation out of extreme poverty. Hundreds of thousands of people in Bangladesh. Lots of them children.

R: *Sounds expensive.*

G: It's not cheap. You give them some cash every month for a couple of years, and a productive asset like a cow that generates flows of income for them, and some training, and access to savings facilities …

R: *Sounds very expensive!*

G: In India the programme costs between US$350 and $650 per participant (Hashemi and de Montesquiou, 2011).

R: *$650 for hundreds of thousands of people! How many governments can afford that?*

http://dx.doi.org/10.3362/9781780448879.005

G: Think of it as an investment in poverty reduction. As you know, donor agencies and NGOs spend millions on development projects in poor countries every year, so governments are getting plenty of financial support for these projects. Donors see graduation programmes as good value for money.

R: *But governments cannot rely on international aid. It's not sustainable and it doesn't build national ownership. If social protection is rights-based – which it should be – it must be built on a social contract between governments and citizens. Donors are not accountable to poor people in foreign countries!*

G: That's true. But there are many creative ways that even the poorest governments can raise money to pay for social protection programmes, such as reallocating public spending or levying ring-fenced taxes (Ortiz et al., 2015). Ultimately, it's a political choice – the main constraint on social protection is not lack of money but lack of political will.

R: *Well, if it has positive impacts on poor people, that probably justifies the expense, though I wonder how cost-effective graduation programmes are compared to other, cheaper interventions.*

G: Cheaper, maybe, but less effective – how many success stories do you know of, where people get out of poverty thanks to a development project? Anyway, what's worse: giving poor people the means to make a living, or leaving them in poverty and dependent on handouts like food aid indefinitely?

R: *Okay, I can see the logic. Teaching a man to fish – or maybe giving a woman microcredit to sell fish! But isn't there a risk that giving all these goodies to people for free will make them dependent on the programme? Why would they bother to work if they know they can rely on handouts from the state?*

G: On the contrary – the whole point is to break 'dependency syndrome', not to create it. Giving people the tools they need to help themselves.

R: *But you often hear stories about unemployed men drinking away their welfare money, or teenage girls deliberately getting pregnant to get child grants, or even parents keeping their babies malnourished to stay eligible for support from the state ...*

G: Anecdotes are not evidence. Of course there are cases of abuse. But there are no rigorous studies proving that this happens on a large scale (Devereux, 2010). We hear these stories because the media loves bad news. The fact is, most social protection beneficiaries are 'good news' stories, so they don't get reported.

R: *And you're saying that graduation programmes are different, because they don't keep giving support indefinitely; they actually aim to get people out of the programme as quickly as possible?*

G: Exactly. Once participants get onto the graduation pathway you can leave them to their own devices and they'll be fine. They get self-reliant and resilient livelihoods. You no longer have to spend any public money on them.

R: *That sounds like an excuse for governments to abandon their poor citizens. Help them for a while and then it's 'goodbye and good luck – you're on your own now'. Isn't social protection supposed to be a right?*

G: People often get this confused. Everyone has a right to social protection when they need it. That's not the same as saying everybody has a right to get free cash from their government. Like the Social Protection Floor says, everyone has a right to income security – not to free income.

R: *Now you're splitting hairs. What's the difference?*

G: All the difference in the world. If you have enough income you don't need free social assistance from the state. If you have a private pension or enough savings for your retirement you don't need subsidized social insurance.

R: *So what if your graduates fall back into extreme poverty again – what happens then?*

G: Most of them don't. It's remarkable – surveys done two years after support from the programme stops found that most of the graduates stayed at the income level they achieved at graduation, and many kept improving. Very few fell back (BRAC, 2013).

R: *And what about those who did? Isn't the whole point of social protection to guarantee a safety net precisely for such situations?*

G: Fair point – these programmes tend to be a 'one-way door', so once you're out, you're out. But you can build safety nets into the system and some programmes do regular re-targeting, so you could in theory go through the revolving door every year.

R: *Anyway, what about the children? How do these graduation programmes help them?*

G: Well, obviously if you're a child in a family benefiting from these programmes and the family gets better off, the child will be better off also.

R: *'Obviously'? What about all that research that was done back in the day on intra-household allocations, which found that girls often get less than boys?*

G: 'Less than' in what way?

R: *In many contexts girls get less food, they are less likely to go to school, they won't be sent to a clinic when they are sick …*

G: Well, these sweeping generalizations are often made, but is there any hard evidence?

R: *Plenty! Amartya Sen, who won the Nobel Prize for economics, once calculated that there are over 100 million 'missing women' in Asia, due to neglect of daughters, female infanticide, gender selective abortion, and other practices that discriminate against women and girls (Sen, 1990). So we should never assume that children, especially girls, will automatically benefit from programmes that target households.*

G: That's probably why many programmes, including graduation programmes, target women as recipients. Not only because women need to be economically empowered, but because giving cash and other resources directly to women usually improves outcomes for children more than if you give this support to men.

R: *That's the same argument that is made about conditional cash transfer programmes.*

G: And they've been effective, haven't they? Good for children, and good for women.

R: *Yes, the impact evaluations are generally positive. But they are controversial.*

G: Why?

R: *Well, if you take a rights-based approach then you have to question whether it is appropriate to make social protection conditional on people behaving in certain ways.*

G: Hang on. All they have to do is send their children to school and clinics – what's so terrible about that?

R: *Shouldn't all parents send their children to school? Surely primary education should be free and compulsory for everybody, not just for poor people?*

G: Yes, but maybe some people need an incentive.

R: *Maybe poor people need an incentive, you mean! The poor are so irresponsible, aren't they?*

G: That's not fair. I thought you would approve of giving money to women and enforcing children's right to education and healthcare.

R: *Of course I do, but not if giving money to women reinforces stereotypical gender roles and makes mothers responsible for meeting punitive conditions, then taking the money away from them if they don't behave.*

G: Actually the conditionalities are often 'soft' – if families fail to comply a social worker or case manager tries to find out what the problem is and offers appropriate support.

R: *'Cuddly conditionalities' – now I've heard everything!*

G: Anyway, what about the rights of the child that you always like to go on and on about? Doesn't that justify insisting that parents treat their children well?

R: *It's a balancing act, isn't it? There's the right of the household to social protection, and then there's the right of the child to education and health. Do we have the 'right' – pardon the pun – to make the one conditional on the other?*

G: Are these trade-offs inevitable?

R: *Sometimes it looks like it. Take the Productive Safety Net Programme in Ethiopia, which tries to graduate poor rural families out of food insecurity by offering employment on public works projects to men and women, and asset packages that promote secondary livelihood activities. What do you think happened to children's well-being in these families?*

G: Hmm. Economics 101 predicts that higher incomes should lead to more investment in children's education and less need for children to work to contribute to the household's income, so I would deduce that school attendance increased and child labour decreased.

R: *That's the income effect, but economic theory also identifies a substitution effect. If you think about it, public works programmes and asset transfers that promote income-generating activities both increase the demand for household labour, and child labour and adult labour are substitutes. So which effect do you think dominated: the income effect or the substitution effect?*

G: As you know, I believe in graduation programmes, so I have to say the income effect dominated. Please tell me I'm right.

R: *It's not that straightforward. You have to disaggregate the children by age cohort and sex. Boys and older girls benefited by working fewer hours, but girls aged 6 to 10 had to do more work and they went to school less often* (Hoddinott et al., 2011).

G: And how do we explain that?

R: *Probably the girls had to stay home and look after their younger siblings while their mother was out doing public works or other livelihood activities.*

G: So now you're arguing that women should stay at home and look after the children? Not very progressive, Mr Rights!

R: *Not at all. We just need to make livelihood programmes more gender- and child-sensitive, by providing childcare facilities on public works sites, for instance* (Holmes and Jones, 2013).

G: Even so, it's worrying that there are these trade-offs.

R: *Yes, and it has led some people to argue that graduation programmes focus too much on achieving short-term improvements and not enough on transforming lives and livelihoods in a sustainable way.*

G: How do you mean?

R: *Surely the real test for graduation is whether children grow up less poor than their parents, which means investing in their development, not creating incentives for their parents to take them out of school. Graduation isn't truly sustainable unless it's 'intergenerational graduation'* (Roelen, 2015).

G: Let's agree on that then. Graduation for all – long may it last!

References

Hashemi, S. and de Montesquiou, A. (2011) 'Reaching the poorest: lessons from the graduation model', *Focus Note* 69, Washington, DC: CGAP.

Ortiz, I., Cummins, M. and Karunanethy, K. (2015) 'Fiscal space for social protection: options to expand social investments in 187 countries', *ESS Working Paper,* no. 48, Geneva: ILO.

Devereux, S. (2010) 'Dependency and graduation', *Frontiers of Social Protection Brief,* Number 5. Johannesburg: Regional Hunger and Vulnerability Programme (RHVP).

BRAC (2013) 'An end in sight for ultra-poverty: scaling up BRAC's Graduation Model for the poorest', *Briefing Note 1: Ending Extreme Poverty,* Dhaka: BRAC.

Sen, A. (1990) 'More than 100 million women are missing', *New York Review of Books,* 20 December, pp. 61–6.

Hoddinott, J., Gilligan, D. and Taffesse, A.S. (2011) 'The impact of Ethiopia's Productive Safety Net Program on schooling and child labor', in S. Handa,

S. Devereux and D. Webb (eds), *Social Protection for Africa's Children*, pp. 71–95, London: Routledge.

Holmes, R. and Jones, N. (2013) *Gender and Social Protection in the Developing World: Beyond Mothers and Safety Nets*. London: Zed Books.

Roelen, K. (2015) 'The 'twofold investment trap': children and their role in sustainable graduation', *IDS Bulletin* 46(2): 25–34.

About the author

Stephen Devereux (s.devereux@ids.ac.uk) is a development economist working predominantly on food security, famine, rural livelihoods, social protection and poverty reduction issues. He is a research fellow at the Institute of Development Studies, University of Sussex.

CHAPTER 6

Does wealth increase affect school enrolment in ultra-poor households: evidence from an experiment in Bangladesh

Munshi Sulaiman

Abstract

Access to education is usually found to be highly correlated with household income and wealth. This correlation often instigates an expectation that increasing income of the poor households will lead to greater human capital accumulation. This paper exploits randomized roll-out of a large-scale livelihood development programme for the ultra-poor in Bangladesh to measure the effect of asset transfer and livelihood supports on children's schooling. We find limited impact on enrolment although this programme has been extremely successful in transforming the economic lives of the ultra-poor and causing substantial increases in their income and productive assets. The beneficiary households are also found to have increased their expenditures on education. This increase in educational investment, however, has not affected educational attainment during the evaluation period. We also find that the programme increased the extent of child labour immediately after asset transfers. The level of this impact on children's work declines two years after the interventions ended. The increases in child labour are concentrated in activities related to livestock rearing, which is the primary type of asset transferred in this programme. However, we do not find evidence indicating a trade-off between children's enrolment and work. The evidence suggests that asset transfer programmes can be more effective by including additional components focusing on improvement in educational outcomes instead of relying primarily on spillover effects through income gain.

Keywords: asset transfer, school enrolment, programme evaluation, Bangladesh

FOSTERING HUMAN CAPITAL ACCUMULATION by the poor is one of the key priorities in development. Besides its intrinsic value, human capital accumulation through education is important for breaking intergenerational poverty traps (Barham et al., 1995; Solon, 1999; Chadwick and Solon, 2002; Levine and Jellema, 2007). Therefore, how to increase school enrolment and educational achievements, especially for children from poorer socio-economic backgrounds, is an important policy question for developing countries. Since educational achievement is often strongly associated with household income and wealth

http://dx.doi.org/10.3362/9781780448879.006

(Glewwe and Jacoby, 2004; Grimm, 2011; UNESCO, 2011), anti-poverty programmes that are successful in increasing income of poor households have the potential to create a positive spillover effect on school enrolment of their children. On the other hand, such programmes can also have adverse effects on children's education depending on the form of support in these programmes. For example, an increase in productive assets of the poor can increase the demand for child labour and a large enough increase in child labour can reduce school enrolment (Cockburn and Dostie, 2007). This paper provides experimental evidence on the impact of an asset transfer programme for the ultra-poor in Bangladesh on children's schooling.

The programme is called 'Challenging the Frontier of Poverty Reduction/ Targeting Ultra-Poor' (CFPR/TUP), which was designed and implemented by an NGO called BRAC in Bangladesh since 2002. This programme is also known as the 'graduation model'. In this programme, ultra-poor households are provided with income-generating assets (mostly livestock) along with a range of other supports – including training, stipends, free health care facility, and input supports for their livestock for a specified period – in order to enable them to obtain a more stable livelihood. Evaluations of this approach in Bangladesh indicate that the programme has substantial effects on increasing wealth and income of the participant households (Emran et al., 2014; Ahmed et al., 2009; Rabbani et al., 2006). In a randomized evaluation, Bandiera et al. (2013) confirm large positive impacts of the programme on wealth and income, and transformational effects on livelihood security at the end of the 2-year intervention. More importantly, the sizes of impact on several key indicators have increased further after 4 years (i.e. 2 years after end of programme), clearly demonstrating sustainability of these gains.

In this paper, we use data from the experimental evaluation to assess whether the increase in wealth has also caused any intra-household spillover effect on school enrolment of the children. We do not find any significant impact on school enrolment rates for either boys or girls at the end of the programme. This lack of impact is observed at both primary and secondary school age levels. The only positive effect on enrolment rate is observed for secondary school-aged boys after 4 years with an effect size of 7.7 per cent. In terms of new enrolment, there is also a positive impact of 4.7 per cent after 4 years on children who were 3–5 years old at baseline. Besides these modest long-term effects on enrolment, the intervention households are also found to have been spending more on children's education than the control group. In terms of grade repetition, a crude measure of quality of education, there is no major effect. Although girls of primary school age were 7 per cent more likely to have repeated a grade during the intervention phase, this negative effect is no longer observed after 4 years.

On the other hand, programme participation had significant immediate impact on increasing the amount of child work for both boys and girls, especially of secondary school age. Concentration of this effect in livestock-rearing activities indicates that the increased demand for child labour is related to livestock transfers. The magnitude of effects on child work, however, decreased after 4 years. We do not find any effect on children's engagement in household chores as a result of their households' being in the programme. Changes in child work also do not show any clear association with the change in their enrolment status after 4 years. We observe statistically significant increases in child labour in beneficiary households irrespective of whether they were enrolled or not. We conclude that these effects on child work do not explain the limited effects on school enrolment.

Given that the particular approach of asset transfer followed in TUP has been very successful in creating greater economic opportunities for the ultra-poor and pathways out of extreme poverty, this slow progress in human capital accumulation by their children needs to be considered for further improvement in the model's effectiveness. This is even more important considering the inter-generational persistence of extreme poverty. There are a number of similar graduation programmes being initiated in several countries encouraged by the successes of this model on the livelihood front. These initiatives may benefit by looking beyond the current graduation models in designing interventions, and aiming to impact livelihood and children's welfare simultaneously. For instance, the transfers in TUP are not conditional on school enrolment of the children. Using the case of PROGRESA, de Brauw and Hoddinott (2011) have shown that it is the conditionality rather than the transfers per se that influences investment in human capital. Therefore, applying conditionality or providing other educational supports targeting school enrolment for the ultra-poor households should be tested in new graduation initiatives.

The paper is organized as follows. The next section briefly describes the context in terms of inequality in access to education across different income groups in Bangladesh. There follows a discussion of the TUP programme, the experiment design, and data. The results of average effects on school enrolment and child labour are then presented followed by a conclusion with policy implications of the findings.

Poverty and school enrolment in Bangladesh

Access to education is usually associated with the economic well-being of the households. In this section, we briefly examine the variations in school enrolment across different poverty groups in Bangladesh. For this, we rank the households in the national Household Income and Expenditure Survey (HIES-2005) into quintiles by their per capita adult-equivalent expenditure. BRAC sometimes uses the term 'ultra-poor' to refer to the poorest 10 per cent in income distribution. Therefore, we also separate the households of the poorest quintile into two deciles to observe existence of any inequality in access to education within the poorest end of this welfare distribution.

Table 1 shows the net primary and secondary enrolment rates for boys and girls across different expenditure quintiles. We observe significant differences in the net enrolment rates, at both primary and secondary levels, between children living in the poorest and the second poorest quintiles. Boys belonging to households of the poorest quintile had a net primary enrolment rate of 57 per cent, which was significantly lower than the second poorest quintile (65 per cent) in 2005. Despite government initiatives for universal primary education since the early 1990s, this difference in access to education at primary level is quite noteworthy. Significant differences are observed within the bottom quintile as well. When these households are split into two deciles, enrolment rates for the bottom decile are found to be lower (at 53 per cent) compared to the second poorest decile (61 per cent). Similar differences are observed for net primary enrolment rates of girls (60 per cent vs. 66 per cent), and for net secondary enrolment of boys (14 per cent and 27 per cent) and girls (27 per cent and 35 per cent). This pattern of inequality in access to education is sometimes presented to argue that increasing household income for the ultra-poor will lead to an increase in the school enrolment rates of their children (e.g. Maitra, 2003). Using impact evaluation data, we demonstrate that this association does not necessarily imply an automatic chain of impacts.

BRAC's ultra-poor programme and evaluation design

Programme description

BRAC has been a pioneer NGO in implementing programmes that target the extreme poor in Bangladesh, and the ultra-poor programme is one of their more recent initiatives. This paper focuses on the second phase of this programme, which started in 2007 with the aim of reaching over 800,000 households in 40 districts of the country by 2011. The programme targets

Table 1 Net enrolment rates among household expenditure groups (2005)

Household category	Net primary		Net secondary	
	Boys	**Girls**	**Boys**	**Girls**
Poorest quintile	57	63	20	31
2nd quintile	65	68	31	43
3rd quintile	72	70	38	54
4th quintile	74	77	54	63
Richest quintile	81	80	69	72
Total	68	71	41	51
t-test (bottom two quintiles)	3.09***	1.88**	4.71***	4.47***
2nd decile	61	66	27	35
Bottom decile	53	60	14	27
t-test (bottom two deciles)	2.58**	1.69*	4.14***	2.24**

Note: *** $p<0.01$, ** $p<0.05$, * $p<0.1$
Source: Estimates from HIES-2005

ultra-poor women in rural areas who are unable to access mainstream social protection programmes.

This programme aims to empower the poorest women economically, socially, and psychologically through a multi-faceted intervention package. Participant women are provided with a combination of productive assets (usually cows, goats, poultry, or seeds for vegetable cultivation) as the main entry point. Although some of the other services, such as healthcare, are provided to all the members of beneficiary households and the programme is viewed as a household-level intervention, all the transfers are made through a woman member of each household. They commit to retain and manage the asset for two years but they are allowed to sell it or exchange it for another income-generating asset within that period.

The asset transfer is accompanied with skills training, specific to the type of asset provided. A trained asset specialist visits each beneficiary household every 1–2 months during the first year of the programme. In addition, BRAC programme officers visit them weekly for about 18 months to ensure that these ultra-poor women, who have limited prior experience of running a business on their own, are fully supported.

To compensate for any short-run fall in income due to the occupational shift, a weekly subsistence allowance is provided for the first 40 weeks, which is until the participants learn to manage the assets well enough to generate a regular flow of income. Between 18 and 24 months into the programme, the beneficiaries also take part in confidence building sessions about how to use microfinance and are enrolled in village-level microfinance groups.

Other components of the programme include savings facility, preventive and curative health care services, and social development support involving training on legal, social, and political rights. The ultra-poor households receive monthly visits from a health volunteer and get access to BRAC's legal services. There are also provisions for full cost of treatment if any member of the beneficiary households suffers a major illness. These health supports are designed to reduce costly morbidity and distress sales of assets. In addition, BRAC initiates the establishment of village committees that bring together representatives from the village elite and ultra-poor households. These committees extend social and financial supports to all the beneficiary households. Matin et al. (2008) give a more elaborate explanation of the programme components and their purposes.

Targeting

At the first step, geographical targeting is done to determine which district and sub-districts are to be selected for the programme. These are chosen to be the most vulnerable parts of the country in terms of food insecurity mapping conducted by the World Food Programme (WFP). After this site selection, teams from respective local BRAC branch offices select the relatively poorer communities within their operational area.

The programme uses a combination of participatory wealth ranking and survey methods to identify the ultra-poor households in each community. A participatory rural appraisal (PRA) is conducted to list all the households in a village and to divide them into 4–5 community-defined wealth categories. Households ranked in the lowest wealth group become the 'community-defined ultra-poor'.

In the final stage of targeting, the BRAC team visits these community-defined ultra-poor households and conducts a brief survey. This data is used to determine programme eligibility based on pre-defined selection criteria. There are three exclusion criteria, all of which are binding. Households who are already borrowing from a microfinance institute, who are recipients of any government anti-poverty programmes, and who have no adult woman in their members, are excluded from the programme. Furthermore, to be selected into the programme, a household has to satisfy at least three of the following five inclusion criteria: 1) total land owned including homestead is not more than 10 decimals; 2) there is no adult male income earner in the household; 3) adult women in the household work outside the homestead; 4) school-aged children have to work; and 5) the household has no productive assets. After further cross-checks by branch managers, to make sure that the information provided in the survey is correct, the households satisfying at least three of these inclusion criteria and none of the exclusion criteria are defined as the Specially Targeted Ultra-Poor (STUP) households. All these STUP households are targeted by the programme and receive the full intervention package.

Evaluation strategy and survey design

The roll-out of the programme was randomized to identify the effects of the programme by comparing the changes in treated to control households before and after the interventions. Details of the randomization protocol are available in the main impact evaluation paper by Bandiera et al. (2013). Randomization was done at branch office level so that all selected communities within a branch were treated either in 2007 or after 2011. We survey all ultra-poor households selected by the programme in these branches at baseline and every two years, and the programme rolled-out in control areas after the second follow-up survey. Data used in this paper covers a total of 40 branches (of which 20 are treated), 1,409 villages and 6,814 STUP households who have been interviewed both in the baseline (in 2007) and in the two follow-up surveys (in 2009 and 2011).

Ultra-poor households were selected, using the targeting method outlined above, at the same time in both treatment and control branches. The only difference between them is that the ultra-poor in treated branches received the assets and other interventions immediately after baseline whereas the ultra-poor in control branches received those after 2011. The baseline survey was carried out to measure the pre-programme characteristics of treatment and control households. Bandiera et al. (2013) find that the STUP households from treatment and control branches had very similar characteristics at baseline. Imbens and Wooldridge (2009) suggest the normalized differences between treatment and control groups should be less than 0.25, as a rule of thumb, for consistency of estimates. Normalized differences between the two groups are found to be lower than 0.15 for a range of baseline characteristics for this evaluation.

The first follow-up survey was carried out on the same households during January–December 2009. There were on average 800 (minimum 511, maximum 987) days in between the baseline and follow-up surveys for a household. This implies that by the time we observed the treated households at follow-up the most intensive part of the programme was just completed. The second follow-up in 2011 was done to measure the sustainability of the effects 2 years after the end of all interventions.

Findings

In this section we present the estimates of average effects of programme participation on school enrolment, a few other education-related indicators, and extent of child labour. We measure the average impact using the following difference-in-difference estimate

$$y_{ijt} = \beta_0 + \beta_1 treat_j + \beta_2 followup_t + \beta_3 treat_j \times followup_t + u_{ijt} \qquad (1)$$

where y_{it} is a dummy equal to 1 if the individual i from household j in time t is enrolled in school and 0 otherwise. $Treat_j$ is a dummy for household j being assigned to treatment in the randomized experiment, $followup_t$ is a dummy equal to 1 for each follow-up survey period and u_{ijt} is the error term. The coefficient of the interactions between treatment and follow-up surveys (β_3) identify the impacts of the programme under two key assumptions of: 1) common trend between treatment and control groups; and 2) no spillover effect on the control group. Since the control households come from villages located within control branch offices, there is no concern about spillover effect on them. We also look into the average effects after controlling for individual and household characteristics at baseline. While the baseline characteristics are uncorrelated with treatment status, thanks to randomization, and unlikely to affect the coefficients, inclusion of these controls can improve precision of the estimated impacts. We, however, do not find any qualitative difference between the estimates with and without the baseline controls and, therefore, present only the estimates without controls.

Before presenting the estimates of the impact on the children's outcomes, Figure 1 graphically presents the impact of the programme on household wealth. In this graph, average values of total household assets at baseline and follow-up surveys (in 2007 price) are presented by their intervention status. This shows that these two groups of households owned a similar level of assets at baseline. While the households in control branches experienced some growth

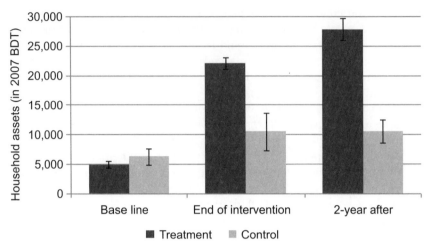

Figure 1 Average asset growth between treatment and control

in assets between baseline and follow-up, the growth was substantially higher for the treatment households. By the end of programme interventions at first follow-up, treatment households owned about twice the amount of assets of the control group. This impact on asset ownership increases further at the second follow-up, and the impacts are substantially larger than the amount of assets they received from the programme. This shows that the beneficiary households have not only managed to retain the assets but also have accumulated further assets. Bandiera et al. (2013) critically evaluate the impact of the programme on income, economic activities, and assets. They find very large effects on all these dimensions, and the graph is presented to put the main effects of the programme into perspective.

Effects on schooling

Table 2 presents impact estimates on school enrolment for the cohorts of boys and girls who are of primary (6–10 years) and secondary (11–15 years) school age during the three survey rounds. Enrolment rate for boys of primary school age in control households was 73 per cent at baseline (Column 1). There was no significant difference between the children in treatment and control groups at baseline. There was also no significant change in these enrolment rates between the baseline and the follow-up surveys for control group. The difference-in-difference estimate on the enrolment rate of primary school age boys after 2 years (at the first follow-up) is –0.04 and statistically not significant. Average effect of 2 per cent for this cohort after 4 years is also not significant. This implies that the programme did not have a significant impact on enrolment rate of these boys.

The same average effects have been measured separately for girls of primary school age (Column 2), and for secondary school age boys (Column 3) and

Table 2 Average effect on school enrolment

	Primary school age		Secondary school age		All children of school going age
	Boys	Girls	Boys	Girls	
	(1)	(2)	(3)	(4)	(5)
Treatment (1=Yes, 0=No)	0.028 (0.02)	0.038 (0.02)	−0.038 (0.03)	0.029 (0.03)	0.017 (0.02)
Follow-up 1 (2 years after)	0.014 (0.02)	0.028 (0.02)	0.046 (0.03)*	0.053 (0.03)*	0.021 (0.01)*
Follow-up 2 (4 years after)	0.039 (0.02)	0.064 (0.02)***	0.182 (0.03)***	0.165 (0.03)***	0.082 (0.01)***
Programme effect after 2 years	−0.041 (0.03)	−0.018 (0.03)	0.052 (0.03)	−0.053 (0.04)	−0.014 (0.02)
Programme effect after 4 years	0.017 (0.03)	−0.030 (0.03)	0.077 (0.04)**	−0.023 (0.04)	0.010 (0.02)
Constant (control group at baseline)	0.725 (0.02)***	0.736 (0.02)***	0.400 (0.02)***	0.515 (0.02)***	0.620 (0.01)***
Observations	5,190	4,669	4,205	3,811	17,875
R-squared	0.005	0.003	0.037	0.019	0.007

Note: Children categorized by their age in survey years. Standard errors in parenthesis clustered at village level; *** $p<0.01$, ** $p<0.05$, * $p<0.1$

girls (Column 4). Column 5 gives the average effects estimated for all the children in the 6–15 years age cohorts. The results show that none of these impacts is statistically significant, except for the effect on boys of secondary school age after 4 years. There is a 7.7 per cent increase in enrolment for these boys in intervention households compared to the control group at the second follow-up. Most of these not significant effects are quite precisely estimated. For instance, we can reject any positive effect of least 4 per cent on enrolment of girls at 5 per cent significance level after both 2 and 4 years. The evidence clearly shows that the programme did not have any impact on enrolment after 2 years, but there is a long-term positive effect on secondary school enrolment of boys. Boys of secondary school age had a lower enrolment rate (40 per cent) than the girls of the same age group (51 per cent). Both boys and girls of this age bracket have experienced similar general improvement, shown by the changes in control groups, during the 4 years (18 vs. 17 per cent). The interventions impacting enrolment of only secondary school-aged boys (and not the girls) can be a potential 'catch-up' effect. Greater emphasis by the government on secondary school scholarships for girls than for boys can also be a reason for this difference. Further investigation of this scholarship programme hypothesis would require collecting data on scholarships available in these communities. Figure 2 gives a visual depiction of this general lack of impact on enrolment rates for all school-aged children.

Despite the huge successes of the programme in increasing income and assets of the beneficiaries, the lack of impact on enrolment is a cause of concern. It is possible that it takes longer than 2 or 4 years for the increases in asset or income to influence children's education-related outcomes and here we look at relatively short-run effects. However, using non-participant ultra-poor households from the treatment villages as a comparison group in an evaluation of the previous phase of this programme, Sulaiman (2010) does not find any significant effect on children's school enrolment after 3 to 6 years of programme participation.

Although enrolment rate is the most common measure of access to education, there are other aspects of education that could potentially be influenced by wealth. More importantly, enrolment does not reflect the students' performance in schools or education attainments. It is possible that the programme may have affected achievement of the students if households invested more in quality of education than in its quantity. Table 3 looks into the effect on three different indicators related to access and household investments in education. Columns 1 and 2 measure the effect on new enrolment for boys and girls who are 3–5 years old and not enrolled at baseline. Among these boys, 43 per cent and 80 per cent in the control group get enrolled 2 and 4 years later, respectively. There is no statistical difference between treatment and control group after 2 years, but it is 4.7 per cent higher for treatment group after 4 years. It indicates that the programme may have some influence on household decisions for fresh enrolments for boys. However, this difference is not statistically strong with 10 per cent level of significance. We do not find any positive effect on this indicator for girls.

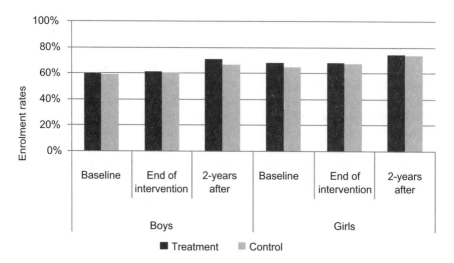

Figure 2 Enrolment rates of all school-aged (primary and secondary) children

Table 3 Average effects on new enrolment, private tutoring, and education expenses

	New enrolment of children aged 3–5 years at baseline		Private supplementary tutoring		Household expenses on education	
	Boys	Girls	Primary	Secondary	All eligible	Trimmed
	(1)	(2)	(3)	(4)	(5)	(6)
Treatment (1=Yes, 0=No)	—	—	−0.019 (0.02)	−0.011 (0.03)	−3.568 (56.12)	29.601 (38.50)
Follow-up 1 (2-years after)	0.429 (0.03)***	0.462 (0.03)***	−0.023 (0.02)	−0.010 (0.02)	220.554 (85.65)**	89.353 (33.26)***
Follow-up 2 (4-years after)	0.804 (0.02)***	0.826 (0.02)***	0.035 (0.02)*	0.121 (0.03)***	120.647 (45.76)***	173.363 (36.84)***
Programme effect after 2 years	−0.010 (0.03)	−0.024 (0.04)	0.035 (0.02)*	0.034 (0.03)	−45.800 (101.94)	16.260 (44.51)
Programme effect after 4 years	0.047 (0.03)*	−0.004 (0.03)	0.035 (0.02)	0.008 (0.04)	498.059 (95.45)***	152.872 (52.11)***
Constant (control group at baseline)	—	—	0.136 (0.01)***	0.186 (0.02)***	589.491 (37.24)***	504.942 (25.32)***
Observations	2,977	2,769	7,528	4,314	8,428	8,343
R-squared	0.688	0.684	0.006	0.020	0.011	0.017

Note: Columns 1 and 2 compare enrolment rates of children who were below schooling age at baseline and were not enrolled. Columns 3 and 4 are children of school age groups in survey years and are enrolled in the respective survey rounds. Column 5 includes all households with at least one child of school-going age, and column 6 drops the 1 per cent observations with the highest amounts spent for education. Standard errors in parenthesis clustered at village level; *** $p<0.01$, ** $p<0.05$, * $p<0.1$

Columns 3 and 4 measure the programme effects on the extent of supplementary private tutoring for students at primary and secondary schools. Private tutoring has been becoming a norm in Bangladesh even at primary level (Nath, 2008). Given that a large portion of the students in these ultra-poor households are first generation learners, they need such tutoring the most although their parents can least afford it. The point estimates of effects on this indicator are positive although have weak statistical significance only for boys in primary schools (3.5 per cent) after 2 years. Therefore, we can rule out any consistent effect on increasing supplementary private tutoring. In terms of household expenses for education, Table 3 shows positive effects after 4 years in households with at least one child attending primary or secondary schools. The effect sizes are substantial compared to the baseline mean of control group – about 85 per cent impact if all the households are included and 30 per cent impact when the outliers (5 per cent observations with the highest amounts spent) are dropped. These results suggest that the increase in wealth and income could influence households' educational investments in the long run although we do not see strong short-term impacts on enrolments.

Data on test scores and other schooling outcomes were not collected in this study. As a proxy for school achievement, we can measure the effects of the programme on grade repetition (attending the same grade for more than one year) by the enrolled in schools. Table 4 presents the estimated impacts on grade repetition for children who were enrolled both at baseline and the respective follow-up surveys. We find that the programme did not have any significant impact on grade repetition for boys. The likelihoods of grade repetition significantly increased (by 7 per cent) for girls of primary school age (Column 3) after 2 years. One explanation for this increase in grade repetition could have been that more households in the intervention group are letting their poorly performing girls stay in schools who would otherwise drop out. This explanation implies that we would see a positive effect on net enrolment, which is not the case. Therefore, there is a short-term effect on lower educational attainment for girls. This negative effect on school attainment is no longer observed after 4 years.

Our analysis could potentially go beyond these average effects. For instance, it is possible that influence of asset or income increase on human capital accumulation is determined by the quality of schools that they can access. However, there are many such dimensions that one could possibly look at for heterogeneity of impacts. Without very strong prior reasoning, such analyses are susceptible to false discoveries. With this important caution, we also looked at heterogeneity of impacts on enrolment by distance to the nearest primary/secondary schools, sex of household head, and the number of siblings of schooling age (results not presented). We do not find any significantly consistent pattern from this analysis.

Effects on children's work

Table 5 presents the impact estimates on child labour using the same difference-in-difference specification, where the dependent variables are total hours spent in the last year in any earning activities, in livestock rearing, and in household chores. For simplicity, we present only the effect sizes and control group average at baseline.

Point estimates of the impacts on total hours of work are between 38 and 66 hours for children of primary school age after 2 years (Columns 1 and 4 in Panel A). Quite understandably, the effects are relatively larger for older children (between 157 and 239 hours in Panel B). These average effects translate to about 25 to 40 minutes of total work per day. This does not appear to be extremely high. The magnitudes of the effects also reduce substantially after 4 years for secondary school-age girls, who had the highest increase in 2 years. However, an important question related to this child work and welfare is the type of activities that they are engaged in.

Columns 2 and 5 show that the major portion of the effects on overall child labour comes from increase in activities related to livestock rearing, especially by secondary school-aged children. The level of increase in hours spent on livestock-related activities does not vary significantly between boys and girls. Similar to the pattern of impacts on total hours of work in any earning activity, there are significant drops in the effect sizes after 4 years. Using household level aggregates of children's work as an indicator, Bandiera et al. (2013) also show the same pattern in declining effects on child labour. While it is encouraging for the programme, there is a lack of adequate explanation of this decline. We can rule out this being a potential cohort effect, whereby the intervention effects decline as the children get older and stop doing particular types of work. If this were a cohort effect, we would have observed such a decline when measuring impacts by comparing intervention and control children by their baseline age cohorts, but less sharper declines by comparing children in the same age groups of the survey years. We do not see any difference in the impact estimates by these two alternative cohort analyses (results available upon request). One conjecture based on anecdotal evidence is that some children start helping their families with livestock rearing out of excitement, which may subside over time (Sulaiman, 2010). Finally, we do not find any programme effect on children's engagement in household chores. Although these results show that transfer of assets for livelihood promotion can have an immediate increase in child labour for the ultra-poor households and this effect may taper off gradually, these do not necessarily imply a trade-off between child labour and school enrolment.

To explore how the changes in time spent for earning activities are associated with the changes in enrolment, Figure 3 shows the average changes in hours spent in livestock rearing by the changes in enrolment status of the

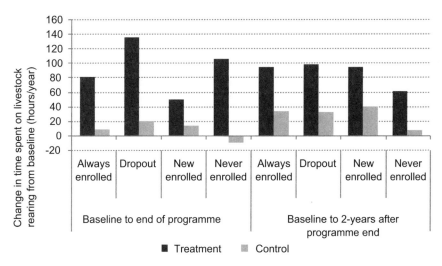

Figure 3 Association between change in enrolment and change in livestock hours

children. Since these changes happen simultaneously after the programme interventions, we cannot assess causality between the changes in these two indicators. However, there are three key patterns that we observe in this graph. First, conforming to the previous average effects, the graph shows that the treatment households had larger increases in the amount of child labour in livestock rearing compared to control. Second, there are noticeable differences across the four enrolment groups in treatment households after 2 years. Children from treatment households who dropped out between the two survey rounds had the highest increase in time spent on livestock rearing. On the other hand, the newly enrolled children experienced the lowest increase in their hours of work in this activity. Always enrolled and never enrolled children observed a similar increase in their work hours between the two rounds. Finally, these associations between change in enrolment and change in children's work hours in livestock rearing become far less prominent after 4 years.

The extent of the increase in work hours for always enrolled children in treatment households implies that increased child labour cannot be the main explanation for lack of impact on enrolment. Overall it seems that the increase in work hours is most likely to be happening through reduced leisure. Nonetheless, this increase in demand for children's work, albeit small, is an aspect to be aware of in designing and implementing livelihood promotion programmes.

Policy implications and conclusion

The results presented in this paper show that the asset transfers in this graduation model did not have any major immediate impact on school enrolment of children and increased the extent of child labour. Despite its laudable successes in accelerating growth in income of the ultra-poor households, this is an important concern in measuring success of this approach to poverty reduction, especially in the context of breaking inter generational poverty traps through increased human capital accumulation. Since household poverty is found to be a key determinant of access to education, progress in poverty reduction is often expected to yield improvement in education. For example, Maitra (2003) claims that educational attainment of children increases with an increased permanent income of the household in Bangladesh. This paper has demonstrated that improvement in schooling does not automatically follow an increase in income and wealth.

The Consultative Group to Assist the Poor (CGAP), in association with Ford Foundation, has undertaken major initiatives to test and scale-up this livelihood approach in over 10 countries. Experimental evaluations under their Graduation programme show large effects of the model on income and assets of the ultra-poor beneficiaries in India, Pakistan, Ethiopia, Ghana, and Peru (Banerjee et al., forthcoming). The magnitudes and sustainability of the effects on livelihood outcomes make the model a potentially attractive tool in social protection programmes in many developing countries. Although improving educational outcomes is usually not a primary objective of this model, there is scope for making future initiatives more effective by incorporating new aspects in the package. The findings presented in this paper have similar implications also for other livelihood promotion programmes.

One particular avenue to explore for improving educational outcomes is making (parts of) the transfer conditional on schooling. In recent years, there has been a surge in the number of conditional transfer programmes to promote schooling and other human capital accumulation by the poor. Triggered by the success of PROGRESA, a number of conditional cash transfer (CCT) programmes have been initiated in many developing countries. A large and growing literature has demonstrated the positive effects of CCTs on school enrolment (e.g. Skoufias, 2005; Attanasio et al., 2006). While there is a general consensus across studies about the positive effects on enrolment, there is relatively less consistency in the evidence on children's performance in schools (Garcia and Hill, 2010). Barham et al. (2013) find that even the short-term impacts on enrolment achieved by a 3-year CCT could result in significant difference in learning outcomes after 10 years. Given the differences in effects on school enrolment between the two types of programmes, the conditionality aspect of cash transfer can be tested within the graduation model. In fact, using the case of PROGRESA, de Brauw and Hoddinott (2011) show that it is the conditionality, rather than the transfer itself, that influences investment in human capital. Baird et al. (2011), in their experimental study of conditionality with cash transfers in Malawi, also find significant influence of conditionality on school attendance and learning outcomes for adolescent girls. This study, however, also finds that unconditional transfer reduces teenage pregnancy and marriage rates for school dropouts, which is naturally not feasible to achieve with conditionality of school attendance. Despite this debate on outcomes beyond education for non-enrolled children, the existing evidence supports a policy suggestion of piloting conditionality in livelihood programmes that involve transfers.

These two approaches, graduation vs. CCT, are different not only in imposing conditionality but also in many other important aspects. The form of transfer (cash vs. productive assets) is one of the other key important differences. While asset transfer in the ultra-poor programme has been found successful in increasing income of the poor, this approach has also increased the demand for child labour in the beneficiary households. Change in the demand for child labour is often identified as an important link in the 'poverty-education nexus' (Amin et al., 2004) although there is weak correlation between child labour and school enrolment (Ravallion and Wodon, 2000) in Bangladesh. Using detailed information of time use by the children in rural Ethiopia, Cockburn and Dostie (2007) find that demand for child labour increases with asset accumulation. According to their findings, an increase in the ownership of livestock increases demand for child labour while an increase in income reduces child labour and increases demand for education. The net effect is determined by the relative magnitudes of these two effects. However, the findings in this paper do not indicate increased child labour as a key constraint in achieving impact on education.

Evaluations of CCTs, in general, observe a decrease in child labour (Schultz, 2004; Skoufias, 2005). In their evaluation of a CCT programme in rural Colombia, Attanasio et al. (2006) find that time spent in education and work are not complete substitutes for each other. Children may draw some of their time from leisure to increase time spent in schools. It is likely that a similar reallocation of time between leisure and work happens because of asset transfers, especially when the asset management requires work that can be done by a child. Therefore, through adding conditionality in asset transfer programmes, it might be possible to influence enrolment with/without a simultaneous increase in child labour. Given that the largest effect on children's work observed is about 40 minutes per day and these effects decline significantly after 4 years, a direct focus on education seems to hold more promise than trying to avoid any increase in children's work. The process of imposing conditionality, however, needs to be thought through. While cash transfers can stop when the household fails to meet the conditionality, asset transfers are mostly done in one go and may not have the same level of enforceability. Alternatively, other supports in this graduation model (such as the weekly allowance) can potentially be tied to children's school attendance.

It is also important to highlight that the programme participants in this evaluation are found to have increased their investments in education after 4 years. This shows that the increase in wealth does have some spillover effects on education. The main argument is that the process can be very slow, and livelihood programmes can be more proactive in influencing inter generational poverty dynamics by focusing on greater human capital accumulation.

References

Ahmed, A.U., Rabbani, M., Sulaiman, M. and Das, N. (2009) *The Impact of Asset Transfer on Livelihoods of the Ultra Poor in Bangladesh*, Research Monograph Series no. 39, Dhaka: Research and Evaluation Division, BRAC.

Amin, S., Quayes, M.S. and Rives, J.M. (2004) 'Poverty and other determinants of child labor in Bangladesh', *Southern Economic Journal* 70(4): 876–92.

Attanasio, O., Emla, F., Ana, G., Diana, L., Costas, M. and Alice, M. (2006) *Child Education and Work Choices in the Presence of a Conditional Cash Transfer Programme in Rural Colombia*, Working Paper No. 06/13, London: Institute for Fiscal Studies (IFS).

Baird, S., McIntosh, C. and Ozler, B. (2011) 'Cash or condition? Evidence from a cash transfer experiment', *Quarterly Journal of Economics* 126: 1709–53 <http://dx.doi.org/10.1093/qje/qjr032>.

Banerjee. A., Duflo, E., Goldberge, N., Karlan, D., Osei, R., Pariente, W., Shapiro, J., Thuysbaert, B. and Udry, C. (2015) 'A multi-faceted livelihood program leads to sustained improvements in the lives of the poorest of the poor: Evidence from randomized controlled trials in six countries', *Science*, 348(6236): 1–16 <dx.doi.org/10.1126/science.1260799>.

Bandiera, O., Burgess, R., Gulesci, S., Rasult, I. and Sulaiman, M. (2013) *Can Entrepreneurship Programs Transform the Economic Lives of the Poor?* Economic Organisation and Public Policy Discussion Papers, EOPP 043, London: London School of Economics.

Barham, V., Boadway, R., Marchand, M. and Pestieau, P. (1995) 'Education and the poverty trap', *European Economic Review* 39(7): 1257–75 <http://dx.doi.org/10.1016/0014-2921(94)00040-7>.

Barham, T., Macrous, K. and Maluccio, J.A. (2013) *More Schooling and More Learning? Effects of a Three-Year Conditional Cash Transfer Program in Nicaragua after 10 Years*, Working paper no. 432, Washington, DC: Inter-American Development Bank.

Chadwick, L. and Solon, G. (2002) 'Intergenerational income mobility among daughters', *American Economic Review* 92(1): 335–44 <http://dx.doi.org/10.1257/000282802760015766>.

Cockburn, J. and Dostie, B. (2007) 'Child work and schooling: the role of household asset profile and poverty in Ethiopia', *Journal of African Economies* 16(4): 519–63 <http://dx.doi.org/10.1093/jae/ejl045>.

de Brauw, A. and Hoddinott, J. (2011) 'Must conditional cash transfer programs be conditioned to be effective? The impact of conditioning transfers on school enrolment in Mexico', *Journal of Development Economics* 96(2): 359–70. <http://dx.doi.org/10.1016/j.jdeveco.2010.08.014>.

Emran, M.S., Robano, V. and Smith, S.C. (2014) 'Assessing the frontier of ultra-poverty reduction: Evidence from CFPR/TUP, an innovative program in Bangladesh', *Economic Development and Cultural Change* 62(2): 339–80 <http://dx.doi.org/10.1086/674110>.

Garcia, S. and Hill, J. (2010) 'Impact of conditional cash transfers on children's school achievement: evidence from Colombia', *Journal of Development Effectiveness* 2(1): 117–37 <http://dx.doi.org/10.1080/19439341003628681>.

Glewwe, P. and Jacoby, H.G. (2004) 'Economic growth and the demand for education: Is there a wealth effect?' *Journal of Development Economics* 74 (1): 33–51 <http://dx.doi.org/10.1016/j.jdeveco.2003.12.003>.

Grimm, M. (2011) 'Does household income matter for children's schooling? Evidence for rural sub-Saharan Africa', *Economics of Education Review* 30(4): 740–54 <http://dx.doi.org/10.1016/j.econedurev.2011.03.002>.

Imbens, G.W. and Wooldridge, J.M. (2009) 'Recent developments in the econometrics of program evaluation', *Journal of Economic Literature* 47(1): 5–86 <http://dx.doi.org/10.1257/jel.47.1.5>.

Levine, D.I. and Jellema, J.R. (2007) 'Growth, industrialization, and the intergenerational correlation of advantage', *Industrial Relations* 46(1): 130–70.

Maitra, P. (2003) 'Schooling and educational attainment: evidence from Bangladesh', *Education Economics* 11(2): 129–53 <http://dx.doi.org/10.1080/09645290210131665>.

Matin, I., Sulaiman, M. and Rabbani, M. (2008) *Crafting a Graduation Pathway for the Ultra Poor: Lessons and Evidence from a BRAC Programme*, Working Paper no. 109, Manchester: Chronic Poverty Research Centre.

Nath, S. R. (2008) 'Private supplementary tutoring among primary students in Bangladesh', *Educational Studies* 34(1): 55–72 <http://dx.doi.org/10.1080/03055690701785285>.

Rabbani, M., Prakash, V.A. and Sulaiman, M. (2006) *Impact Assessment of CFPR/TUP: A Descriptive Analysis Based on 2002–2005 Panel Data*, CFPR/TUP working paper no. 13, Dhaka: BRAC.

Ravallion, M. and Wodon, Q. (2000) 'Does child labor displace schooling? Evidence from behavioral responses to an enrollment subsidy', *Economic Journal* 110(462): 158–75 <http://dx.doi.org/10.1111/1468-0297.00527>.

Schultz, T.P. (2004) 'School subsidies for the poor: evaluating the Mexican Progresa poverty program', *Journal of Development Economics* 74(1): 199–250 <http://dx.doi.org/10.1016/j.jdeveco.2003.12.009>.

Skoufias, E. (2005) *Progresa and its Impacts on the Welfare of Rural Households in Mexico*, Research Report No. 139, Washington, DC: International Food Policy Research Institute.

Solon, G. (1999) 'Intergenerational mobility in labor market', in O. Ashenfelter and D. Card (eds), *Handbook of Labor Economics*, Vol. 3A, pp. 1761–800, Amsterdam: North-Holland <http://dx.doi.org/10.1016/S1573-4463(99)03010-2>.

Sulaiman, M. (2010) *Assessing Impact of Asset Transfer on Children's Education: A Case of BRAC's Ultra-Poor Programme in Bangladesh*, Background paper for Education for All Global Monitoring Report-2010, Paris: UNESCO.

UNESCO (2011) *The Hidden Crisis: The Armed Conflict and Education*, Education for All Global Monitoring Report-2011, Paris: UNESCO.

About the author

Munshi Sulaiman (munshi.sulaiman@yale.edu) is a post-doctoral associate at Yale University, New Haven, CT. I thank Oriana Bandiera, Selim Gulesci, Imran Matin, Imran Rasul, and Robin Burgess for their extensive support, and the anonymous reviewers for their constructive feedback. Special thanks to BRAC for full cooperation in implementing the research project. Any remaining errors are mine. This research benefited from funding by the UK Department for International Development (DFID) as part of the iiG, a research programme to study how to improve institutions for pro-poor growth in Africa and South Asia. The views expressed are not necessarily those of DFID or BRAC.

CHAPTER 7

Responsible finance and child labour: *quo vadis* microfinance?

Patricia Richter and Sophie de Coninck

Abstract

Despite a remarkable downward trend since 2000, child labour remains a reality for 168 million children worldwide (from 245 million in 2000). Of those children, more than half are engaged in hazardous work that directly endangers their health, safety, and moral development. These latest statistics from the International Labour Organization illustrate a pressing concern for today's world and call for integrated efforts to tackle them. This article proposes a framework for development practitioners and policymakers to help them design interventions with a particular focus on financial service providers. We briefly describe root causes of child labour – including demand, social norms, access, costs and quality of education, vulnerability and risk exposure, and income poverty – and then propose innovative interventions that financial service providers can engage in to address, where possible, each of the causes. The article then presents evidence from recent experimental research in Pakistan which shows the significant positive effect that an innovative health and accidental death insurance product had on reducing child labour. Further evidence from experimental research with an associated school fees loan and an awareness campaign in Nigeria, and an integrated training package and sensitization programme in Mali, illustrate that the impact of interventions on child labour, education, and poverty are not always straightforward.

Keywords: microfinance, child labour, impact, responsible finance, social performance

OVER THE LAST DECADE, the microfinance industry was confronted with allegations of not fulfilling its social mission, not lifting clients out of poverty, and instead making money off the poor. It answered to these serious charges with inclusive industry consultations and, together, industry stakeholders worked hard to put the client at centre stage again and gradually emerged as a responsible finance movement. Many challenging issues have been addressed during these recent years, including protecting clients, strengthening social performance management, and carving out standards for microfinance investors and donors. However, one responsible finance issue has not received much attention: child labour among microfinance clients. This article addresses the issue by first clarifying what

http://dx.doi.org/10.3362/9781780448879.007

child labour is and providing a reality check about its extent worldwide. It then briefly presents the root causes of child labour that are relevant for the microfinance industry and suggests entry points to address these root causes. Finally, the article unveils findings from a recent research effort of the International Labour Organization (ILO) showing the actual extent of child labour among microfinance clients and highlights the experience of three microfinance institutions (MFIs) that innovated in product delivery with the goal to reduce child labour. The article closes by drawing lessons for a responsible microfinance industry that acknowledges the challenge and need of addressing child labour among clients.

What is child labour? Some clarifications first

Enterprises in the informal economy are often exposed to challenging work environments. Child labour still features as one of these challenges. Despite improvements, working children of all ages who are sometimes active under questionable conditions, remain a component of informal employment patterns. However, not all *work* that *children* (defined as young people below the age of 18 years) (United Nations Convention on the Rights of the Child 1989; ILO Worst Forms of Child Labour Convention 1999) undertake is negative. In fact, work that is appropriate to their age and development and that does not interfere with learning can provide children and young people with skills and experience, which can help them prepare to be useful and productive members of society during their adult life, as well as contribute positively to their development and welfare, and the welfare of their families.

In sharp contrast, *child labour* is a significant violation of children's rights, fundamental labour rights, and human rights. Therefore, the international community has established standards on how child labour should be defined by outlining the type of work, the conditions under which work is performed, the working hours, and the age of employed children. These factors determine the type and length of permissible activities. Together, these dimensions distinguish between children in employment, child labour, and hazardous work and other worst forms of child labour as illustrated in Figure 1.

Children in employment encompasses all children in any economic activity for at least one hour on any day, or during a reference period (for instance seasonal work). Economic activity covers all market production and certain types of non-market production (principally the production of goods and services for own use). It includes work in the formal and informal economy, inside and outside family settings, work for pay or profit (in cash or in kind, part-time or full-time), or as a domestic worker outside the child's own household for an employer (with or without pay).

Child labour is a subset of children in employment. Child labour refers to work performed by children who are under the minimum age legally specified

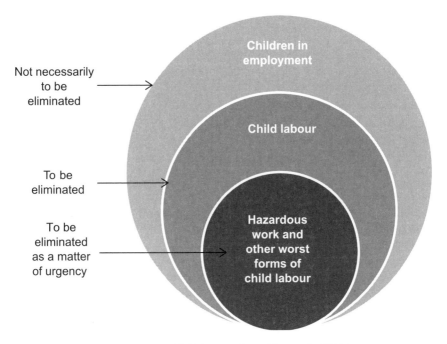

Not necessarily
to be
eliminated

To be
eliminated

To be
eliminated
as a matter
of urgency

Figure 1 Children in employment, child labour, and worst forms of child labour
Source: ILO (2013a: 46)

for such work. The ILO Minimum Age Convention No. 138 (1973) marks out minimum age limits for different types of employment: 13 for light work, 15 for ordinary work, and 18 for hazardous work (see Table 1). The minimum ages applicable in each country are set by national legislation. The minimum working age cannot be less than the age set for completion of compulsory schooling. Characteristics of child labour are that it is mentally, physically, socially, or morally dangerous and harmful to children and that it interferes with their schooling by depriving them of the opportunity to attend school, obliging them to leave school prematurely, or requiring them to attempt to combine school attendance with excessively long and heavy work.

The ILO Worst Forms of Child Labour Convention No. 182 (1999) defines the *worst forms of child labour* and calls for their elimination as a matter of urgency. These include slavery or practices similar to slavery (e.g. trafficking, debt bondage, and use in armed conflict), sexual exploitation, illicit work, or other work which, by its nature or the circumstances in which it is carried out, is likely to harm the health, safety, or morals of children. The latter category is commonly referred to as hazardous work. *Hazardous child labour* is work that is performed by children in dangerous and unhealthy conditions that can lead to a child being killed, injured, or made ill. Girls and boys in this type of employment can experience work-related ill-health, including psycho-social problems, which can result in permanent disability, impairment, or

Table 1 Minimum ages for admission to employment according to ILO Convention 138

	General	Exceptions for developing countries
Minimum age for light work	13 years	12 years
Minimum age for ordinary work[1]	15 years	14 years
Minimum age for hazardous work	18 years	No exception

Note: [1]A ratifying state has the option to designate a higher age at 16 (e.g. China and the Democratic Republic of the Congo)

illness later in life, which in turn can impede their accessing decent work opportunities as adults. Hazardous child labour represents the largest category of children working in the worst forms of child labour, and occurs in sectors as diverse as agriculture, mining, construction, manufacturing, the service industries, and domestic work.

The latest statistics from the ILO show that since 2000 when child labour was estimated to be as high as 245 million, the number of child labourers has since been reduced by almost 78 million. However, child labour still remains a reality for 168 million children worldwide accounting for almost 11 per cent of the world's children (ILO, 2013a). Out of those children, more than half are engaged in hazardous work that directly endangers their health, safety, and moral development (see Table 2). The overall reduction in child labour since 2000 benefited girls (minus 40 per cent) more than boys (minus 25 per cent).

While absolute numbers are largest in Asia and the Pacific, the highest incidence of child labour is found in Africa with more than one in five children in child labour. At 73 million or 44 per cent, children aged 5–11, who should not be engaged in *any* employment, still account for the largest share of child labour (ILO, 2013a).

Child labour impedes children's education and children enter adulthood lacking the skills needed for decent work, leaving them much more vulnerable to joblessness or to low-productivity, insecure jobs throughout their working lives. In addition to the individual consequences, child labour also results in broader concerns for national development. Whereas governments have the primary responsibility for setting out national protection for children in their countries through national law, employers' and workers' organizations, the private sector, civil society, and others play an essential role in promoting and supporting such action. This article looks in particular at the role that the microfinance industry can play therein. Before outlining this role, the next section lays the basis for understanding why children work.

Causes of child labour are multidimensional

The reasons why children work are manifold. Typically, a child's parents or guardians have the responsibility to decide how a child allocates their time between school, work, and leisure. The factors influencing this decision are

Table 2 Children in employment, child labour, and hazardous work by sex, 5–17 years age group, 2000–2012

Sex	Year	Children in employment		Child labour		Hazardous work	
		('000)	%	('000)	%	('000)	%
Boys	2000	184,000	23.4	132,200	16.8	95,700	12.2
	2012	148,327	18.1	99,766	12.2	55,048	6.7
Girls	2000	167,700	22.5	113,300	15.2	74,800	10.0
	2012	116,100	15.2	68,190	8.9	30,296	4.0
Total boys & girls	2012	264,427	16.7	167,956	10.6	85,344	5.4

Source: ILO (2013a)

triggers for child labour. Literature typically mentions income poverty as the first root cause and, indeed, analysis of available data has shown that child labour is more pervasive in poor countries (Siddiqi and Patrinos, 1995; ILO, 2013b). For poor households to guarantee sufficient income, child labour may be the only way to increase revenues and hence ensure the survival of the family. However, poverty is not the only cause of child labour. Blume and Breyer (2011) provide an in-depth analysis of five root causes of child labour potentially relevant for the microfinance industry: demand; social norms; access, costs, and quality of education; vulnerability and risk exposure; and income poverty.

Demand

The demand for child labour is not a negligible root cause. Typical demand arguments include the lower wages paid to children, their weaker power to demand improvements in working conditions, or their assumed willingness to follow orders more easily than adults.

For the typical microfinance client who runs a family business, the decisions regarding labour supply and demand are taken by the same person. Under such circumstances, the cost argument becomes further pronounced as family businesses have easier access to their own children who are perceived to be considerably cheaper than hired external labour. In addition, time of one's own children can be allocated more flexibly and parents have better control over them (e.g. to prevent theft). Also, it cannot be ignored that some parents may see their children as human capital investment, to which technical, business, and life skills can be transferred to carry on family tradition (Blume and Breyer, 2011).

Social norms

Communities may view work as a valuable experience and as skills training for life. Hence, parents may have a positive attitude towards child work. At the same time, parents may be unaware of the detrimental effects of child labour including abuse (physical or emotional) and work-related injuries among many others. A long-term negative consequence is the propagation of child labour to future generations. Children who forgo education in order to work will also grow up to be poor as adults, and as such are more likely to send their own children to work. Emerson and Souza (2003) describes this 'dynastic trap' of intergenerational persistence of child labour both theoretically and with empirical support from Brazil. All such consequences of child labour are amplified by a low quality education system, ignorance towards the benefits of education, or culturally perpetuated structural constraints such as caste. Another contribution to culturally encouraged child labour is the will of children to work in order to gain prestige and independence in their society.

Access, costs, and quality of education

Theory suggests that parents would choose education over work for their children and be prepared to pay upfront for the costs of schooling in the present to generate higher wages in the future. However, if the education system does not live up to the expectation of providing the necessary skills and thus a higher return in the future, parents might send children to work instead of school.

In addition to the lack of access to quality education, the high cost of schooling (fees, uniforms, books, transportation, etc.) prevents parents from sending children to school. This is especially so if large sums need to be paid at once upfront and if a culture for school savings is not established or the financial sector does not allow for borrowing for school fees at reasonable costs. In these cases, the short-term costs may outweigh the long-term benefits of education.

Lastly, children may also work to cover costs associated with their own schooling and thus be at risk of shifting into child labour.

Vulnerability and risk exposure

Vulnerability and poverty often go hand in hand: poor families live and work in environments that are exposed to natural disasters, to disease due to challenges in access to water, sanitation, or health services, or to hazardous working conditions. These conditions make them vulnerable to income and consumption shocks for which they do not have effective coping strategies, such as the choice of a less risky environment, the diversification of economic activities, or the ability to accumulate physical or financial assets including savings and use of insurance. Lacking an alternative strategy, children may work when the household has been hit as an answer to the economic shock. However, once children are integrated into the labour market it is difficult to transition back to school even when the economic shock has been mitigated. Child labour might easily manifest and become irreversible. Koster (2005) provides an example of this phenomenon in Kashmir, Pakistan where the number of child labourers increased following the earthquake in 2005.

Income poverty

As described above, poor households may rely on the earnings of children to ensure sufficient household income. This contribution is more valuable – compared to overall household income – in poorer households and hence the incentive for parents to choose work over school and leisure is higher. With increasing household income, the utility of the additional income generated by the child decreases and with it the incentive for child labour. Nielsen and Dubey (2002) show that child labour in rural India in fact reduced as income increased. Edmonds (2005) obtains similar results from panel data in Vietnam.

Income poverty may be linked to low value and low productivity assets. As poor households lack the means to invest in upgrading assets to increase productivity, children may fill this gap. If a household invests with the intention to increase productivity, income should also rise and consequently reduce the necessity of child labour or at least reduce hours worked.

However, the acquisition of productive assets also has the potential to increase labour demand (e.g. livestock needs supervision), which might be filled by children if no alternative labour is affordably available.

Understanding these five root causes and how they interrelate provides an entry point for development practitioners to effectively address child labour through working with microfinance institutions (MFIs) and their clients. The following sections suggest how the microfinance industry can address each of the root causes described above. This framework is founded on Blume and Breyer (2011).

What can MFIs do to address root causes of child labour?

As MFIs widely serve the informal sector, child labour among their clients is of particular concern to them and the root causes described above are more likely to be at play. Child labour might affect clients' own children or other children that clients employ. The following paragraphs suggest entry points for each cause of child labour. For programme design, it is important to, first, engage in determining the cause(s) of child labour affecting a particular target group and, second, to design an effective access to finance strategy that addresses the identified cause(s). As child labour often has multiple roots which are interlinked, a combination and sequencing of access to finance interventions may be most effective.

The subsequent suggestions purposefully focus on the potential *positive contributions of microfinance*. We do acknowledge, however, that microfinance, when implemented incorrectly, can spur the creation of child labour. For example, Islam and Choe (2009) find that participation in a microfinance programme in rural Bangladesh may increase child labour while decreasing school enrolment as children that were taken out of school were more likely to work in household enterprises that were set up with microcredit. In addition, the negative effects were more profound for girls and for younger children than for boys and older siblings. For more on the negative contributions of microfinance we refer the interested reader to additional literature on the topic, such as Wydick (1999), Kring (2004), and Islam and Choe (2009), which go beyond what this article covered in the previous section.

Demand

MFIs have a very strong position for addressing both demand and supply causes of child labour. This is because their clients typically operate family businesses in which both demand and supply considerations are taken by the same individuals – parents or guardians – that determine the time allocation between school, work, and leisure of children.

Considering this unique position, MFIs that actively want to address child labour can target specific industries or sectors in which child labour is most prevalent. Such targeting would need to be country and region specific. For example, in West Africa, agriculture and in particular cocoa farmers could be a target industry while in the Philippines an entry point could be sugarcane farmers and in Ethiopia, weavers.

Furthermore, the provision of financial services can be linked to education about the causes and effects of child labour. Often, child labour occurs because the negative consequences on children are not known. Educating parents about detrimental effects and children about their rights could significantly reduce both the demand and supply of child labour.

In addition, loans can be conditioned on improvements regarding the employment of children: for example, reduction in hours worked, allocation to non-hazardous activities, and requirement of full-time school attendance for children of compulsory school age. Loan applications that do not meet minimum criteria or do not agree on improvements should not be approved. Some microfinance providers, like ProCredit and Vision Fund, have declared that they will not issue loans to clients that are suspected of engaging child labour (ProCredit, 2012; World Vision, 2009). This being said, it is important that loan officers be sufficiently trained to recognize child labour and to enable them to agree and monitor their clients' improvement activities.

In addition, MFIs can also run awareness campaigns that have the potential to reach not only clients but also the wider community, such as banners at branch offices, radio shows, and theatre plays. In addition to evidence presented later in this article for child labour, Cruz et al. (2009) have shown significant results of education campaigns on clients' knowledge of causes and prevention of, for example, malaria in Ghana.

Social norms

To tackle established beliefs, MFIs need to raise the awareness and sensitivity of management and staff on the causes and forms of child labour. Only then should institutions attempt to raise awareness among clients. For both, MFIs can cooperate with local (NGOs) or international partners (like the ILO) to offer training based on ILO tools against child labour, and develop and broadcast public awareness campaigns via radio. National or regional microfinance associations have a great potential to address social norms as they can facilitate the coordination and cooperation with local and international partners for the microfinance industry.

MFIs can condition the use of their financial services on attending education or training sessions on child labour. Furthermore, they can develop, together with clients or the community, a code of conduct to which microfinance clients shall adhere.

Access, costs, and quality of education

While MFIs are not at the forefront of influencing actual school fees or the quality of education, they may be able to influence the total costs of education. They can offer financial education to make clients understand that school expenditures are by no means unexpected expenses but can be planned in advance. Further nurturing a culture to plan for expected expenses, the institution can provide school savings accounts.

In addition, the institution may also offer educational loans that are targeted at clients that need to cover longer-term educational expenses. Of course, institutions may also provide short-term school fee loans to cover smaller amounts of associated school expenses especially in an environment of free primary or even secondary education.

If government extends social transfers for schooling, MFIs could encourage either government or clients to deposit these transfers into accounts to avoid misuse of such funds. For first-time clients, this also offers the opportunity to gain access to a broader range of financial and related non-financial (e.g. financial education) services.

Vulnerability and risk exposure

Exposure to risk and the inability of poor households to employ effective coping strategies when faced by a shock appears to be the most prevalent cause for child labour. While use of a range of financial services could tremendously help poor households to overcome temporary cash flow shortfalls and better manage risks without resorting to child labour, they often do not have sufficient access. Consequently, providing access to *protective* financial services has the highest potential for an MFI to have a positive impact as it can provide the safety nets necessary against income and expenditure shocks. The effect can be even larger if protective financial services are linked to financial education or business development services to address vulnerability with a longer-term strategy.

Insurance plays an essential role to protect households against losses due to insurable events like death, illness, destruction of property, or theft. Especially if MFIs partner with insurance providers that offer affordable multiple coverage, they could fill an important gap in improving the risk managing strategies of poor households. Programmes that incentivize innovative distribution channels for insurance and the use of technology to minimize administrative costs could help experiment and show the great potential of insurance on reducing child labour.

Savings are of high importance, especially when they are accessible, secure, and liquid. If clients can access their savings for planned expenses (e.g. wedding), investment opportunities (e.g. productive equipment), and emergencies (e.g. funerals, illness, theft), they do not need to resort to an additional pair of hands to earn extra income. Building up assets instead of putting a vulnerable household in more debt is a much more empowering strategy.

To meet unexpected expenses of smaller amounts, emergency loans may also be an appropriate tool. However, for large losses, especially if they affect many people at once, development programmes should rather think about relief and grants (van Doorn and Churchill, 2004).

The last decade has seen numerous innovations in branchless banking, mobile money, or technology solutions for bringing protective financial services closer to vulnerable households – all of which can intensify their impacts if included in child labour elimination strategies.

Income poverty

The typical intervention to increase income through MFIs is extending productive loans. The argument is that such an investment increases productivity which in turn yields higher income. A number of studies have shown such positive results (Khandker, 1998; Nelly and Dunford, 1999; Littlefield et al., 2003). However, literature has also produced mixed results on the actual income effect of loans to microfinance clients and suggests that only borrowers with sufficient entrepreneurial skills, capacities, and investment opportunities may succeed in generating additional income (see Bauchet et al., 2011 for a summary; or Augsburg et al., 2012).

However, providing loans is not the only entry point for MFIs to increase income. In particular, MFIs can work towards empowering women with responsibilities for monetary decision-making and hence allocation of additional income, for example, towards schooling. The new role of women as economic decision-makers 'enables them to increase expenditure on the well-being of themselves and their children' (Mayoux 2000) since they are more likely to do so than men (Mosley and Rock 2004). Furthermore, financial education can help clients plan household and business budgets realistically and with enough foresight to avoid foreseeable income shortages. Productive loans could be linked to business and management training to increase the survival of business ventures and sustain positive income increases by supporting income diversification and identifying new business branches with potential higher business returns. Leasing products can also have a positive effect on income generation as they avoid diverting funds into non-productive assets.

It should be noted that an increase in productive assets may also incentivize clients to employ children and reduce schooling. This negative effect would follow the arguments sketched in the previous section and MFIs should purposefully observe whether this materializes in order to reverse unintended impacts.

Evidence from systematically implementing the microfinance–child labour framework at the ILO

Based on this framework, the ILO launched a specific child labour segment as part of its global Microfinance for Decent Work (MF4DW) action research programme (2008–2012) (ILO, n.d.). This programme aimed to assess whether MFIs could enhance their impact on improving clients' work-related challenges through innovative packages of financial and/or non-financial services. Evidence was generated by quantitative impact evaluations mainly using a difference-in-differences methodology.

At the outset of the action research in 2008, the ILO conducted a diagnostic survey to assess the most pressing work-related challenges among microfinance clients (ILO, 2009a). The survey, implemented in collaboration with 22 MFIs covering nearly 5,000 clients worldwide, revealed that child labour is a reality among microfinance clients: counting the 5–14 years age bracket only, children contributed to 5 per cent of the work force. However, the number of children employed per microentrepreneur varied greatly from 1 to 65. On average, slightly more than half of all children (55 per cent) were boys and 45 per cent were girls. Of the sample, one-fifth did not attend school at all, while half attended school full-time. On average, child labourers worked a little less than 6 hours per day. Interestingly, child labourers in more urban settings tended to work longer hours, regardless of the region. The diagnostic also quantified that most employment of children was through their own children or the children of relatives (two-thirds). So indeed, the diagnostic survey provided evidence that child labour is an issue among clients of MFIs. Interestingly, this result came as a surprise to a number of MFIs. This finding emphasizes the need to increase awareness and capacity within the microfinance industry for identifying and tackling child labour.

The diagnostic study also showed that *vulnerability* was one of the most serious challenges among microfinance clients and hence a major root cause for child labour. Across the sample, 43 per cent of respondents were confronted with large, unforeseen expenses in the year preceding the survey. The study identified accidents and illnesses as the main causes. Consequently, half of the unforeseen expenses were related to medicine, hospitalization, and surgery; another 10 per cent related to death and funeral costs. While indeed these causes were unforeseen (contrary to school fees which are often mistakenly

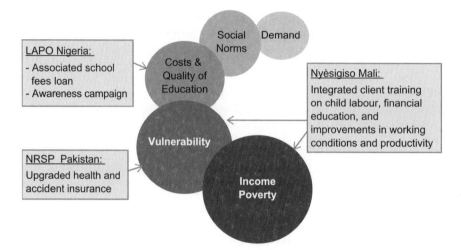

Figure 2 Root causes of child labour and MF4DW interventions

perceived as unforeseen expenses), only 2–3 per cent of respondents used insurance or social security to cover the related costs. The latter fact might link to another finding of the diagnostic that more than half of the clients operated their businesses in the informal sector. This meant that they did not have access to the social security system due to their informal status. In addition, *income poverty* also emerged as a challenge as 14 per cent of clients indicated that they had repayment difficulties, and 8 per cent had borrowed from the MFI to repay another outstanding loan.

Based on the diagnostic results, three MFIs decided to design innovations to address prevalent child labour among their clients: NRSP in Pakistan, Nyèsigiso in Mali, and LAPO in Nigeria (see Figure 2). The following sections describe the interventions of the institutions and the results they achieved.

Can health and accident insurance reduce vulnerability and affect child labour and schooling? An example from Pakistan

The National Rural Support Programme (NRSP), an MFI in Pakistan, works with about 2 million poor households in 56 districts of all four provinces as well as Azad Jammu and Kashmir. In 2008, NRSP conducted a diagnostic in the area of Hyderabad in the south of Pakistan where more than 9 per cent of the population is organized through the MFI (Landmann and Froelich, 2013). The diagnostic indicated high prevalence of child labour especially in the glass bangles industry. Furthermore, it identified high vulnerability to health costs. The following figures illustrate the extent:

- 6.5 per cent of clients reported employing children;
- average age of child labourers: 12 years;
- average working hours per day of children <8 years: 7 hours, often forgoing school, or combining schooling with their work;

- 12 per cent of respondents had been confronted with a large unforeseen expense in the last year;
- most common reasons for large unforeseen expenses: death, accident, surgery, or illness.

Responding to the high incidence of child labour and vulnerability among clients, NRSP upgraded its health and accidental death insurance product by making it available to all non-nuclear family members (aged 18–65) in the client's household. The underlying logic was that the extended insurance would mitigate the household's medical and hospitalization expenses which otherwise may push children into work. NRSP implemented the innovation in three steps:

1. *Orientation training.* 40 NRSP staff were introduced to child labour concepts and trained on identifying child labour among clients.
2. *Product roll-out.* 1,300 clients were sensitized to the new voluntary health and accidental death insurance covering non-nuclear family members living in the client's household for a premium of Rs100/year per adult + spouse + underage children (approx. US$1/year). Insurance benefits per individual: hospital stays more than 20 hours covered with ceiling of Rs15,000 (US$175) and accidents leading to death or permanent disability up to Rs15,000.
3. *Informal client guidance.* Loan officers regularly inquired whether clients had incurred medical/hospital expenses; if so, loan officers guided clients through the insurance usage process.

In collaboration with the ILO and the University of Mannheim, NRSP accompanied the implementation of the insurance product with data collections on clients that had access (treatment group) and clients that did not have access (control group) to the insurance. Altogether, five rounds of data were collected from 2009 to 2011 including a baseline (total of 2,097 client households) and four follow-up waves (last wave: 1,975 client households). The impact of the insurance product on child labour outcomes, including child labour incidence, schooling, and insurance use as risk mitigation strategy, was estimated using a difference-in-difference methodology. For more details see Landmann et al. (2014) and Landmann and Froelich (2013).

The evaluation produced robust evidence that the upgraded insurance product decreased child labour incidence by almost 7 per cent. The prevalence of hazardous occupations dropped by 5.7–6.5 per cent. The main driver for this reduction was a shift from dangerous work in shops and factories towards less intensive work around the house. When separating by gender, the largest effects were observed for boys. However, boys started off as a higher percentage of child labourers (20.2 per cent) than girls (13.2 per cent) except for the incidence of hazardous occupations which were similar at around 9 per cent. Remembering that the explicit goal of the insurance was to prevent children transitioning into child labour after an economic shock in the household, the analysis showed that it is indeed consistently lower for clients with insurance.

On schooling, the analysis did not yield significant results. While school attendance of children aged 5–14 (with girls attending slightly more often [72 per cent] than boys [68 per cent]) showed a slight upward trend, none of the results was significant. The analysis also produced interesting evidence on poverty: households *with* child labour generally scored lower on the Progress out of Poverty Index (27 versus 32), had lower levels of education, lower per capita income, and more household members.

Based on the positive results of the innovation, NRSP decided to continue offering the product and to increase research efforts in collaboration with the same research partner. As part of ILO's exit strategy and in an effort to support continuous sustainable implementation, ILO offered NRSP the following advice:

- Continue to train NRSP loan officers in promoting awareness around the characteristics of the insurance product and its use.
- Carry on negotiations with the primary service provider to ensure that the insurance product is offered in a financially sustainable manner that is still affordable to NRSP clients.
- Track progress in reducing child labour among clients as part of NRSP's social performance agenda.
- Introduce sensitization sessions on child labour for staff so that NRSP loan officers can identify child labour among the clients they serve.
- Investigate how insurance can impact the child labour situation in other parts of the country, in rural areas, and in different economic sectors.

Can integrated client training reduce child labour? An example from rural Mali

Another institution that joined the MF4DW action research was Nyèsigiso, a savings and credit cooperative operating in Mali since 1990. Nyèsigiso is the second largest MFI in Mali, reaching almost 200,000 members and covering five administrative regions. In 2008, the institution conducted a diagnostic study among 269 of its clients and found that child labour featured as a serious work challenge:

- 11 per cent of self-employed clients reported employing at least one child;
- 56 per cent of the employed children were own children;
- three-quarters of the employed children were boys;
- three-quarters of the employed children were at least 12 years old;
- almost half (44 per cent) of the employed children did not go to school;
- almost all (92 per cent) of these children that did not go to school were boys;
- 55 per cent of the employed children worked at least 7 hours per day.

Furthermore, *vulnerability* appeared widespread and clients were confronted with *income poverty*:

- 54 per cent of clients experienced an unforeseen expense with more than half related to illness, accident, and maternity;

- 20 per cent of clients experienced repayment problems mainly due to economic difficulties related to business (50 per cent) and illness (20 per cent) (ILO, 2009b).

These diagnostic findings, backed by national statistics showing a heavy reliance on child labour in the agricultural sector, encouraged Nyèsigiso to step up efforts to reduce child labour among clients by developing a sectoral intervention strategy. Nyèsigiso combined three relevant topics – reducing child labour, improving working conditions and enhancing productivity in agriculture, and financial education – into one training package and integrated the package into a broader sensitization programme.

As a result of the innovation, Nyèsigiso hoped to see a change in the type of work that children conducted (from hazardous to non-hazardous), a reduction in the hours that children worked, and an appreciation of the advantages of schooling compared with child labour (Froelich et al., 2012a). In particular, the child labour and working conditions training were aimed at reducing the demand for child labour, financial education was aimed at addressing vulnerability, and training on productivity was aimed at addressing income poverty.

Nyèsigiso implemented the innovation in four steps:

1. *Staff orientation.* 48 Nyèsigiso staff were familiarized with child labour concepts (including specific regulations in Mali) and how working conditions and agricultural productivity interrelate. Following the orientation workshop, staff developed training modules and trained trainers on the respective modules to be rolled out to clients.
2. *Client training roll-out.* 514 clients were sensitized to child labour, productivity, working conditions, and financial education in one-day training sessions.
3. *Client sensitization.* Posters and flyers were disseminated that reinforced the anti-child labour messages.
4. *Informal client guidance.* After the training, volunteers visited trained clients to follow up whether training lessons were well understood and applied.

The impact of the client training and sensitization on four child labour outcomes (child labour incidence, schooling, awareness of child labour, and household welfare) were measured by a difference-in-difference methodology. In total, 1,578 client households were included in the study (covering 4,069 children). Unfortunately, data quality challenged the analysis mainly due to difficulties matching clients across data waves and hence results are not as strong as in the NRSP case.

However, one significant outcome is that the combined strategy resulted in a reduction of 26 per cent in child labour incidence among girls. While the same variable also decreased for boys (2.7 per cent), the effect was not significant (ILO, 2015). Other positive outcomes include an increase in the perceived acceptable age for children to start contributing to household income (by roughly one year for boys and girls) as well as an increase in the perceived importance of attaining education levels above primary education (Froelich et al., 2012a).

As part of ILO's exit strategy and in an effort to support Nyèsigiso to continue the important work done, the MFI received the following advice on how to facilitate further implementation:

- Review the gender dimension of the child labour training.
- Tailor financial services, including savings, for school-related costs.
- Investigate how a similar training package can impact the child labour situation in other parts of the country and in different economic sectors apart from agriculture.
- Continue to track performance indicators around child labour, working conditions, and productivity.

Can an associated school fees loan and awareness raising reduce child labour? An example from Nigeria

The third MFI that worked on reducing child labour in the MF4DW action research was Lift Above Poverty Organization (LAPO) in Nigeria. Established in 1988, LAPO is the largest microfinance bank in the country with 269 branches in 26 out of 36 states. LAPO has more than 590,000 active clients (Froelich et al., 2012b). An initial diagnostic identified several work-related challenges among 198 clients in 2008, among them *child labour* and *income poverty*:

- 33 per cent of clients had children (aged 5–14) working for them;
- 73 per cent of the working children were girls;
- 96 per cent of reported child labourers were clients' own children;
- 99 per cent of working children combined work with schooling;
- most children worked between 2 and 4 hours per day;
- less than half of the clients (48.5 per cent) could cover household expenses with household incomes.

Considering that Nigeria had one of the highest prevalences of reported child labour in the world, with nearly 15 million children (mainly involved in street vending or hawking) in 2003, LAPO promoted schooling for the children of clients through a scholarship programme which, however, remained unsustainable. Therefore, LAPO decided to implement a school fees loan through the MF4DW and complemented it with an awareness raising campaign on the topic of child labour and schooling of children. The soft loan could be offered to mature clients to cover the annual cost of associated school attendance.

LAPO implemented the innovation in four steps:

1. *Orientation training.* 20 LAPO staff were introduced to child labour concepts and trained to identify child labour among clients and promote alternative options in an initial three day orientation training. Additional LAPO staff members were trained in participating branches.

2. *Client training roll-out.* Approximately 2,500 clients were sensitized to the effects of child labour.
3. *Product roll-out.* Approximately 2,500 clients got access to the associated school fees loan (at 1 per cent per month), which was intended to help struggling parents to diffuse the initial lump sum school payment due at the beginning of each school year over a monthly repayment schedule, and to cover other school-related costs, such as uniforms, transportation, and books.
4. *School attendance monitoring.* Clients who received associated school fees loans were randomly selected and visited by regional managers or monitoring staff to observe whether children were found in the workplaces of clients or at school.

The impact of the associated school fees loan and the awareness campaign was measured on three outcome variables – child labour incidence, schooling, and awareness of child labour – by using a difference-in-difference methodology. In total, 2,269 client households were included in the study. Similar to Nyèsigiso, data quality challenged the analysis. For LAPO, difficulties emerged from identifying and matching clients across data waves and inconsistencies in data with the consequence that the results were less robust. Marginal impact on school attendance could be established for clients that were exposed to the awareness campaign (ILO, 2015). No significant impact could be found for the other two outcome variables, neither for child labour incidence nor child labour awareness.

As with the other two MFIs, LAPO also received advice at the end of the research project on how to continue the chosen path towards addressing child labour among clients:

- Review the awareness campaign material that may be giving unclear messages regarding child work and child schooling.
- Review client data for errors. This might help to explain the unusual findings for such a straightforward innovation in terms of its direct approach to lessening child labour.
- An analysis could be undertaken looking specifically at clients who dropped out, reasons for dropping out, or reasons for not taking the survey or school fees loan.
- Examine attrition rates in the sample. It is possible that some inconclusiveness in the data is due to too few clients being observed in sequence.
- Based on the inconclusiveness of the data, continue to review child labour among its clients, particularly if the innovations are to continue. All persons involved in the survey process should undergo thorough re-training and be incentivized for quality of work. Internally capacitated staff can then continue this important work and hopefully reach a more positive impact on incidence of child labour in the future.

Way forward for development practitioners including donors and microfinance service providers

This article presented a framework for development practitioners and microfinance providers to effectively address child labour. It first provided a statistical reality check about child labour in today's world based on the latest estimates from the International Labour Organization. It then introduced the five main root causes for child labour – demand, social norms, access, costs and quality of education, vulnerability and risk exposure, and income poverty – before linking concrete interventions to each of the root causes. Lastly, the article presented evidence from implementing the framework through three microfinance experiments in Pakistan, Mali, and Nigeria tested through the ILO Microfinance for Decent Work action research. While the results from Pakistan showed a significant positive effect on reducing child labour, the results from Nigeria and Mali were more ambiguous. From the experience presented, we can draw a set of lessons:

First, child labour is a challenge among microfinance clients in many countries. Child labour is a serious human rights violation which contradicts several international conventions and needs to be addressed.

Second, child labour has multidimensional root causes. Consequently, every intervention or programme aiming at addressing child labour needs to consider the manifold reasons in order to achieve a positive change. The decision of which financial or related non-financial service to use is heavily dependent on the situation that causes child labour to occur in that specific circumstance. For example, access to savings, insurance, and emergency loans seem best suited for clients who use child labour due to their inability to manage risks. Any development effort that works in isolation on limited root causes will hardly yield sustainable results in the long run. Programmes need to keep in mind that microfinance is not a one-size-fits-all solution.

Third, microfinance can contribute to reducing child labour among clients especially when offering a range of financial services including insurance, savings, leasing products, emergency loans, and productive loans as well as related non-financial services such as financial education, business and management training, or child labour sensitization. Because the root causes of child labour are interlinked, it is the interplay between the different services that has the highest potential to yield positive results by addressing the multidimensional causes of child labour.

Fourth, without increased awareness and capacity within the microfinance industry to identify and address child labour, neither financial nor non-financial services can unfold their positive impact. Conditional loans are a constructive way of ensuring that entrepreneurs do not use child labour *only* if loan officers are able to identify child labour. Therefore, awareness raising and capacity building of microfinance staff, management, and board of directors is long overdue. These cannot be one-off efforts, but they need to be ingrained in the moral DNA of institutions.

Fifth, child labour is a potentially broader issue that also needs to be tackled at the global level. So far, it has not received sufficient attention in industry-wide standard setting undertakings such as the Universal Standards for Social Performance Management or the Client Protection Principles.

Sixth, microfinance stakeholders should share innovative approaches, lessons learned, challenges faced, and findings discovered from research and experimentation in order to illustrate how the industry may have stronger effects in the fight against child labour or how to avoid unintended negative outcomes. MFIs that have walked the talk, such as those that participated in the Microfinance for Decent Work action research, are a rich resource the industry can draw from. The potential for sharing tools is especially high at a national level where the same legal child labour frameworks apply.

Seventh, the industry can improve research efforts by following lessons learnt from this article spanning the planning, design, and implementation of the research:

- Involve impact evaluators from the beginning to get the best possible evaluation design given an MFI-specific context (e.g. for the experimental evaluation design, design of client sample, design of questionnaires).
- Carefully articulate the theories linking interventions to outcomes, and develop the channels at work between the innovation and the intended outcomes.
- One follow-up survey will measure short-term impact, whereas several follow-up surveys will give medium- and long-term impact.
- Questionnaires should be streamlined across time and space. It is important that the same survey instruments are used for the control and target group.
- Carefully consider who is collecting data. If loans officers have to collect data on top of their regular work, the quality of interviews might suffer. Clients might feel uncomfortable when loan officers visit them as neighbours might think that they are having repayment difficulties. Also, clients might answer some questions more truthfully when asked by a third party who guarantees confidentiality.
- During data collection, note extraordinary events taking place that might affect the clients (e.g. droughts, major elections, the building of a dam).
- All clients need a unique ID to identify them over different waves.
- Minimizing attrition is important. Questionnaires could record clients' mobile numbers or precise descriptions of where they live to find them for subsequent interviews.

Lastly, further research on effective approaches remains essential. Research should include cost-benefit analyses to contribute to the double bottom line literature and evidence of a 'business case' for microfinance-led child labour interventions may encourage more MFIs to pursue a sustainable business alternative mainstreaming child labour initiatives. The ILO Microfinance for

Decent Work action research has started innovating along these lines. The ILO welcomes opportunities to engage with financial institutions to share their experience and advance the child labour agenda in the microfinance industry.

References

Augsburg, B., Haas, R.D., Harmgart, H. and Meghir, C. (2012) *Microfinance, Poverty and Education*, IFS working paper, London: Institute for Fiscal Studies.

Bauchet, J., Marshall, C., Starita, L., Thomas, J., and Yalouris, A. (2011) *Latest Findings from Randomized Evaluations of Microfinance*, Washington, DC: CGAP.

Blume, J. and Breyer, J. (2011) *Microfinance and Child Labour*, Employment Working Paper No. 89, Geneva: International Labour Organization.

De La Cruz, N., Crookston, B., Gray, B., Alder, S., and Dearden, K. (2009) 'Microfinance against malaria: impact of Freedom from Hunger's malaria education when delivered by rural banks in Ghana', *Transactions of the Royal Society of Tropical Medicine and Hygiene* 103(12): 1229–36 <http://dx.doi.org/10.1016/j.trstmh.2009.03.018>.

Edmonds, E.V. (2005) 'Does child labour decline with improving economic status?' *The Journal of Human Resources* 40(1): 77–99.

Emerson, P.M. and Souza, A.P. (2003) 'Is there a child labor trap? Inter-generational persistence of child labor in Brazil', *Economic Development and Cultural Change* 51(2): 375–98.

Froelich, M., Landmann, A., Poppe, R., Unte, P., van Doorn, J. and Midkiff, H. (2012a) 'Améliorer les conditions de travail et la productivité en milieu agricole pour réduire le travail des enfants: Etude d'impact de l'innovation de Nyèsigiso en matière de formation et sensibilisation', internal report, Geneva: International Labour Organization, Social Finance Programme.

Froelich, M., Landmann, A., Midkiff, H. and van Doorn, J. (2012b) 'School Support Initiative: an impact evaluation of LAPO, Nigeria's school fees loan and awareness campaign innovation against child labour', internal report, Geneva: International Labour Organization, Social Finance Programme.

International Labour Organization (ILO) (2009a) 'Microfinance for Decent Work: results of diagnostic client survey', internal report, Geneva: International Labour Organization, Social Finance Programme.

ILO (2009b) 'Micro-finance au service du Travail Décent – Analyse des résultats de l'enquête auprès des clients de Nyèsigiso, Mali', internal report, Geneva: International Labour Organization, Social Finance Programme.

ILO (2013a) *Making Progress Against Child Labour: Global Estimates and Trends 2000-2012*, Geneva: International Labour Organization, International Programme on the Elimination of Child Labour (IPEC).

ILO (2013b) *World Report on Child Labour: Economic Vulnerability, Social Protection and the Fight Against Child Labour*, Geneva: International Labour Organization.

ILO (2015) *Microfinance for Decent Work: Enhancing the Impact of Microfinance – Evidence from an Action Research Programme*, Geneva: International Labour Organization, Social Finance Programme.

ILO (n.d.) 'Microfinance for decent work: action research' [online] <www. ilo.org/empent/areas/social-finance/WCMS_168033/lang--en/index.htm> [accessed 15 April 2105].

Islam, A. and Choe, C. (2009) *Child Labour and Schooling Responses to Access to Microcredit in Rural Bangladesh* [pdf], MPRA Paper 16842, Munich Personal RePEc Archive <http://mpra.ub.uni-muenchen.de/16842/1/MPRA_ paper_16842.pdf> [accessed 8 April 2015].

Khandker, S. R. (1998) *Fighting Poverty with Microcredit*, Oxford: Oxford University Press.

Koster, S. (2005) 'Pakistan: UNICEF fears increased child labour in quake area' [online], Relief Web, 6 December 2005 <http://reliefweb.int/report/ pakistan/pakistan-unicef-fears-increased-child-labour-quake-area> [accessed 8 April 2015].

Kring, T. (2004) *Microfinance as an Intervention Against Child Labour in Footwear Production in the Philippines*, Working Paper No. 12, Melbourne: School of Development Studies, University of Melbourne.

Landmann, A. and Froelich, M. (2013) *Can Microinsurance Help Prevent Child Labour? An Impact Evaluation from Pakistan*, Microinsurance Research Paper No. 32, Geneva: International Labour Organization.

Landmann, A., Froelich, M., Midkiff, H., and Breda, V. (2014) *Microinsurance and Child Labour: An Impact Evaluation of NRSP's (Pakistan) Microinsurance Innovation*, Social Finance Working Paper No. 58, Geneva: International Labour Organization.

Littlefield, E., Murdoch, J. and Hashemi, S. (2003) *Is Microfinance an Effective Strategy to Reach the Millennium Development Goals?* CGAP Focus Note No. 24, Washington, DC: CGAP.

Mayoux, L. (2000) *Microfinance and the Empowerment of Women: A Review of Key Issues*, ILO SFP Working Paper 23, Geneva: International Labour Organization, Social Finance Programme.

Mosley, P. and Rock, J. (2004) 'Microfinance, labour markets and poverty in Africa: a study of six institutions', *Journal of International Development* 16(3): 467–500 <http://dx.doi.org/10.1002/jid.1090>.

Nelly, B. and Dunford, D. (1999) *Impact of Credit with Education on Mothers and their Young Children's Nutrition: CRECER Credit with Education Program in Bolivia*, Freedom from Hunger Research Paper No. 5, Davis, CA: Freedom from Hunger.

Nielsen, H.S. and Dubey, A. (2002) 'Child labour in rural India: a micro-economic perspective', *The Indian Journal of Labour Economics* 45(3): 479–96.

ProCredit (2012) *Code of Conduct* [pdf], ProCredit Bank <www.procreditbank-kos.com/repository/docs/Code_of_Conduct_eng.pdf> [accessed 8 May 2015].

Siddiqi, F. and Patrinos, H. (1995) *Child Labour: Issues, Causes and Interventions*, Human Capital Development and Operations Policy Working Paper No. 56, Washington, DC: World Bank.

Van Doorn, J. and Churchill, C. (2004) *Microfinance against Child Labour: Technical Guidelines*, Geneva: International Labour Organization, International Programme on the Elimination of Child Labour (IPEC) and Social Finance Programme (SPF).

World Vision (2009) *Fact Sheet: Child Labour* [pdf], World Vision <www. worldvision.com.au/libraries/dtl_fact_sheets/factsheet_child_labour.pdf> [accessed 8 May 2015].

Wydick, B. (1999) 'The effect of microenterprise lending on child schooling in Guatemala', *Economic Development and Cultural Change* 47(4): 853–69.

Relevant conventions

ILO Worst Forms of Child Labour Convention, 1999 (No. 182)
United Nations Convention on the Rights of the Child (CRC), 1989
ILO Minimum Age Convention, 1973 (No. 138)

About the authors

Patricia Richter (richter@ilo.org) is a technical officer at the Social Finance Programme of the International Labour Organization, Geneva.

Sophie de Coninck (deconinck@ilo.org) is a technical specialist on child labour at the ILO International Programme on the Elimination of Child Labour, Geneva.

CHAPTER 8

Recognizing and supporting working children through microfinance programming

Richard Carothers

Abstract

Microfinance programmes can help low-income and poor families improve their earnings and begin the process of moving out of poverty, but young children often join the workforce of these microenterprises as credit becomes available. Experiences gained from Egypt and several other countries have shown that children from as young as six years of age can play an important role in helping their families meet the initial increase in labour demands of their growing business. This paper points out that microfinance institutions are well-placed to support working children within their client businesses and help these children improve their lives both within and outside of their work. By drawing on the UN Convention on the Rights of the Child, microfinance practitioners in Egypt were able to improve children's working conditions and learning opportunities through a series of nine intervention tools that could be integrated into standard microfinance programmes. The paper describes the tools and explains how they were developed and implemented in collaboration with working children themselves, their families, and business owners. The paper also describes some of the opportunities and challenges that would face those intending to replicate this type of programming from the perspective of both microfinance institutions and children's rights/child protection agencies.

Keywords: children's work, child labour, microfinance, child rights, occupational safety and health

WE HAD BEEN INVITED for dinner at the home of our Canadian International Development Agency (CIDA) project officer in the Maadi suburb of Cairo. After dinner we had the chance to look at some of the video clips we had made as part of the micro and small enterprise projects we were implementing in Upper Egypt. The videos featured some small business start-ups including plastic recycling, printing, automotive repair, and other businesses that employed up to a dozen workers. As we were pointing out the new technology and production processes involved, our CIDA colleague surprised us with a question: 'what are those kids doing?' We explained that children often showed up when we came to visit the businesses and they liked to be part

http://dx.doi.org/10.3362/9781780448879.008

of any videos that we made but we did not think that the children actually worked in any of the businesses. Still by the end of the evening we agreed to take a closer look. This was the beginning of what became the CIDA-funded project, 'Promoting and Protecting the Interests of Children who Work' or 'PPIC-Work'.

Discovering children working in microfinance client businesses

Our initial survey of children working in our client businesses began in the southern governorate of Aswan, Egypt, where our partner agency, the Egyptian Association for Community Initiatives and Development (EACID), had recently formed as a microfinance institution and was implementing programmes with micro and small business owners. EACID's loan officers helped design and implement a survey but the results showed that none of the businesses acknowledged that they employed children. Following some discussion we decided to use a less structured interview format and begin again. The senior management of EACID along with Canadian field staff joined the loan officers as an expanded survey team and with the loan officers still present, the clients were comfortable discussing the issue of children and work. The team used a structured interview guide but were also able to ask probing questions about how children spent their time over a typical day and clarify what was considered to be work done by children. When asked about their own family situation, clients responded that 'of course we have children' and later 'of course our children do help out with family businesses', but they did not consider the children to be employed. In some instances non-family children also 'helped out' either in client businesses or nearby businesses and clients explained that this was sometimes done as a favour to other families and children who needed to earn extra income. Children worked six days a week, the time spent varying significantly from two hours up to eight hours per day after school. Those children who worked longer hours had little time for play, homework, or sleeping but they and their families still considered attending school to be important. A typical day for these children could include five hours of schooling, eight hours of work, two hours for travelling to and from school and work, two hours for meals, ablutions, and any other activities, and seven hours for sleeping. The second survey had helped clarify the misunderstanding in the previous survey about whether children were actually employed and showed that about half of the businesses involved children who were 'helping out' in various capacities.

We began discussions with business owners, parents, and the children themselves and started to realize some of the complexities around children's work and how we as microfinance practitioners might respond. Children worked to help support themselves and their families and it was not clear to us that trying to prevent the children from working would be in their best interest.

Egyptian microfinance programmes were not the only ones finding children working in client businesses. This became evident when CIDA (2007: 12–14) funded a study to see how microfinance programmes were affecting children. The study, entitled *Impacts of Microfinance Initiatives on Children*, took place in Bolivia, Tanzania, India, and Egypt. It found that not only did children work in client businesses but the length of the children's workday increased as credit became available. Children were providing the additional labour to support initial business growth and either helped their parents directly in the business or took over parental responsibilities within the home. Results from Egypt showed that as loan size continued to increase the requirement for children's work in the business or in the home eventually decreased as larger loans were used to purchase productive machinery or employ adult workers. Details of the study methodology are included in the CIDA report.

Forming the PPIC-Work concept and finding allies

The PPIC-Work project began in early 2002 with the aim of improving the working conditions and learning opportunities of children working in the client businesses of microfinance institutions. The project itself ran from 2002 to 2011 with a budget of C\$4.5 m covering four components. Approximately 40 per cent of the budget was used for the work carried out with EACID and covered the costs of developing the various intervention tools with support from national and international experts. EACID had already become operationally sustainable before the beginning of the PPIC-Work project and continued to cover its own operating costs throughout the project period. EACID did receive a contribution of \$200,000 to its loan fund with the understanding that EACID would initially undertake greater risks in lending to businesses that employed children. EACID did find some higher losses in the early stages of the programme as the interventions were being developed but repayment rates soon returned to the 98 per cent range that was typical for EACID.

The project team felt that operating with and through microfinance institutions had a number of advantages and would make use of:

- the positive relationship between loan officers and business owners that would facilitate connecting with working children;
- the ability for business owners to access loans when additional funds were needed to improve children's working conditions or learning opportunities;
- the ability to monitor children's working conditions through loan officers' routine visits;
- multiple loans for continued improvements in children's working conditions and learning opportunities over time;
- sustained financing of loan officers from loan revenues.

These initial assumptions were supported by experience as the project unfolded. While there are several advantages to working through microfinance institutions, there are some limitations. The approach is applicable in those instances where children are working in the informal sector businesses that are clients of microfinance institutions. While this excludes children who work in businesses that are not interested in or eligible for microfinance loans, there are over 100 million active microfinance clients throughout the world (Daley-Harris, 2009), making it possible to reach large numbers of working children through microfinance programmes. Interventions to help working children however can only be made through clients who have been successfully managing their businesses and continuing to repay their loans on time. Any interventions undertaken by loan officers have to be limited so as not to significantly affect their overall workload and not influence decisions about the viability of a particular loan.

Prior to beginning PPIC-Work we had expected that children would not be directly involved in the microfinance activity of their parent(s) and would benefit through improved family income. However through the second survey we found that some children were directly involved in productive activities and were helping the business to grow, repay loans, and generate income for the business and themselves. The benefits from microfinance for these children would be more complex and difficult to assess. The working children could still benefit through improved levels of family or their own income and learn new skills through their work, but they could also be exposed to a range of possible harms. To ensure that we would be able to properly analyse and protect the working children we expanded the PPIC-Work team to include both local and international specialists in child rights, children's participation, gender equality, and occupational safety and health. We also sought out assistance from other agencies that worked with children and were able to provide advice on child protection programming including: the Child Rights Unit of CIDA, the International Labour Organization (ILO), UNICEF Egypt, Save the Children, Plan International, Terre des Hommes, and others.

Children and work

We considered children to be working if they were contributing to the productive activities of a business whether they were paid or not. We also recognized that the discussion of children's work has continued to generate considerable debate as there are both positive and negative aspects of work. There are three major conventions that set out conditions under which children can work. The ILO's Convention 138 from 1973 emphasized children's age and industrial sectors as the main determinants for children's work. These minimum age standards form the basis of many national child labour laws but have been challenged as not taking into consideration the nature of the work that children actually perform and not being in children's best interests. There have been instances where enforcement of this type of legislation has resulted in younger children leaving one form of work and migrating to other, less visible and more harmful forms of work (Bourdillon et al., 2009). The Convention on the Rights of the Child in 1989 placed the emphasis on ensuring that children were not exploited through work. More recently still, in 1999, the ILO Convention 182 on the Worst Forms of Child Labour states that children should not be harmed through work. While ensuring children do not work in exploitative or harmful situations remains an important goal, many children work in situations that are not considered exploitative or harmful. The ILO now states:

> Not all work done by children should be classified as child labour that is to be targeted for elimination. Children's or adolescents' participation in work that does not affect their health and personal development or interfere with their schooling is generally regarded as being something positive (ILO, 2014).

As the PPIC-Work team became more involved in discussions about children's work and child labour we began to recognize three categories of children's work:

- *'Worst forms'*. Work that is inherently hazardous and/or exploitative and from which children should be removed.
- *'Hazardous work'*. Work in which hazards can be mitigated; once this is accomplished, children may participate in such work without a violation of rights.
- *'Benign/educational work'*. Work in which children will not be harmed and from which they may benefit or learn.

Developing the PPIC-Work interventions

We found little evidence of inherently hazardous work (hazards that could not be mitigated) among EACID clients, but many of the workplaces did expose children to harm whether in the form of long working hours, use of unsafe machinery or production practices, exposure to unhealthy chemicals or environmental conditions, physical or psychological abuse, or other factors. The PPIC-Work team felt that many of these problems could be mitigated or eliminated and began to develop a series of intervention tools in collaboration with the working children and the business owners who employed them.

Dual-purpose loans

We found that many business owners were ready to help working children but they also wanted to know 'what's in it for me?' At the core of the PPIC-Work approach is the dual-purpose loan intervention that continues to provide regular loans to businesses but then provides additional loans in instances where children are working. Both loans are provided under the normal lending conditions of the microfinance institution and must be viable, meaning that the business owner has to have a good credit history and have sufficient revenues to repay both loans. The particular improvements for children's working conditions or learning opportunities are agreed upon by the loan officer and business owner (often consulting with the working children) and included in the loan contract. In some cases it was clear that not all of the problems affecting children's work could be eliminated through a single loan but these would be addressed through multiple loans over a period of time. As business owners found that they could get both the regular loan for the business and an additional loan to improve children's work they became more interested in the programme. There wasn't so much of a 'should' behind their decisions but rather from their point of view an opportunity to further improve their business while helping children. In developing the dual-purpose loan programme it was important that this did not become a reason for businesses to seek out and employ children as a way of accessing larger loans. Under EACID's programme business owners who did not employ children could also negotiate larger loans for their businesses provided they had a viable business plan, a good credit history, and sufficient revenues to repay the larger loan.

While most business owners who received the dual-purpose loans did follow through with the improvements for children, this was not always the case. In one instance a mechanic who worked with his three young sons (aged 16, 14, and 10 years) had agreed to use his additional loan to purchase safety equipment (steel ramps) so that when he and his sons were working under vehicles the work could be carried out safely. By the time the loan was repaid the business owner had still not purchased the safety equipment and began arguing with the loan officer that it was unnecessary. The loan officer disagreed and informed the mechanic that he would not be eligible for future loans until the safety equipment was in place. Within two weeks the mechanic had purchased the safety equipment and was back to negotiate the next loan. The interest of clients in gaining access to future loans provides the loan officer with an easy mechanism for encouraging compliance with minimal additional workload.

Key processes

In order to learn more about working children's issues in general and children's rights, gender equality, and children's participation in particular, we adapted the UNICEF Canada training materials on children's rights as well as other materials on gender equality and children's participation. We also provided training for the senior project team and the microfinance staff including loan officers (the training manuals for these programmes are available through the PPIC-Work (2009b) website).

Children's rights

The UN General Assembly adopted the Convention on the Rights of the Child in 1989 and in 54 Articles, set out the rights that all children have. In the case of working children there are several rights that we found to be of particular relevance including Articles 3, 12, 28 and 32, listed below:

- Best interest – in all actions concerning children ... the best interests of the child shall be of primary consideration.
- Participation – the child who is capable of forming his or her own views (has) the right to express those views freely in all matters affecting the child.
- Education – all children have a right to education.
- Economic exploitation – children have a right to be protected from economic exploitation and from performing any work that is likely to be hazardous ... (OHCHR, 1989).

Receiving training on children's rights helped staff understand the challenges working children face so they would be better prepared to engage in conversations with business owners about how children's rights could be respected and fulfilled. EACID staff were able to convert the training materials for use with the working children themselves and enlisted a local trainer to provide a two-day children's training workshop. Once working children themselves learned about their rights they were ready to advocate for change knowing that the loan officers would be there to support them if needed.

The loan officers and working children both recognized that any improvements for children could not jeopardize the survival of the business and in practice most changes benefited both the children and the business.

Gender equality

CIDA is recognized internationally for its work on gender equality and has published training manuals for development practitioners. We adapted these materials for microfinance institutions and eventually for working children (these materials are also available through the PPIC-Work (2009b) website).

In some of the early meetings with working children we met young boys who were working as informal apprentices where, under the guidance of the business owner and older workers, they learned the technical, business, and life skills related to the operation of small workshops such as: auto mechanics, metalworking, carpentry, and plumbing. These workshops were male owned and since EACID provided loans mainly to women there were only a few of these businesses within the loan portfolio. As the boys often began their apprenticeships between the ages of eight and twelve years and were exposed to a variety of hazards, we considered it important to include these children within the programme. Thus EACID began to expand its lending to male-owned businesses. In a subsequent study 'Gender, Hazards and Children's Work', we recognized that both the work children performed and the hazards children faced within their work were differentiated by gender (Zibani, 2009). Girls were more likely to be exposed to verbal abuse and sexual harassment while boys were exposed to physical hazards and in some instances male attitudes increased the level of risk. Senior male workers showed their bravado by deliberately avoiding the use of safety equipment and procedures. Boys who wanted to emulate the senior workers would also choose to ignore safety but be less experienced and more prone to injury when they did so.

Another gender-differentiated hazard for girls was a lack of learning opportunity or career path through their work. Whereas boys were able to learn technical and business skills and prepare for careers as senior workers or business owners, girls found it difficult to advance in their work. Families and working girls themselves often viewed their work as a way of saving money for marriage. It was common for girls to be involved with retail sales or mundane, repetitive work that provided little chance for growth. Business owners, whether male or female, explained that they were reluctant to promote girls to more senior positions and provide them with higher-level training even when they were good workers because it was assumed the girls would soon leave.

Loan officers became aware of the need to look for different types of problems and solutions to meet the needs of working girls and boys. While it was possible to mitigate some gender-differentiated workplace hazards, there were other gender issues that were beyond the reach of a microfinance programme.

In developing a children's advisory group for the PPIC-Work project we included an even number of girls and boys to make sure that gender issues were adequately reflected, despite the fact that there were more boys than girls working within the overall portfolio of clients. The children who became part of the advisory group represented the variety of business types served by EACID and lived close enough to the EACID offices so that they could attend meetings without interfering with their schooling or work.

The approach used by EACID to bring girls and boys together was supported and welcomed by parents and families. EACID formed a small team of two senior female staff who led the programme and were assisted part time by two younger male loan officers. The children were always supervised and group meetings were held at the EACID offices and were open to parents and other family members. The timing of the meetings was set so that children could attend the meetings and return home safely.

Children's participation

In developing the original PPIC-Work concept the project team began reaching out to working children in the Aswan governorate to find out more about children's work. Some of these children were working within EACID client businesses, others were not, but at this stage of the project development we wanted to connect with as many working children as possible. The project team found working children were 'just normal kids' who enjoyed sports, games, and other children's activities but they also had their work experience and understood why they were working, the role work played in supporting themselves and their families, the problems they faced in work, and possible solutions. Even before learning about children's rights we had come to respect the views of working children and realized that they would be important partners for us in developing and implementing the PPIC-Work project. Eventually a group of about 50 girls and boys became the advisory group and helped develop many of the PPIC-Work interventions.

To help working children analyse some of the problems that they raised we adapted community development tools that had been used with adults and began working with children who were street vendors. A common problem cited by these children was the disrespect and sometimes abuse they were shown by their adult customers. To help review and analyse the problem the project team adapted the adult literacy methodology of Paulo Freire (1968). Freire's approach helped communities identify but deperson-alize social problems and then discuss these objectively. This process that Freire referred to as 'conscientization' included: identification of a problem theme; translation of the problem into a depersonalized format or code (photograph, song, drama or other form); re-presentation of the code to the original group; objective discussion of the code; and development of an action plan to bring about social change. Through discussions with the children we had identified a problem theme – the mistreatment of working children by adult customers – and then shaped this into a problem 'code' that could be presented back to the children for analysis. In our case the problem code became a simple puppet drama that portrayed the experiences that the children had described. We re-presented the drama back to the children with initially four of the EACID staff operating the puppets and later the children taking turns as the puppeteers. The drama became much more animated as the children modified parts of the basic script and added some of their own experiences. The children were then asked whether the drama actually reflected their own experience and, if so, what was the problem in the drama, what were the causes, and what were the possible solutions. In the analysis that followed children identified that customers became disrespectful when they felt that children had deliberately been dishonest in handling money and had given less change than was due. The children acknowledged that this happened at times but they explained this was a result of their poor maths skills rather than attempts at dishonesty and a solution would be for EACID and the PPIC-Work project to help them improve their maths and literacy skills. The project team was impressed with the analytical skills of the children and agreed to help implement what became the Education Support Programme (see the following section). While over 90 per cent of the children working in EACID client businesses combined their work with formal, full-time education, the length of their workday meant that they did not have much time for study or homework and as a result their performance in school suffered.

While popular theatre continued to be used as an analytical tool along with photo and art documentation of work and life experiences, the children also took part in focus group discussions similar to adult learning workshops. In these types of discussions it was possible for the children to work in smaller groups based on gender or age or both. This helped ensure that all children were able to express their views and that the views of girls and boys as well as older and younger children were included.

The children's advisory group evolved over the project period with older children graduating out and younger children joining. The children's group continued to help develop the various intervention tools, develop training materials, and prepare project reports and documentation as well as monitoring and evaluation.

Education support programme

The education support programme was developed with the support of Caritas Egypt who had extensive experience in adult literacy and numeracy programmes. While most of the children were attending primary or middle school, many were not able to read or write at a basic level. As the educational support programme was implemented over the following months the curriculum was broadened at the request of the children to include coaching on other school subjects beyond literacy and numeracy. The emphasis of the programme was on learning and progressed at the children's pace.

As the programme continued working children improved their academic performance but they were also more self-confident, better behaved in class, and less bothered by the types of bullying that was sometimes directed towards working children by other students. In the education support programme all children were respected by their classmates and their adult instructors. Later on when they were dealing with customers they were able to avoid some of their previous mistakes with money and were more resilient when faced with occasional insults from some adults.

Code of conduct

As EACID became more familiar with the business owners who were employing children they arranged to bring a group of business men and business women to see what conditions should be applied when children are working. The meeting began with a presentation by an occupation and health specialist who explained some of the hazards that are specific to children's levels of physical development and maturity. The male and female business owners then worked first separately and then collectively to come up with their own set of suggestions for appropriate conditions that should apply when children work.

EACID then asked the children's advisory group to review the recommendations from the adults and make any changes that were necessary. At the time of these discussions the children were already aware of children's rights and gender equality principles. The children worked in groups divided by age and gender and eventually accepted most of the adult suggestions. They did however want to modify the length of workday from six hours as suggested by the adults to eight hours during school holidays to avoid a loss of income.

The children were then asked whether there were any further problems in their work that had not been addressed. One 10-year-old boy raised the issue of psychological abuse (insulting a child during work particularly when other workers were present). All of the children in the advisory group agreed that this did occur and was one of the most difficult experiences for working children. This type of abuse was not only directly hurtful but undermined the child's self-esteem and encouraged other workers to use similar insults towards the child. While the adults had identified the importance of avoiding physical abuse the children felt that psychological abuse was even more harmful and should not be allowed. As the children became aware of their rights they were ready to ask for these types of changes and when necessary enlist the support of the loan officer.

The children and adults met together to review the updated recommendations. None of the children worked for any of the business owners who were taking part so the children were comfortable with the meeting. EACID staff had combined recommendations coming from adults and children into a single list that did not attribute the recommendations to a particular group. All of the recommendations were reviewed and the revisions made included in a final list. The children's recommendations for the prohibition of psychological as well as physical abuse along with a longer workday during their holidays were all included.

EACID announced that it would use the recommendations as a code of conduct that would become part of future loan contracts with business owners who employed children. EACID considered the code of conduct would be helpful for improving the working conditions of children and would be reasonable for those business owners who would have to comply with the code of conduct. The code of conduct would be appended to the loan contract and a copy pasted on the wall of the business so that business owners, working children, and loan officers would be able to refer to it during future visits to the business. The code of conduct could be revised whenever needed through the same process used to develop it (the EACID code of conduct along with a more detailed discussion of its development are included on the PPIC-Work (2009b) website).

Computer-based learning

With knowledge of their rights many working girls were convincing their parents that they should be able to continue their education and prepare for their own careers. Their work however was mainly in retail operations and did not provide useful career experiences. EACID staff arranged for the girls in the advisory group to visit several of the technical trades businesses where boys were learning skills. At the end of the visits the girls met with the staff and explained that they were not interested in the work the boys were doing but instead would like to learn more about computer technology and the use of computers within business.

In following the interests of the girls the project team met with some computer specialists to see how to respond. We learned about Sugata Mitra's 'Hole in the Wall' experiments from India that were suggesting:

> The acquisition of basic computing skills by any set of children can be achieved through incidental learning provided the learners are given access to a suitable computing facility, with entertaining and motivating content and some minimal (human) guidance (Mitra, 2011).

Assuming that once the girls had access to computers they would be able to learn basic computer skills on their own, the project team decided to develop a computer game that would teach basic business principles and business ethics. Over the following two-year period the computer specialist, project team, and the working girls (eventually boys joined the group) collaborated to develop the Ba'alty (My Shop) computer game. The game allows children to create and grow a business from modest beginnings to a series of shops serving a variety of customers and communities. As the children try to improve the business and maximize their own net worth they are faced with choices. They can choose to focus on short-term profits or take a long-term view and re-invest some revenues back into the business, train workers, improve workplace safety, or promote good community relations. Developing a winning strategy generally requires a longer-term approach but the game includes several randomized variables and does not produce the same results each time. Children have found the game to be quite realistic and when training new children they say, 'decide the way you would in real life, the game works like that'. (The Ba'alty computer game is available as a free download in both Arabic and English (PPIC-Work, 2009a), and further information on the design, development and use of the game can be found on the PPIC-Work (2009b) website.)

Several generations of working girls and boys who have come through the EACID programme have become experts at playing the game. Girls tend to play the game in groups and work collaboratively while boys play the game competitively. Some of the girls who were involved in the original development of the game have gone on to complete post-secondary education and now work with computers in different businesses in Aswan.

Hazard assessment and mitigation

In implementing the dual-purpose loan programme the loan officers worked with business owners and working children to identify, analyse, and mitigate hazards in the work place. To build the capabilities of the loan officers we developed a training programme on occupational safety and health to help them better identify and resolve hazards. From the outset we realized that the loan officers would have to be able to carry out any additional work without adding significantly to the time spent on a routine business visit. Generally discussions with business owners and working children would last about 10 minutes but could be followed up and continued on subsequent monthly visits.

We enlisted the support of international and Egyptian occupational safety and health specialists and worked together to develop a series of practical tools that helped loan officers identify problems and prioritize interventions. While it was preferable to mitigate hazards that could lead to severe or frequent injuries, it was important to begin with practical and affordable changes. More complex issues could be dealt with later and might require an incremental approach over multiple loan cycles. Preferred solutions would be those that eliminated a particular hazard by changing the production process. In other instances the hazard could be mitigated through better-designed machinery or production techniques that reduced risks for children. Where these types of solutions were not possible safety signage and training would be implemented and children assigned to tasks that would not expose them to hazards. The PPIC-Work team learned from the occupational safety and health specialists that the least preferred and least effective safety measures would be the provision of personal protective equipment (masks, hard hats, gloves, safety footwear, etc.) as these place the onus for safety on the child. Children's workplaces should be safe without the requirement for personal protective equipment and children should not work in situations where personal protective equipment is required.

None of the EACID microfinance clients employed children in work that was considered to be inherently hazardous where hazards could not be mitigated. In cases of inherently hazardous work the approach would be to help children relocate to find alternative, safer forms of work (training manuals are available through the PPIC-Work (2009b) website and additional information can be found in Carothers et al. (2010)).

Learning through work

Many working boys along with a few working girls were involved in work that was helping them learn career skills. There are several ways that learning and work are combined including learning *for* work as in vocational education programmes or learning *with* work where literacy or other instruction is provided alongside work. In apprenticeships learning happens *through* work and takes place in the workplace rather than classrooms with guidance from experienced workers. Learning *from* work occurs when knowledge and skills developed from work can be applied outside the workplace.

The PPIC-Work team was particularly interested in learning through work and carried out a study in several technical workshops to find out how learning was taking place and what might be done to improve the learning process.

In technical workshops children begin work between the ages of 8 and 12 years and learn technical, business, and life skills as they progress through four levels. At the *entry level* the children begin to support other workers by cleaning, bringing refreshments, and performing other support tasks. At this level children learn life skills and are expected to follow instructions, understand the importance of timeliness and honesty, recognize the value of teamwork, and respect senior workers. At the *junior level* children begin to prepare working materials, clean tools, and support the technical work of older workers while observing the production process. At the *intermediate level* children become skilled in the various aspects of the technical work, begin to observe business operations, and supervise or train younger workers. At the *senior level* children master the technical skills, become proficient in the creative aspects of the work, and become able to support the business owner in all aspects of the business. Children are usually around 17 to 18 years of age when they reach the senior level as progress depends on their ability to learn and level of maturity as well as the needs of the business and the roles of other workers within the business. Senior workers tend to stay on and work with the business owner as skilled young adults and may later choose to move on and start their own business.

While the majority of children working in EACID client businesses attend school, only half of the children working in the trade businesses were combining their work with ongoing schooling. The project team decided to look for ways of improving the business that would encourage business owners and working children to value and apply skills and knowledge learned through formal education. At the same time the PPIC-Work team was seeing evidence that learning skills through work is a viable and effective way for children to develop long-term careers that in the Egyptian context can provide better levels of earnings than conventional vocational education programmes. Many of the business owners who had learned their skills as working children were earning incomes several times those of university graduates including most of the EACID staff. The effectiveness of learning through work in Egypt has been confirmed through a recent study of the long-term benefits of learning technical skills through formal education programmes and through informal apprenticeships (Krafft, 2013).

To improve the learning within the technical workshops EACID helped business owners visit similar but larger-scale facilities that used modern production methods. EACID then helped business owners identify and acquire new types of technologies that would improve their business performance and improve the learning environment for working children. One example involved the introduction of computerized diagnostic scanners into small automotive repair workshops. The scanners allowed mechanics to properly repair modern vehicles but required the workers using the equipment to be literate, numerate, and have a basic understanding of computer technology. Working children in these businesses were often the quickest in learning the new technology and both they and the business owners recognized the importance of formal education when using this level of technology. EACID has been able to make these types of technologies available through loans and has also developed a rental programme for instances where business owners would only need the new equipment occasionally.

Through the use of the PPIC-Work intervention tools EACID and other microfinance institutions have been able to improve the working conditions and learning opportunities for working children.

- The dual-purpose loans, the code of conduct, and hazard mitigation applied together can help improve working conditions.
- The education support programme, the Ba'alty computer game, and improvements to the learning through work process can help working children continue to learn technical, business, and life skills as well as achieve better academic results and more self-esteem.
- Learning about children's rights, gender equality, and children's participation have helped both microfinance staff and working children to better understand the complexities around children's work and how improvements can be achieved.

Costs associated with implementing the PPIC-Work programme

Most of the work involved in implementing the PPIC-Work programme is done by the loan officers and is included within their normal work. EACID found that this could be done with little or no additional operating costs. EACID found the cost of training the loans officers on occupational safety and health (2 days), gender equality (3 days), child rights (3 days), and children's participation (2 days) to be relatively modest. Groups of 40 staff could be trained at local training venues by local trainers who had become familiar with the training materials. The original cost of developing the training materials had been covered through the PPIC-Work project.

To implement the ongoing programmes with working children EACID assigned two senior female staff to conduct the education support programme and the children's training on child rights, gender equality, and safe workplaces. The female staff were assisted part time by two younger male loan officers. These programmes were designed for groups of 40 children at a time and held for 3 hours twice weekly and continued for approximately 7 months. During these sessions the children had access to the Ba'alty computer game where the children learned from each other. EACID again found the costs of these training programmes to be inexpensive and affordable from its own resources.

Impacts on children

Working children who have been part of the PPIC-Work programme have reported a variety of changes within their work and lives. An internal study carried out towards the end of the project found that children were generally aware of the code of conduct as well as other interventions and have been able to reduce their working hours, have time for breaks and holidays, and are generally able to schedule work so that it doesn't interfere with school. They have also reported improvements in their levels of pay and workplace safety and engage in discussions with business owners to achieve further improvements. A randomized survey carried out in Aswan as part of a CIDA evaluation (see Carothers et al. (2010) for more details including the study methodology) examined EACID clients and similar businesses that also employed children but were not part of the EACID programmes. The survey found that 97 per cent of the EACID clients were involved in improving safety within workplaces while only 27 per cent of non-EACID clients were at this level.

The internal study also found that children recognized the learning they had achieved through their work and explained their appreciation of the Ba'alty computer game as a way of learning more about business principles including access to and use of credit in setting up and growing a business.

The book entitled *Rights and Wrongs of Children's Work* cites the PPIC-Work project as an example of a child-centred approach that has been more effective in addressing the needs of working children than other child labour interventions that have attempted to remove children from work and focus on labour inspection and law enforcement (Bourdillon et al., 2010: 195–200). While not all problems of working children can be solved through a microfinance programme, in the case of EACID 'responses from both [working] children and business owners suggested that very significant progress had been made in many establishments' (Bourdillon et al., 2010: 200).

Why would businesses and microfinance institutions be interested in supporting working children?

While *business owners* were ready to assist working children it was neither unexpected nor unusual for them to also ask 'what's in it for me?' The loan officers also wanted to ensure that any loans issued to help children would not jeopardize the viability of the business and its ability to repay loans.

The PPIC-Work approach was generally most effective when businesses and working children both benefited through the changes that were being introduced and financed through loans. There were many examples of these 'win–win' situations:

- By increasing his working capital loan, a father who was operating a community grocery shop was able to negotiate for home delivery of his supplies. This meant that his teenage daughters no longer had to go to the market in the early morning to bring back the heavy supplies of fruits and vegetables while contending with traffic on the street and harassment from passers-by in the dark morning hours. The business and family income were able to grow and while the girls continued to perform light work serving customers in the shop, they worked for shorter hours and had more time for school and studying.
- A loan to expand a restaurant and separate the kitchen from the eating area allowed the boy who served customers to collect the food orders

through a serving window rather than having to enter the kitchen and negotiate his way around the hot stove and boiling oil.

- Another boy working in a restaurant has decided that he will open his own group of restaurants based on the business skills he has learned through the Ba'alty computer game and his real life experience.
- In other cases the installation of safer electrical wiring, better lighting and ventilation, proper tables and seating facilities for work, carts to reduce the need for heavy lifting, guarded machinery, and shorter working hours all helped to improve children's work.

As a *microfinance institution* that was developing and implementing the PPIC-Work project, EACID found that supporting working children was consistent with its own social mandate and objectives. The PPIC-Work programme also assisted EACID in its relations with the local and national levels of government which had criticized the high interest rates associated with microfinance but approved of EACID's support for working children.

As many of the clients employed their own children or the children of close family members they appreciated the programming that EACID was developing. EACID's ability to offer business loans and support programmes for working children became a competitive advantage for EACID when other microfinance institutions began to operate in the Aswan governorate.

Working children within EACID's PPIC-Work programme will be well placed to operate their own businesses and at that time will require access to the types of financial services provided by EACID. The support that EACID has provided to these children will help ensure that they will become future clients and successful business operators.

In 2010 EACID presented the results of the PPIC-Work programme at the annual conference of the Social Investment Organization (now the Responsible Investment Association) in Canada. EACID presented its results as an example of a microfinance programme that can provide good rates of return while achieving positive social outcomes for marginalized groups such as working children. Some investors represented large pension funds; they explained that while they had only 10 per cent of their current investments in socially responsible funds, the majority of their clients invested with them because of that 10 per cent. Expanding investment into opportunities like microfinance would provide a competitive advantage when attracting clients. Supporting working children could help microfinance institutions demonstrate the positive social impacts that are of interest to socially responsible investors.

Next steps

The issue of children working within microfinance client businesses provides an opportunity for microfinance practitioners and child protection agencies to work together to improve the lives of children and at the same time support business development programming. Many of the PPIC-Work interventions can be implemented at minimal cost and the ability of microfinance programmes to reach large numbers of the informal businesses where children do work would mean that the lives of many millions of working children could be improved through a collaborative approach. At the same time it would be possible to enhance the social impact of microfinance programming and perhaps help open up new forms of investment capital.

Working together would require microfinance institutions to become familiar with children's rights and gender equality and be able to facilitate children's participation in the development and implementation of programming. Training materials on these topics from the perspective of microfinance institutions have been developed and are available through the PPIC-Work (2009b) website. At the same time child protection and child rights agencies would have to become familiar with the realities of small businesses and business support programmes such as microfinance. The development of a collaborative programme would have to be based on both the empirical realities of working children within a given context and the local realities of the micro and small businesses where they work. There would be a need to agree on the types of outcomes that could be achieved through this type of programming so that suitable indicators could be developed and used to measure progress. Agreement at this level would be an important step in further discussions with socially responsible investors that could provide significant levels of investment in microfinance provided positive social impacts are achieved and verified and the security of assets and reasonable returns on investments are maintained.

References

Bourdillon, M., Myers, M. and White, B. (2009) 'Reassessing minimum-age standards for children's work', *International Journal of Sociology and Social Policy* 29(3): 106–17.

Bourdillon, M., Levison, D., Myers, M. and White, B. (2010) *Rights and Wrongs of Children's Work*, Piscataway, NJ: Rutgers University Press.

Canadian International Development Agency (CIDA) (2007) *Impacts of Microfinance Initiatives on Children* [pdf], Gatineau: CIDA <www.acdi-cida.gc.ca/INET/IMAGES.NSF/vLUImages/Childprotection/$file/impactsofmicrofinanceinitiativesonchildren-en.pdf> [accessed 23 April 2015].

Carothers, R., Breslin, C., Denomy, J. and Foad, M. (2010) 'Promoting occupational safety and health for working children through microfinance programming', *International Journal of Environmental and Occupational Health* 16(2): 164–74.

Daley-Harris, S. (2009) *State of the Microcredit Summit Campaign Report*. Washington, DC: Microcredit Summit Campaign.

Freire, P. (1968) *Pedagogy of the Oppressed*, New York: Seabury.

International Labour Organization (ILO) (2014) 'What is child labour' [online], ILO <www.ilo.org/ipec/facts/lang--en/index.htm> [accessed 29 December 2014].

Krafft, J. (2013) *Is School the Best Route to Skills? Returns to Vocational School and Vocational Skills in Egypt* [pdf], St Paul, MN: Minnesota Population Centre, University of Minnesota Working Paper No. 2013-09 <www.pop.umn.edu/sites/www.pop.umn.edu/files/WorkingPaper_VocationalEducation_09.pdf> [accessed 15 January 2015].

Mitra, S. (2011) 'Beginnings' [webpage], New Delhi: Hole-in-the-Wall Education Ltd <www.hole-in-the-wall.com/Beginnings.html> [accessed 29 December 2014].

Office of the High Commissioner for Human Rights (OHCHR) (1989) 'Convention on the rights of the child' [webpage], United Nations Human Rights <www.ohchr.org/en/professionalinterest/pages/crc.aspx> [accessed 15 January 2015].

PPIC-Work (2009a) *Ba'alty Computer Game* [online] <www.baalty.org/en/index.html> [accessed 15 January 2015].

PPIC-Work (2009b) 'PPIC-Work: manuals and field guides' [webpage], Egypt: PPIC-Work <www.ppic-work.org/resources.htm> [accessed 15 January 2015].

Zibani, N. (2009) *Hazards and Gender in Children's Work: An Egyptian Perspective*, Cairo: Population Council.

About the author

Richard Carothers (richardcarothers@rogers.com) is president of Partners in Technology Exchange Ltd, Ontario, Canada.

CHAPTER 9

Independent child migrants in developing countries: a literature review

Shahin Yaqub[1]

Abstract

Independent child migrants are aged below 18 years, and migrate without a parent or formal adult guardian. Often related to schooling, work, and lifecycle transition, this independent movement of children could be part of a wider debate linking migration and development, but is often unrecognized or conflated with concerns about child trafficking. Across the world many children are independent migrants who actively participate in their movements, are substantially self-dependent, and often are depended upon by relatives left behind. This paper synthesizes quantitative and qualitative research to shed light on: (1) the numerical scale; (2) characteristics of migrant children; (3) decision-making processes; (4) why it happens; (5) modes of movements; and (6) situations of children at destinations.

Keywords: migration, child poverty, children's work, trafficking, urbanization, socioeconomic mobility

CHILDREN HAVE BEEN CONSIDERED in migration mainly as dependents accompanying migrant parents, or left behind by them. Until recently trafficking or asylum-seeking, rather than migration, were thought to account for most of the independent movements of children. Less understood are the independent movements whereby children migrate for work, school, or other reasons.

The contexts, manner, and implications of migration can differ between child and adult migrants because of age-specific biological vulnerabilities and resiliencies; and age-specific responses to incentives and risks at origins and destinations. Children's lower consumption needs can influence their 'reservation wages' and employment choices, but this is balanced against their needs for care, development, and protection. Children are subject to particular legal and social norms, restrictions, and expectations, which influence the age-appropriateness of work, opportunities for migration, and access to shelter, livelihoods, healthcare, and schooling at destination.

In this review, the terms 'children', 'migration', and 'independent' are defined as follows:

- Children are aged below 18 years, following the United Nations Convention on the Rights of the Child. Additionally 12 years and 15 years are relevant cut-offs for children's work under ILO Conventions.[2]

http://dx.doi.org/10.3362/9781780448879.009

- Migration is a chosen change in 'usual residence' (defined as place of daily rest) from birthplace or country (UN, 1978, 1998).
- Independent children are without a parent or legal/customary adult guardian.[3] This comprises separated children (with relatives apart from parents and adult guardians) and unaccompanied children (with no adults).

The review covers around 40 studies with quantitative and qualitative field evidence (sample sizes are reported in brackets as 'N'). It shows that independent child migration is a major issue in developing countries, often involving poor, rural children, occasionally as young as 7–10 years (but generally older). Often it is motivated by children themselves, with their own reasons and financing, inter-linked to family ones, such that many children's independent movements would need to be seen in a broader migration–development lens, rather than child trafficking.

Quantitative evidence on independent child migration

This section reviews data on numerical scale and characteristics. Is independent child migration uncommon (e.g. hundreds), and if not, how many are involved and in what sorts of places? Is it only male youth, and if not, are many young children and girls involved? Other assumptions examined are that it is mostly internal migration by poor and unschooled children. Official data from governments and international organizations rarely distinguish independent child migrants, and instead the studies draw on surveys at border-points, families at origins, places of employment, informal sector surveys, and national censuses.

Asia

A survey of over 17,000 children at the Nepali border in 2004 found two-thirds were travelling to India independently (Adhikari and Pradhan, 2005). The majority were seeking work (60 per cent), and a third had been to India before. Summarizing six surveys in Nepal, Gurung (2004) argues poverty as the dominant reason for leaving home; as well as parental influence, domestic problems, and personal choice. Gurung estimates around 1.6 per cent of 5–17-year-olds work away from home, totalling 121,000, of whom 44 per cent were girls.

In Bihar and Uttar Pradesh 1 million children, 3 per cent of 5–14-year-olds, reside away from their mothers (Edmonds and Salinger, 2007). Children living away on average were 10 years old; twice as likely to be boys; and more likely from asset-poor families. In Mumbai, of around 5,000 independent child workers located by a NGO, nearly all were migrants and over half were under 12 years old (Edmonds and Salinger, 2007). In the Philippines, official statistics estimate 400,000 children live and work away from home (Camacho, 2006).

One-third of migrants from 22 Laotian villages bordering Thailand were independent migrant children, some 30,000 children (Phetsiriseng, 2003). Cycles of repatriation and remigration are common. Lack of jobs and schooling were major push factors. Seasonal migration remains important, but villagers reported that children increasingly preferred to migrate to avoid agricultural work. Additionally, Phetsiriseng argues children may prefer migrant work because this can give them more control of income than on a family farm or enterprise.

In Cambodian villages bordering Thailand, ILO (2005) reports that over half of 10–17-year-olds (N=163) were not in school and 36 per cent were working (half of whom were 10–14 years old). Among currently or previously working children, nearly a quarter of 10–14-year-olds, and half of 15–17-year-olds, worked outside the village. Most went to Thailand, with working 10–14-year-olds at roughly the same rate as working 15–17-year-olds. All children working outside the village were independent migrants.

Africa

In Benin 100,000 children (22 per cent of 6–16-year-olds) migrated independently (Kielland, 2008). Boys were on average aged 11 years at departure, and girls 10 years. Close proximity of schools reduces boys' migration, but has no effect on girls' migration, which may reflect gendered access to education. Children of wealthier households are more likely to be in school and less likely to be migrants (particularly girls). Greater maternal education increases the likelihood of girls migrating (but has no effect on boys), and female headedness increases the likelihood of boys migrating (but has no effect on girls).

In Burkina Faso 330,000 children (9.5 per cent of rural 6–17-year-olds), migrated independently (Kielland and Sanogo, 2002). Around 30 per cent went to another rural area, 40 per cent to a city, and 30 per cent abroad. Parents said 18 per cent of boys and 16 per cent of girls migrated entirely on their own initiative. Less remoteness, better transport, and greater access to media are thought to increase children's independent migration.

Erulkar et al. (2006) surveyed 1,076 children in Addis Ababa, and found one-third were migrants. Only 17 per cent lived with parents. Girl migrants were four times as likely as boys to be living without parents. Around one-third migrated when younger than 10 years, 47 per cent between 10 and 14 years, and just under a fifth between 15 and 18 years. Half migrated for schooling, although 13 per cent did not enter school. Nearly a quarter of girls said they migrated to escape early marriage. Death of a parent and parental divorce were also commonly cited.

In Uganda, a survey of 433 working children found that 40 per cent were not living with a parent and 63 per cent were migrants (ILO, 2004). Of migrants, 70 per cent were aged 15–17 years, 28 per cent 10–14 years, and 2 per cent 5–9 years. Of children under the ILO definition of child labour (rather than merely economically active), 80 per cent were migrants.

Hatloy and Huser (2005) surveyed street children in Bamako (N=340), of whom migrants composed 80 per cent. Some 13 per cent were aged 6–11 years, 41 per cent 12–14 years, and 46 per cent 15–17 years. The main reason for leaving home was money; but around a tenth cited mistreatment. Only a quarter of children said that life was better than at home; but only a tenth wished to return home, two-thirds wished for a better job, and 11 per cent wished for schooling.

Hatloy and Huser (2005) surveyed street children also in Accra (N=1,341), of whom migrants composed 98 per cent. Some 10 per cent were aged 6–11 years, 27 per cent 12–14 years, and 63 per cent 15–17 years. Nearly all reported money as the reason for leaving home. A fifth of the 6–11-year-old children travelled to Accra alone. Little involvement of recruiting agents or unknown adults was reported (11 cases in the sample). Nearly three-quarters were in contact with parents, mainly through telephone, letter, or oral messages, rather than visits. Three-quarters of the children said they saved in informal savings schemes. While only 27 per cent said life was better than at home, returning home was wished by 23 per cent, getting a better job by 46 per cent, and going to school by 18 per cent.

A quarter of street children in Lusaka were migrants (N=1,150), with one-third aged 15–17 years, 40 per cent 12–14 years, and 27 per cent 4–11 years (Lemba, 2002). Fewer than 30 per cent spent the night on the streets. A third resided with non-relatives or alone. Half cited work, money, and helping family as to why they were street working. Girls earned more, mainly because average earnings in prostitution were four times higher than for other activities. Returning to school was cited by 70 per cent as help most wanted; capital to start a business or employment by 13 per cent; housing, food, or clothes by over 8 per cent; money for repatriation by 1 per cent; and assistance reconciling with parents by nearly 1 per cent.

In Kigali 65 per cent of street children were migrants (N=290), perhaps up to a quarter were living independently, and 53 per cent were aged under 15 years (Veale and Dona, 2003). The authors found that compared with non-migrant children, migrants were statistically more likely to be sleeping on the streets, out of school, and reporting nightmares. For reasons for being on the street, nearly 46 per cent cited poverty or economic motives; 17 per cent family disharmony; and 27 per cent parental death, parental remarriage, or loss of parents.

A longitudinal survey over two years in one rural district of South Africa recorded 39,163 episodes of children's out/in-migration (Ford and Hosegood, 2005). Around 21 per cent of children migrated, and over 80 per cent did so independently. Around 60 per cent migrated out of the district. Children in households with more assets were less likely to migrate. Death of the mother increased the chances of a child's migration, unless death was due to HIV/AIDS, in which case it lowered the chances of migration. Father's death increased migration, whether due to HIV/AIDS or not.

Americas

Quiteno and Rivas (2002) surveyed 110 working children in cities in El Salvador, of whom two-thirds were boys, and 19 per cent were aged 16–17 years, 36 per cent 13–15 years, and 45 per cent 7–12 years. Around 41 per cent were migrants, of whom 9 per cent said they lived with neither parent. Asked why they had migrated, parental push was cited by 8 per cent, wanting to help the family by 23 per cent, wanting to earn money by 63 per cent, and survival needs by 5 per cent. Half the children spent their earnings on themselves, and the others remitted some.

Mexico is seen mainly as an origin or a transit country to the USA, but Mexico is a major destination as well. Migration across Mexico's 1,000 km southern border, for example, sustains a range of fruit and other production. Sin Fronteras (2005) estimate 10 per cent of agricultural migrants are 14–17 years old, mostly boys. Younger children are involved – Sin Fronteras cites official data on independent Guatemalan children repatriated from Mexico, and around 1.5 per cent were below 11 years old and nearly 23 per cent aged 11–15 years (April 2004 – April 2005).

Romero et al. (2006) report data on Mexico's internal migration. Of around 3.1 million agricultural wage workers, half are migrant and a fifth children. While mostly with families, around 1 per cent of agricultural wage workers were migrant and independent under 14-year-olds. Around 58 per cent of migrant children aged 6–14 years worked, of which: 1.2 per cent were alone, 66 per cent were with both parents, 14 per cent were with one parent, and others were with village members. All independent migrant children worked, compared with 53 per cent when with both parents.

Cross-national census studies

McKenzie (2008) estimated the number of foreign-born children who recently migrated (<5 years) from countries with gross national income per capita below US$11,116 in 2006. The proportion of migrant children living without a parent at destination ranged from 5 to 82 per cent of girls and 7 to 75 per cent of boys, as shown in Table 1. The unweighted average across countries was 25 per cent of 12–14-year-old girls, 49 per cent of 15–17-year-old girls, 21 per cent of 12–14-year-old boys, and 46 per cent of 15–17-year-old boys. The net-of- marriage figures remain high in several countries, even among girls.

Yaqub (2009a) uses population censuses in one of the few estimates of independent migrant children versus dependent migrant and non-migrant children. Independent children were defined as not co-residing with parents, step-parents, adopted parents, or adult siblings. There were 143,240 international and internal independent migrant children in Argentina, 154,560 in Chile, and 116,781 in South Africa – which was nearly a fifth of the child migrant population in the three countries, and 1.2 per cent of the child population (see Table 2). Independent migrant children had

Table 1 Recently migrated (<5 years) foreign-born children: percentage living without a parent and percentage married

		Girls				Boys			
		Living without a parent, %		Married, %		Living without a parent, %		Married, %	
		12–14-year-old	15–17-year-old	12–14-year-old	15–17-year-old	12–14-year-old	15–17-year-old	12–14-year-old	15–17-year-old
Argentina	1996–2001	19	50	na	2	19	35	na	1
Canada	1999–2001	7	13	na	2	7	7	na	0
Costa Rica	1998–2000	31	60	3	29	20	49	1	5
Greece	1999–2001	14	41	2	19	27	60	0	1
Ivory Coast	1997–2002	55	82	5	41	ss	67	ss	3
Kenya	1998–1999	34	52	2	12	29	47	0	3
Mexico	1995–2000	25	48	2	14	12	29	0	2
Portugal	2000–2001	29	42	0	6	21	50	0	2
South Africa	1999–2001	41	66	0	11	45	75	0	3
Spain	1999–2001	19	34	0	7	21	30	0	2
United Kingdom	2000–2001	5	61	0	5	8	58	0	2
United States	1998–2000	17	39	na	10	18	49	na	4

Note: ss, small sample size; na, not available
Source: McKenzie (2008)

Table 2 Recently migrated (<5 years) independent child migrants in Argentina, Chile, and South Africa

	All children			Independent children		
	Argentina	Chile	South Africa	Argentina	Chile	South Africa
Non-migrant	11,252,440	3,810,340	16,801,111			
International migrant	51,820	29,430	33,987	8,990	5,430	6,924
Inter-province migrant	384,850	396,570	462,526	58,640	81,680	109,857
Intra-province migrant	467,140	340,400	na	75,610	67,450	na

Note: na, not available
Source: Yaqub (2009a)

worse shelter at destinations, whereas dependent migrant children's shelter was no worse than for non-migrant children. Average schooling was around 6 years for independent migrant children, which was nearly two years more than dependent migrant children and similar to non-migrants. Over a fifth of international independent migrant children aged over 15 years were employed, compared with under 4 per cent of non-migrant children. Employment of internal migrant children was lower than international migrant children.

Qualitative evidence on independent child migration

This section examines children's participation in migration. How is children's independent migration decided and organized? What motives might children have for migrating independently? How do children migrate independently given their limited formal opportunities? What are children's situations at destination? The in-depth, multiple sourced and contextualized accounts from ethnography and participatory research methods have helped address the research challenge that decisions are multi-layered and uncovering them is difficult.

How is children's independent migration decided and organized?

In Iversen (2002) children and parents separately provided accounts of migration decisions in Karnataka, India (N=169 under 15-year-olds). Independent child migration was defined strictly as an unambiguous wish to leave home, without any parental involvement in decisions or arrangements (such as for employment or shelter). Some 25 per cent of children's migration aged 10–14 years was strictly independent (with parental involvement in 75 per cent). All were boys, accounting for 3.6 per cent of the village population of 10–14-year-old boys.

Over two-thirds did not seek parental consent and three-quarters overrode parental wishes (however these were not runaways because family relationships were maintained). Boys aged 12–14 years regularly made labour migration decisions independently. Children took responsibility for the organization (or lack of it) of their migration. Around 58 per cent migrated without prearranged work, 29 per cent arranged work via older migrants, and 12 per cent arranged work via relatives. Most travelled with peers or relatives, and few travelled alone.

Orgocka and Jasini (2007) surveyed 150 children and 150 adults in Albania. Large majorities cited children and parents as facilitators of children's independent migration. While older children reported the importance of peers and emigrants (those currently abroad) as facilitators, adults failed to do so. The proportions wanting to migrate were 10 per cent of 10–12-year-olds, 15 per cent of 13–15-year-olds, and 26 per cent of 16–18-year-olds. Almost all children believed work at destination would be necessary, and the majority knew about exploitation risks (sexual, organ sale, crime, or labour). Fake papers and walking over the mountains were cited by children as possible modes of travel.

Beauchemin (1999) reports similar results in rural Ghana (N=805 schoolchildren). Two-thirds had relatives and friends aged below 20 years who migrated. Girls said migration helped to avoid early marriage and to prepare for eventual marriage. Over 80 per cent would like to migrate to seek new opportunities. Of 282 parents interviewed, 81 per cent approved or thought their child's decision to migrate was a good idea. Half had more than one migrant child. When they migrated, 14 per cent of children were aged under 10 years, and 64 per cent between 12 and 17 years. Most parents knew where their children had gone (8 per cent had no contact). Many migrated for around half the year in the low season, and returned to continue schooling with their earnings.

The following illustrates the migration process:

> One day I told my father I had to get some clothes altered. I bought a bus ticket and told my brother to take the bike back home. I knew by the time he got there, it would be too late for my father to do anything. I wasn't afraid when I left. I had cedi 30,000 and the bus ticket cost cedi 10,000. I arrived in Kumasi around 6am. I didn't know anyone here. [He found a job via a clansman he met on the street.] In the beginning it was really hard because people cheat you. Sometimes I earn cedi 10,000 a day, sometimes nothing. So you have to save (Beauchemin, 1999).

De Lange (2006) found that in Burkina Faso boys aged 10 and above migrated up to 200 km, on employment contracts lasting normally a year (N=40 returnees at origin and 14 at destination). Children nearly always undertook the migration decision. Parents worried about children's safety and health, and the loss of family labour and company, but few attempted to prevent migration. At destination children relied on employers, who usually provided room and board. Some were paid less than promised. Returning without money was considered shameful, forcing some to stay. Some had migrated several times despite knowing the hardships. Some continued school after returning, having earned their school fees. Children who were recruited and children who migrated without recruiters were no different from each other in their experiences at destination.

A study of 4,500 cocoa farms in Cameroon, Côte d'Ivoire, Ghana, and Nigeria found an intermediary involved in recruiting 30–40 per cent of the child workers, with the rest recruited by other workers, children making contacts themselves, or by the farmer directly (IITA, 2002). In the cases of recruitment by intermediaries, none of the children reported their parents being paid, none reported being forced against their will to leave home, and most claimed to know the recruiter. In Côte d'Ivoire alone over 22,000 children work in the sector, around 12,000 of whom are independent and over three-quarters were migrants (IITA, 2002).

Camacho (1999) found that many domestic workers aged 14–17 years in Manila had started as provincial migrants when younger (N=50). Over half were under 15 years old at first migration. For the majority, parents and siblings participated in the decisions. Camacho describes how families try (not always successfully) to use social networks to provide protective environments at destination. The Manila job was located by an agency for 8 per cent, by parents for 6 per cent, by themselves for 4 per cent, and the rest by friends or relatives. Around 80 per cent said the decision to work was theirs, and 14 per cent consulted neither parent. Brown (2007) found that domestic workers in Cambodia often used their own social networks to place themselves into work. Relatives and friends were part of the network, but also neighbours and market sellers.

Heissler (2008) interviewed 58 independent child migrants in Dhaka, and 105 parents and community members at origins. Heissler argues that wider education has raised aspirations for salaried work that is accessible only for the wealthiest. High landlessness and abandonment or death of the male breadwinner put migratory pressure on children. Heissler noted that migration allows some children to work beneath their social status, while other children refused to migrate because migration would mark their family as low status.

What are the motives for children's independent migration?

Broadly there are three sets of motives: 1) income generation, fulfilling family obligations, and positioning themselves within their families; 2) accumulation of assets and human capital as part of their own goals of progress, independence, and lifecycle transition into adulthood ('future seeking'); and 3) self-protection to escape domestic abuse, violence, early marriage, and economic and health shocks.

Motive set 1: consumption, family roles, and intrahousehold positioning

While consumption and earnings objectives are important, the research suggests this motivation is linked to children's social relations within the family. Camacho (2006) argues that migrant children in the Philippines often perceive an improved position in their families, depending on their social networks and access to work. Punch (2002) proposes the notion of 'negotiated interdependence' to understand how independent migrant children fulfil family needs while asserting influence over their life. Punch (2007) argues that among Bolivian independent child migrants in rural Argentina work and training can increase their 'generational power', and that migration can be simultaneously empowering (back home) and disempowering (at destinations).

Some studies have found that migration was used to secure specific possessions that could enhance autonomy, such as bikes (De Lange, 2006) and sewing machines (Hashim, 2005). Castle and Diarra's (2003) study of 10–18-year-old independent migrants from rural Mali found girls wanted articles for their marriage, while boys wanted articles to increase their status. In Heissler's (2008) study in Bangladesh, some independent girl migrants said they were saving for their marriage dowry.

In Burkina Faso, 40 per cent of adults surveyed felt 10–14-year-olds should do the same tasks as adults (TdH, 2003). Migrant children in Ghana and the Gambia state '...strong expectations that children should start "giving back" to their parents as soon as they can, usually by their early teens' (Chant and Jones, 2005: 191). Omokhodion et al.'s (2006) survey of 225 migrant and non-migrant children aged 8–17 years working in a market in Nigeria, of whom half were also in school, found that 46 per cent felt that children should not work and a quarter thought it signalled deprivation, but also that work was beneficial for providing incomes, and helping their parents, and was good training for becoming responsible adults.

Independent migrant children send remittances. Anarfi et al. (2005) documents an 18-year-old migrant farm worker in Ghana who had been remitting to his parents since the age of 14; a 14-year-old migrant in Dhaka remitting to his mother; and a 13-year-old girl porter in Accra who remitted cash and household utensils, some for her marriage. Several cases underlined independent migrant children's need for a safe means of saving.

Motive set 2: accumulation of assets and human capital as part of lifecycle 'future-seeking'

Some research suggests migration may be seen within lifecycle stages as one of the few routes to socio-economic mobility for children endowed with limited opportunities. Beauchemin (1999) quotes a 15-year-old migrant in Kumasi: 'I've saved cedi 200,000. I'd have a lot more but I've been robbed often. I want to go back home for a while. But I'll come back. My dream is to set up a television repair shop here.' Heissler (2008) cites a girl domestic worker from a landless family in Bangladesh whose earnings helped buy land, and according to village members the resulting upward economic mobility kept siblings from migrating. Land aspirations were cited by Liviga and Mekacha (1998) in Tanzania and Touray (2006) in semi-arid areas in Asia and Africa.

Schooling is another sought-after 'asset'. Camacho (1999) found that in Manila 30 per cent of independent migrant children paid for their own or siblings' education. In Ghana, Hashim (2005) found that some independent migrant children combined work with schooling, informal apprenticeships, or skills training, in a context where schooling was seen as just one of several determinants of a child's future. Curran (1996) found that family decisions concerning 12–21-year-olds and their education versus migration depended on gender and sibling order in study villages in Thailand that had high poverty, migration rates, fertility, and land scarcity. Sons were preferred for education, both sons and daughters migrated, but daughters were more likely to remit wages.

A survey of 313 child migrants in a Thai town close to Myanmar found just 12 per cent living with a parent (FTUB, 2006). Around 85 per cent cited an economic motive for being in Thailand. Almost all had completed at least primary school, but only a few continued schooling in Thailand (only a fifth said they did not want to study). The children originated from all over Myanmar, some as far as provinces bordering Bangladesh on the other side. Around 60 per cent had arrived within 12 months, suggesting a high turnover, which is argued to help keep wages low. Despite harsh working conditions, around 60 per cent said they liked living in Thailand.

Motive set 3: escape from abuse and shocks as part of self-protection

Adugna (2006) quotes a 15-year-old independent migrant in Ethiopia: 'My parents didn't want to send me to town ... I said I better go somewhere and try my best instead of dying of hunger there.' Adugna found that work was overwhelmingly the main reason for migration, but domestic violence and escaping marriage were also cited. Half maintained contact with their families, visiting home once or twice a year. Police and the fear of arrest were cited as serious problems.

Ansell and Blerk (2004) found that in communities with high rates of HIV, children migrated for work, to care for sick relatives, and be cared for; directions of migration included all four rural/urban combinations; and a third migrated more than once, mainly due to instabilities in their circumstances. Akresh (2004) shows that income shocks trigger informal child fostering in West Africa. Some authors argue that children's work may be a form of 'insurance' against income shocks (Beegle et al., 2006).

Conticini and Hulme (2006) found that in Dhaka domestic abuse contributed to children's independent migration to the streets (N=93). Children stated that economic independence was a means to free themselves from abuse and excessive control. Just 5 per cent of boys and no girls reported that in the year before leaving home they were free of physical, emotional, or sexual violence (11 per cent of boys and 24 per cent of girls were subject to all three). Perpetrators ranged from parents, step-parents, relatives, to school teachers. 'The child learns to consider migration as a concrete alternative to acceptance of violence. Migration to the street … is a decision that develops over time' (Conticini and Hulme, 2006: 35).

Brown's (2007) study of independent child domestic workers in Cambodia found several children came from abusive or dysfunctional backgrounds. Sizeable family debt was present in over half the cases. Age at first entry into work was under 12 years for 12 per cent, and 12–14 years for 26 per cent. Around 70 per cent of the sample (N=123) were migrants, sometimes seasonally. In recruitment, no child was promised different work and the work was as expected before migrating. Children living with relatives were less likely to be recognized as workers and paid. Brown argues that demand for children's work in garments, tourism, and sex work, and across the border in Thailand, may account for regional differences in children's earnings in domestic service, and possibly increase participation by younger children (since the other sectors attract older children).

Stites et al. (2007) found that in Uganda domestic abuse, hunger, and abandonment were reasons for children's migration independently. A steady decline in family livelihoods or health preceded a more discrete trigger for children's migration. Some children sold firewood to pay for their transport, and others had their fare paid at destination by prospective employers. In several cases, young migrants returned with food and cash, and took siblings with them when they re-migrated.

How do independent migrant children move?

Movement seems to occur mainly in two modes: 1) through the kinship network or other social mechanisms; and 2) modes similar to adult labour-market movements and routes. Independent migrant children's modes of movement can lead to non-migrant labels, such as fostered, street children, or runaways.

Mode 1: kinship routes

Fostering often involves independent migration by children. Across West Africa, between a fifth and a third of households (varying by country) include other people's children under 15 years, and most are not orphans (Pilon, 2003). Fostering away from surviving parents can be high even among young children: in Benin, 1.5 per cent of 0–2-year-olds, 9.5 per cent of 3–5-year-olds, 14.3 per cent of 6–9-year-olds and 18.4 per cent of 10–14-year-olds (Kielland, 2008). The causes of fostering include parental illness, death, economic hardship, divorce, and separation; labour needs in the destination household; and broadening children's experiences and schooling. Although fostering commonly requires adult arrangement, children frequently help decide and sometimes initiate it.

Leinaweaver (2007) argues that fostering in Peru is part of kinship strengthening, and almost all parties have an interest: sending parents may have obligations towards the recipient family, or wish to strengthen a relationship, or wish to promote their child's life chances; the receiving household may want the child for reciprocal social reasons or household help; and the child may want to ease parental consumption burdens and find new opportunities, particularly schooling. Leinaweaver argues the more distant the social relationship between receiving adult and migrant child the more possible that exploitation could occur.

Mode 2: labour-market routes

Some children's independent migration resembles adult irregular migration, following similar routes, smugglers, and processes of exclusion at destination. Some cross over fences or rivers marking borders, some cross unchecked at official border points, and others over-stay day passes (Adhikari and Pradhan, 2005; SCF, 2007; FTUB, 2006). Independent child migrants in South Africa crossing from Mozambique have described their travel on foot, and some have had to overnight in territories with wild animals and other dangers (SCF, 2008).

Phetsiriseng (2003) reports that travel costs of independent child migrants in Laos sometimes equal half of the agreed pay. Punch (2007) found Bolivian migrants to rural Argentina often went on contracts covering transport, subsistence, and border crossing, with payment at the end; and this type of contract might be attractive to new migrants. Punch reports a 14-year-old returning after four months with US$600. Generally independent migrant children do not travel alone. For most, the movement seems accompanied, with other children, relatives, or smugglers. Across the Myanmar–Thai border the cost of migration in 80 per cent of cases was zero or under $2, and few travelled with smugglers (FTUB, 2006).

Situations at destination

Kwankye et al. (2007) interviewed in Kumasi and Accra 450 independent migrant children and adults aged 18–24 years who had migrated as children. A quarter had a home, but others slept in markets, shop fronts, stations, and kiosks (for which some paid). This exposed them to uncomfortable sleep, bad weather, sexual harassment, robbery, assault, and morbidity, including malaria, hygiene-related diseases, sexual diseases, and food-related diseases. Children coped by sleeping in groups and with knives. Food had to be purchased, even if costlier and unhealthy. Many were food insecure and missed meals. Fewer than a quarter accessed a clinic ever. Over half were medicated by pharmacists and another 15 per cent self-medicated. Many were sick but went without healthcare. Around three-quarters saved small amounts daily in informal savings schemes. Half said they remit money and goods.

Children – particularly young ones – mostly need adult help to secure housing at their destination, either via social networks or housing markets. Some may arrive at their destination without housing arranged because their parents lacked the economic and social resources, or because they had migrated without parental involvement. Ansell and Blerk (2005) examined migrant housing in Lesotho and Malawi (N=200 children). Most is poor quality and informally provided by small landlords. Ansell and Blerk argue that housing is more than about shelter, because it influences children's care contexts; the indoor environment; the immediate outdoor environment; infrastructure, utilities and services; physical security; and security of tenure. Children's limited independent access to housing may explain why many street children are migrants.

Migration exposes children to new influences on health behaviour (Lane, 2008). While young people are more likely to suffer coercion or sexual violence, they may also be more likely to engage in consensual, unprotected 'survival' sex, such as to access food and shelter. Lane notes that health concerns of children themselves may be more focused on day-to-day considerations such as acne, menstruation, dental care, weight, or psychosocial issues such as relationships, education, and employment.

In a survey of migrants from Myanmar, Laos, and Cambodia in Bangkok (N=696), one in four was a child, and children and unregistered workers were paid less than adult and registered workers (Pearson et al., 2006). Registration was discouraged by employers, the time-consuming process, and the children's lack of understanding of the process. Employers retained the originals of documents, so even when registered, the fear of arrest remained and movement outside the workplace was limited. Employers were more likely to owe money to children than to adults. Few children (<3 per cent) were falsely informed about their type of work or working conditions. A third of those aged 15 years and 14 per cent of 15–17-year-olds had no information on this prior to migration.

Often below the age for work permits, and with little official entitlement to services at destination, independent child migrants have few incentives to identify themselves to authorities. On the streets of Accra (N=35), Orme and Seipel (2007) observed that most independent migrant children seldom used publicly provided social services and were generally sceptical about their ability to meet their needs; social services were either too strict or asked too many questions. In South Africa, independent migrant children from Zimbabwe said they tried to remain invisible to authorities for fear of deportation, making them difficult to reach by social welfare agencies at destinations (UN and IOM, 2007). Deportation can represent lost income, and many children lie about their age and other information to avoid family reunification and to return quickly. Involuntary family reunification may be an additional burden on children not faced by adults.

A quarter of children surveyed in South Africa (N=130) had been previously repatriated, and a further quarter had been arrested but later released

(SCF, 2007). Very few children had ever had contact with a social worker. Some children were as young as seven, and the average age was 14. Crime was mentioned as the worst thing about being in South Africa. When asked what help they most needed in South Africa, the children were equally likely to cite jobs and schooling. In spite of this, 72 per cent of the children felt that their lives in South Africa would be better than their parents' lives.

Hashim (2006) tries to draw out the positives and negatives of independent child migration from study sites in Ghana. Some children end up in abusive and harmful situations at their destination. But migration also allows some of them access to opportunities for income and skills they might not otherwise have. This comes out in the positive way that migrant children spoke about their migration experiences. Also many migrant children expressed that working for others was preferable to working in the family, echoing earlier discussion of children seeking independence and family positioning. Hashim also notes that the positive comments need to be set within the context of the low development situations from which the migrant children originate.

Return child migrants

Studies on returned child migrants help probe children's agency by reporting children's views on migration, after having experienced it. Adhikari and Pradhan (2005) surveyed 8,210 Nepali children returning from India. Half had migrated for work and a tenth for education. Nearly three-quarters had stayed a year or more. A quarter of children intended to migrate to India again within two months, another quarter within a year, and half were unsure if they would re-migrate. One-third had worked as day labourers, especially in construction, and over a quarter worked in hotels, restaurants, and as porters.

ILO (2005) interviewed returned migrants in Cambodia (N=72). Positives of migration were income, work, living conditions, food security, and new skills. Negatives were being arrested, low pay, work conditions, missing family, and being disrespected. Nearly a quarter judged migration to have had a positive impact on their life, 15 per cent mixed impact, and 14 per cent negative. All intended to re-migrate. Only one-third said their return home was to visit family, while others cited problems with employers, police, health, unemployment, or marriage/childbirth.

Iversen (2002) argues that in India a reason that independent migrants return is for marriage; workplace problems can be another reason. In Ghana, Beauchemin (1999) found that while some child migrants return 'successful' with goods and money, others are seen to return home with problems such as debt, sexually transmitted diseases, and babies (children outside marriage may be a barrier to returning). Dezso et al. (2005) found that in Romania returnee child migrants find it hard to readjust to modest living standards and so want to re-migrate.

Conclusions

Some generalizations from the reviewed evidence

Based on the data reviewed, the global scale of children's independent migration might be in the order of tens of millions, perhaps between 1 and 1.5 per cent of the child population in developing countries. Some specific estimates reviewed were 30,000 independent child migrants from 22 Laotian villages; 100,000 in Benin; 121,000 in Nepal; 300,000 in Burkina Faso; 1 million from two Indian states; 143,240 in Argentina, 154,560 in Chile, and 116,781 in South Africa. In Argentina, Costa Rica, Côte d'Ivoire, Kenya, Mexico, and South Africa, between 12 and 82 per cent of migrant children are without a parent at destination. Assumed to be mostly near-adult boys, significant numbers of girls and young children are involved too.

In some cases, migration can be entirely initiated and executed by children – but they are not runaways since parents often support it, or do little to discourage it, and most keep contact with families (which questions a common policy assumption of forced reunification with families). In other cases, some degree of joint decisions exists. Motives reported by children include: 1) boosting consumption, family roles, and intrahousehold positioning; 2) accumulation of assets and human capital to pursue lifecycle transitions (as part of 'future seeking'); and 3) responding to economic and health shocks and intra-family conflict (as part of self-protection). These themes are repeated in different countries.

Several studies found children in hardship who did not want to return home, because they valued independence and the possibility of a better life. Instead, many children want support at their destinations, which requires tackling children's various developmental exclusions at destinations. High economic and social costs of return may prevent some children from returning or circular-migrating, and voluntary repatriation services might be a useful safety net. Research on return child migrants indicates that many were not trapped at their destination, for example by traffickers, and re-migration intentions suggest some children will migrate even having already experienced hardships first-hand.

Economic development seems to be a structural driver, by relocating children to areas of higher employment demand. Similar to what has been shown in adult studies, the process appears gendered. In rural–rural migration, boys can go into farming and plantations; girls migrate less to rural destinations, but do so under informal fostering (escape from marriage usually seems to lead to urban destinations). In rural–urban migration, boys are more likely to migrate onto urban streets than girls; girls and young boys go into domestic service; boys and girls go into gender-differentiated manufacturing jobs; boys are more likely to migrate for schooling, but nearly always work as well; boys and girls can be informally fostered. Low social valuation of female work, generally, could make girls' migration for work less noticed.

Access to shelter, healthcare, schooling, training, safe employment, consumption, physical security, nurture, and visiting their families are prime concerns at destinations. The financing of migration, particularly whether debt was involved, the financial returns to children's work, and the ability to save safely, are likely important determinants here – but remittances and earnings by children are hardly researched. Age-specific restrictions on documents (e.g. residence permits, health permits, labour permits) and children's often limited information, understanding, and abilities regarding these, may push them into riskier activities. Accessing work often requires adult involvement and shelter is even more strongly adult-mediated. Most are disadvantaged without some form of benevolent adult mediation. State agencies, including police, are often hindrances or threats.

Migration, development, and children: some open issues

Children's independent migration, located largely in informal sectors and irregular migration, may be a component of the 'hidden' dimensions of urban poverty, and connect to development agendas on 'unregulated' urbanization. Children's independent migration affects development agendas in poverty, child labour, street children, and 'education for all'.

Research has not yet clarified how policies can respond to the needs of independent migrant children in a safe, substantial, and supportive way. Interventions could be seen as condoning children's labour and exploitation; supporting children's movement into uncertain care; promoting children's moves away from families; or undermining education. Indeed if not well-designed, policies might turn out to fulfil some of these dangers. Moreover the bulk of independent child migrants are in poor- and middle-income countries and places, raising concerns about resources and capacities to effectively address the issues.

Mostly the assumption has been to protect children involved in independent movements against trafficking. Distinguishing independent child migration from child trafficking 'on the ground' is complex. Under the UN Protocol to Prevent, Suppress and Punish Trafficking in Persons, Especially Women and Children, in the case of children, facilitated movement for exploitation is considered sufficient for trafficking to have occurred. It is not necessary to prove duress, deception, abduction, etc. A child's consent is irrelevant in this definition, but both facilitation and exploitation are necessary.

Yet the research indicates that children do wilfully move in order to contribute to their and their families' well-being and development. This raises underexplored issues related to children's influence and participation in development, and the particular support and protections this may require. Such migration–development linkages cannot be adequately considered through a child trafficking lens with its emphasis on 'children in harm', and its necessity by definition of criminal involvement. Bastia (2005) argues that indiscriminate anti-trafficking measures can sometimes complicate children's movements in terms of low-level corruption and employment options, and based on case studies of Bolivian children in Argentina, questions simple categories of 'victims of trafficking' and 'normal labour migrants'.

The 'glitter' of destinations, peer influence, or lack of information loom large in policy positions on children's independent migration, rather than the specific goals that many children report, including their economic motives. Current responses fall into two main types: a communication approach that essentially aims to persuade children and parents out of independent child migration by educating them about its dangers and costs; and a legal approach that assumes all independent movements by children are due to criminal activity, and aims to apprehend the criminals and return children home.

A third approach that has received relatively little policy attention, a developmental approach, would identify migration incentives and disincentives, and offer responses that improve children's developmental outcomes. This would map how low, unequal development opportunities at origins and destinations influence children's independent migration, and recognize that migration could be part of a managed solution, and not only a source of child risks. In the main, the research suggests that children accept independent migration risks at such early ages only because, in the realities in which they live, socio-economic security and prospects disappear early.

Endnotes

1. This is a much shortened version of Yaqub (2009b) which documents more of the literature and discusses independent child migration in economic history, contemporary migration–development links, and underexplored research questions.
2. Following ILO conventions 138 and 182, children 15 years and older can work if it is not hazardous for their safety, physical or mental health, or moral development; and children 12–14 years old can perform certain types of light work a few hours per week. All other economically active children are termed as 'child labourers'. Economic activity encompasses productive activities, except schooling and chores in the child's own household, of at least one hour per week (whether for the market or not, paid or unpaid, casual or regular, or legal or illegal).
3. Children may be independent at destination after travel because of parental death, deportation, or abandonment. Some children may travel independently but not be independent at destination, because their travel is for family reunification.

References

Adhikari, R. and Pradhan, N. (2005) *Increasing Wave of Migration of Nepalese Children to India in the Context of Nepal's Armed Conflict*, Kathmandu: Save the Children.

Adugna, G. (2006) 'Livelihoods and survival strategies among migrant children in Addis Ababa', mimeo, Trondheim, Norway: University of Trondheim.

Akresh, R. (2004) *Risk, Network Quality, and Family Structure: Child Fostering Decisions in Burkina Faso*, Working Paper 65, BREAD, Cambridge, MA: Harvard University.

Anarfi, J., Gent, S., Hashim, I., Iversen, V., Khair, S., Kwankye, S., Addoquaye Tagoe, C., Thorsen, D., and Whitehead, A. (2005) *Voices of Child Migrants*, Brighton, UK: Sussex University.

Ansell, N. and van Blerk, L. (2004) *HIV/AIDS and Children's Migration in Southern Africa*, Cape Town: Idasa and Kingston, Ontario: Queen's University.

Ansell, N. and van Blerk, L. (2005) 'Migrant children's perspectives on life in informal rented accommodation in two southern African cities,' *Environment and Planning* 37(3): 423–40 <http://dx.doi.org/10.1068/a36226>.

Bastia, T. (2005) 'Child trafficking or teenage migration? Bolivian migrants in Argentina', *International Migration* 43(4): 58–89 <http://dx.doi.org/10.1111/j.1468-2435.2005.00333.x>.

Beauchemin, E. (1999) *The Exodus: Growing Migration of Children from Ghana's Rural Areas to the Urban Centres*, New York: UNICEF.

Beegle, K., Dehejia, R.H. and Gatti, R. (2006) 'Child labor and agricultural shocks', *Journal of Development Economics* 81: 80–96 <http://dx.doi.org/10.1016/j.jdeveco.2005.05.003>.

Brown, E. (2007) *Out of Sight, Out of Mind? Child Domestic Workers and Patterns of Trafficking in Cambodia*, Phnom Pen: IOM, Cambodia.

Camacho, A. (1999) 'Family, child labour and migration: child domestic workers in Metro Manila', *Childhood* 6(1): 57–73 <http://dx.doi.org/10.1177/0907568299006001005>.

Camacho, A. (2006) *Understanding the Migration Experiences of Child Domestic Workers in the Philippines*, Quezon City, Philippines: PST CRRC.

Castle, S. and Diarra, A. (2003) *La Migration Internationale des Jeunes Maliens*, London: School of Hygiene and Tropical Medicine, London University.

Chant, S. and Jones, G.A. (2005) 'Youth, gender and livelihoods in West Africa', *Children's Geographies* 3(2): 185–99 <http://dx.doi.org/10.1080/14733280500161602>.

Conticini, A. and Hulme, D. (2006) *Escaping Violence, Seeking Freedom: Why Children in Bangladesh Migrate to the Street*, GPRC-WPS-047, Manchester, UK: Manchester University.

Curran, S. (1996) *Intra-household Exchange Relations: Explanations for Gender Differentials in Education and Migration Outcomes in Thailand*, Working Paper 96-12, Seattle, WA: SPRC, University of Washington.

De Lange, A. (2006) *Study on Child Labour Migration and Trafficking in Burkina Faso's Southeastern Cotton Sector*, Amsterdam: IREWOC.

Dezso, I., Glatz, B., Kerekes, K. and Todea, J. (2005) *Foreignland: Dreamland or Nightmare?* Cluj-Napoca, Romania: Foundation for Children, Community and Family.

Edmonds, E. and Salinger, P. (2007) *Economic Influences on Child Migration Decisions: Evidence from Bihar and Uttar Pradesh*, Discussion Paper 3174, Bonn: Institute for the Study of Labor.

Erulkar, A., Mekbib, T.A., Simie, N., Gulema, T. (2006) 'Migration and vulnerability among adolescents in slum areas of Addis Ababa, Ethiopia', *Journal of Youth Studies* 9(3): 361–74 <http://dx.doi.org/10.1080/13676260600805697>.

Federation of Trade Unions Burma (FTUB) (2006) *Working Day and Night: The Plight of Migrant Child Workers in Mae Sot, Thailand*, Myanmar: Federation of Trade Unions Burma; Bangkok: ILO.

Ford, K. and Hosegood, V. (2005) 'AIDS mortality and the mobility of children in KwaZulu Natal, South Africa', *Demography* 42(4): 757–68 <http://dx.doi.org/10.1353/dem.2005.0029>.

Gurung, Y.B. (2004) 'Nature, extent and forms of child labour in Nepal', *Nepal Population Journal* 11(10): 17–43.

Hashim, I.M. (2005) *Exploring the Linkages Between Children's Independent Migration and Education: Evidence from Ghana*, Working Paper T12, Brighton, UK: Sussex University.

Hashim, I.M. (2006) *Positives and Negatives of Children's Independent Migration*, Working Paper T16, Brighton, UK: Sussex University.

Hatloy, A. and Huser, A. (2005) *Identification of Street Children*, Report 474, Oslo: Fafo.

Heissler, K. (2008) 'Children's migration for work in Bangladesh: the extra- and intra-household factors that shape "choice" and "decision-making"', *Childhoods Today* 2(1): 1–19.

International Institute of Tropical Agriculture (IITA) (2002) *Child Labour in the Cocoa Sector of West Africa*. Ibadan, Nigeria: IITA.

International Labour Organization (ILO) (2004) *Child Labour and the Urban Informal Sector in Uganda*, Uganda: ILO.

ILO (2005) *Destination Thailand: Cross-border Labour Migration Survey in Banteay Meanchey Province, Cambodia*, Bangkok: ILO.

Iversen, V. (2002) 'Autonomy in child labor migrants', *World Development* 30(5): 817–34 <http://dx.doi.org/10.1016/S0305-750X(02)00007-4>.

Kielland, A. (2008) *Child Labor Migration in Benin*, Saarbrücken, Germany: VDM Verlag.

Kielland, A. and Sanogo, I. (2002) *Burkina Faso: Child Labour Migration from Rural Areas*, Washington, DC: World Bank and Geneva: Terre des Hommes.

Kwankye, S., Anarfi, J.K., Addoquaye Tagoe, C. and Castaldo, A. (2007) *Coping Strategies of Independent Child Migrants from Northern Ghana to Southern Cities*, Working Paper T23, Brighton, UK: Sussex University.

Lane, C. (2008) *Adolescent Refugees and Migrants: A Reproductive Health Emergency*, Watertown, MA: Pathfinder International.

Leinaweaver, J. (2007) 'On moving children: the social implications of Andean child circulation', *American Ethnologist* 34(1): 163–80 <http://dx.doi.org/10.1525/ae.2007.34.1.163>.

Lemba, M. (2002) *Rapid Assessment of Street Children in Lusaka*, Zambia: Project Concern International.

Liviga, A. and Mekacha, R. (1998) *Youth Migration and Poverty Alleviation: A Case of Petty Traders in Dar es Salaam*, Research Report 98.5, Dar es Salaam, Tanzania: Research on Poverty Alleviation (REPOA).

McKenzie, D. (2008) 'Profile of the world's young developing country international migrants', *Population and Development Review* 34(1): 115–35 <http://dx.doi.org/10.1111/j.1728-4457.2008.00208.x>.

Omokhodion, F.O., Omokhodion, S.I. and Odusote, T.O. (2006) 'Perceptions of child labour among working children in Ibadan, Nigeria', *Child: Care, Health and Development* 32(3): 281–6 <http://dx.doi.org/10.1111/j.1365-2214.2006.00585.x>.

Orgocka, A. and Jasini, A. (2007) *Assessment of Child Trafficking vis a vis Smuggling in the Northwest of Albania*, Tirana, Albania: Partnere per Femijet.

Orme, J. and Seipel, M.M.O. (2007) 'Survival strategies of street children in Ghana: a qualitative study', *International Social Work* 50: 489–99 <http://dx.doi.org/10.1177/0020872807077909>.

Pearson, E., Punpuing, S., Jampaklay, A., Kittisuksathit, S., and Prohmmo, A. (2006) *Underpaid, Overworked and Overlooked: The Realities of Young Migrant Workers in Thailand*, Bangkok: ILO.

Phetsiriseng, I. (2003) *Lao PDR: Preliminary Assessment of Illegal Labour Migration and Trafficking in Children and Women for Labour Exploitation*, Bangkok: ILO.

Pilon, M. (2003) 'Foster care and schooling in West Africa', Background Paper for EFA Monitoring Report 2003, Paris: UNESCO.

Punch, S. (2002) 'Youth transitions and interdependent adult-child relations in rural Bolivia', *Journal of Rural Studies* 18: 123–33 <http://dx.doi.org/10.1016/S0743-0167(01)00034-1>.

Punch, S. (2007) 'Negotiating migrant identities: young people in Bolivia and Argentina', *Children's Geographies* 5(1): 95–112 <http://dx.doi.org/10.1080/14733280601108213>.

Quiteno, H. and Rivas, W. (2002) *El Salvador: Trabajo Infantil Urbano*, Geneva: ILO.

Romero, S.J.R., Nava, D.P., and Samperio, D.V. (2006) *Diagnostico Sobre la Condición Social de las Niñas y Niños Migrantes Internos, Hijos de Journaleros Agrícolas*, UNICEF México.

Save the Children UK (SCF) (2007) *Children Crossing Borders: Report on Unaccompanied Minors to South Africa*, London: SCF.

SCF (2008) *Our Broken Dreams: Child Migration in Southern Africa*, Maputo, Mozambique: Save the Children.

Sin Fronteras (2005) *Mexico y su Frontera Sur: Sin Fronteras*, Mexico City: IAP.

Stites, E., Mazurana, D. and Akabwai, D. (2007) *Out-migration, Return and the Resettlement in Karamoja, Uganda*, Briefing Paper, Somerville, MA: Feinstein International Center, Tufts University.

Terre de Hommes (TdH) (2003) *Les Filles Domestiques au Burkina Faso: Traite ou Migration?* Burkina Faso: TdH.

Touray, K. (2006) 'Desertification and youth migration: global perspective', presented at the *International Symposium on Desertification and Migration, 25–27 October, Almeria, Spain*.

UN (1978) 'Statistics of internal migration: a technical report', *Studies in Methods*, Series F, No. 23, New York: United Nations Statistics Division.

UN (1998) 'Recommendations on statistics of international migration revision 1', *Statistical Papers* Series M, No. 58, Rev. 1, New York: United Nations Statistical Division.

UN and IOM (International Organization for Migration) (2007) 'Joint assessment report on the situation of migrants from Zimbabwe in South Africa', mimeo, South Africa: UN and IOM.

Veale, A. and Dona, G. (2003) 'Street children and political violence: a socio-demographic analysis of street children in Rwanda', *Child Abuse and Neglect* 27: 253–69 <http://dx.doi.org/10.1016/S0145-2134(03)00005-X>.

Yaqub, S. (2009a) *Child Migrants with and without Parents: Census-based Estimates of Scale and Characteristics in Argentina, Chile and South Africa*, Discussion Paper 2009-02, Florence: Innocenti Research Centre, UNICEF.

Yaqub, S. (2009b) *Independent Child Migrants in Developing Countries: Unexplored Links in Migration and Development'*, IWP 2009-01, Florence: Innocenti Research Centre, UNICEF.

About the author

Shahin Yaqub is a socio-economist specializing in poverty, child development, and social protection, formerly at UNICEF and FAO, and currently at UNDP.

CHAPTER 10

Fostering economic opportunities for youth in Africa: a comprehensive approach

Karen Moore

Abstract

Youth unemployment and working poverty are large and growing development challenges. The barriers faced by young women and men in accessing sustainable livelihoods are many, so supporting their successful transition into employment and entrepreneurship requires a comprehensive and holistic approach. This article reflects on the evolving approach of The MasterCard Foundation-supported programmes in sub-Saharan Africa, within the broader context of wider research and evidence. It suggests that combining training in a range of market-relevant skills, with access to job and business opportunities and appropriate financial services, can foster economic opportunities for youth. It emphasizes the importance of recognizing the role of mixed livelihoods in contexts where formal jobs are lacking, and of supporting youth engagement in agriculture and agribusiness as viable livelihood opportunities. And it highlights that the challenge can only be adequately addressed via the meaningful engagement of a range of stakeholders, including the private sector, government and civil society, and, especially, youth themselves.

Keywords: youth, sub-Saharan Africa, employment, entrepreneurship, skills

ECONOMIC OPPORTUNITIES FOR YOUTH – particularly poor and marginalized youth – are crucial not only to generate an income to support young people and their households today, but also to support their long-term well-being and that of their communities. Successful transitions to jobs and businesses that allow young people to build financial and other assets, knowledge and skills, social networks, and self-confidence, can make the difference between persistent poverty and sustainable livelihoods, between widespread frustrated aspirations and social stability. Yet for millions of youth worldwide, a smooth transition to satisfactory work is a distant dream.

In sub-Saharan Africa, the youth unemployment rate, at almost 12 per cent, is twice that of adults (ILO, 2014). Due to large and growing child and youth populations – those aged below 25 made up over 63 per cent of the population in 2010, expected to remain above 50 per cent by 2050 (UNPD, 2012) – the absolute number of unemployed youth continues to grow. Additionally, vulnerable employment and working poverty are particularly pressing issues

http://dx.doi.org/10.3362/9781780448879.010

in sub-Saharan Africa, with by far the highest rates of both compared with any other region. Estimated at 77 per cent in 2013 (ILO, 2014), 'vulnerable employment' encompasses own-account workers (i.e. those self-employed) and unpaid contributing family workers (i.e. those working on a family farm or for a family business without a wage). These workers are employed under relatively precarious circumstances, with no formal employment arrangements or access to social protection benefits or programmes, putting them at relatively high risk of poverty and vulnerable to the effects of economic cycles. 'Working poverty', estimated at 40 per cent in 2012 at the US$1.25/day level (ILO, 2013), describes those who continue to live in poverty despite their wages or income.

The nature of the challenge can be seen in terms of both risks and opportunities. The large number of African youth who are unemployed or unable to make ends meet through jobs and businesses are often seen as a threat to social stability. But overcoming youth unemployment and working poverty is a chance for significant, positive change. Inclusive growth that fosters economic opportunities for youth, and their meaningful engagement in social and political life, should be seen as an opportunity for innovation, growth, development, and sustainability, at the individual, household, and national levels. Adolescence and young adulthood are key moments to interrupt the intergenerational transmission of poverty (Moore, 2005; Shepherd et al., 2011). Evidence suggests, for example, that long spells of unemployment or underemployment in informal work can have permanent repercussions on future productivity and employment (Guarcello et al., 2007). A lack of early economic opportunities can undermine asset building and life satisfaction (World Bank, 2013). Conversely, smoother and quicker transitions from school to adequate, sustainable jobs or small businesses can have positive, long-lasting effects.

Yet sub-Saharan African youth face a range of barriers to accessing good economic opportunities, constraining their ability to build sustainable livelihoods and escape poverty. Among these are: limited numbers of formal jobs (AEO, 2012); low levels of literacy, education, and work-relevant skills (Sparreboom and Staneva, 2014; UNESCO, 2012, 2013); and a lack of access to assets (Markel and Panetta, 2014), including land (FAO et al., 2014), and to financial services (Demirgüç-Kunt and Klapper, 2012; Demirgüç-Kunt et al., 2013). These barriers are cross-cut by social, economic, and political biases against youth (Banks and Sulaiman, 2012; Markel and Panetta, 2014; MasterCard Foundation, 2013, 2014).

It is important to note the heterogeneity of 'youth' as a group. First, it reflects the same diversity as the population in general. Marginalized youth – including young women, but also youth with disabilities, youth from minority populations, youth living in remote rural areas and urban slums, and others – face particular challenges in accessing work and risk being trapped in vulnerable employment and working poverty. Second, as 'transition' is the defining feature of youthhood, there is additional diversity within the group, whether defined according to the United Nations' 15–24 age range or the wider ranges often adopted by national governments. An 18-year-old may be in school and/or training, and/or working for herself and/or for others. She may be living with parents, alone, or with a partner and/or her own children dependent on her. And transitions are not always uni-directional: a period of self-employment can precede finishing school, for example. This diversity in young people's status and experience adds a layer of complexity to both data-gathering and programming, but understanding 'youth segments' is crucial to successful interventions.

Recent years have seen an increased focus on building youth economic opportunities by many development stakeholders, including The MasterCard Foundation (www.mastercardfdn.org), an independent, global organization based in Toronto, Canada. Through collaboration with partner organizations, the Foundation's programmes promote financial inclusion and advance youth learning, mostly in Africa.

Since 2011, the Foundation has been building partnerships that support economic opportunities for youth, partnering with 22 organizations and investing over \$236 m in this portfolio. As of August 2014, a portfolio review conducted for the Foundation by E.T. Jackson & Associates found that almost 130,000 participants had graduated from training programmes, with almost 59,000 making the transition to employment in a full-time job or internship or to self-employment (MasterCard Foundation, 2015b). This portfolio also includes a Foundation partnership with the ILO to build the evidence base around youth employment and education challenges, resulting in up-to-date, national-level, disaggregated data for 28 developing and transitional countries, including eight in sub-Saharan Africa, to influence youth employment policies and programmes.

In addition, as noted in a portfolio review conducted for The MasterCard Foundation by BCG, the Foundation has invested \$54 m to date in projects centred on financial services for youth, across eight partners working with over 40 financial service providers, including 30 in sub-Saharan Africa (MasterCard Foundation, 2015a). At the beginning of 2015, according to reports consolidated by the Foundation, these projects have provided over 756,000 youth with financial education, and nearly 713,000 with savings services (about 85 per cent through accounts with formal financial service providers). Nearly 111,000 loans have been accessed, to invest in income-generating activities and education, and to cope with emergencies.

The MasterCard Foundation is currently deepening and sharpening its engagement in the economic opportunities for youth space. Initial experience of the Foundation's economic opportunities for youth and youth financial services portfolios suggests that approaches that offer a combination of training in a range of market-relevant skills with access to appropriate financial services and links to job and business opportunities, will be more successful in breaking the barriers faced by youth in accessing work than stand-alone interventions. The Foundation's Economic Opportunities for Youth strategy emphasizes building an understanding of the complexities of Africa's diverse economic development pathways and the barriers that prevent youth from accessing economic opportunities. The overall approach is to identify value chains and markets that offer strong potential to be major sources of employment or entrepreneurship opportunities for youth, and to target market failures or needs of specific youth segments, working with experienced partner organizations to prepare youth to access these opportunities. A current focus is on sustainable livelihoods opportunities for African youth in agricultural value chains and agribusiness, including in the informal sector.

This article reviews the rationale for the Foundation's evolving approach, details the comprehensive, holistic approach its partners take, and concludes with opportunities and challenges, based on early experiences of programme implementation.

Prospects for youth employment in the context of informality, mixed livelihoods, and agriculture

The economic lives of Africans, including African youth, continue to rely heavily on informal labour markets and mixed livelihoods. This often includes farming, especially (but not only) in rural areas, where the majority of Africans continue to live. Recognizing and better understanding this reality, and identifying scope for improvement within this context, may hold some of the answers to youth unemployment and working poverty in the region.

Household enterprises and family farms dominate the African economic landscape. As noted, over three-quarters of African workers are in vulnerable employment: informal work for oneself, or in a household enterprise or farm (ILO, 2014). Across surveys of 13 sub-Saharan African countries during the 2000s, 69 per cent of respondents identified family farming as their primary source of employment, with an additional 15 per cent identifying household enterprises; many more work in household or microenterprises as a secondary activity (Fox and Sohnesen, 2012). A non-farm sector participation rate of 75 per cent for Ghana and 93 per cent for Malawi was reported when both primary and secondary income-generating activities were included (Winters et al., 2009 in Bezu and Holden, 2014).

Combining agricultural and other income-generating activities over time and space to reduce risk and diversify opportunity is common among low-income Africans, including youth. As noted by Murray (2001: 2):

> modes of livelihood that typically prevail both within households and between households are highly diverse. Rural households, for example … may derive a part-livelihood from farming; a part-livelihood from migrant labour undertaken by absent household members in urban areas or other rural areas; and a part-livelihood from a variety of other activities, more or less informal, such as petty trade or beer-brewing. Variable combinations of activities of this kind, likewise gendered in respect of unequal dispositions of labour and appropriations of income between men and women, are often themselves subject to rapid change over time.

Livelihoods are 'mixed' both concurrently and in succession, both in the short term and over the course of a working life (Sumberg and Okali, 2013). And many young people also combine one or more jobs and income-generating activities with investments of time and resources in education or training, to build knowledge and skills in order to grow their business or change their career.

Evidence suggests that such diversification into non-farm enterprises can have positive welfare effects in both rural and urban areas, controlling for levels of education and household characteristics. For those who have completed primary but not secondary education, a household enterprise can be as good an option as wage employment, as private wage incomes are very low for this segment (Fox and Sohnesen, 2012). As such, non-farm economic activities can make up a significant proportion of household income in rural Africa. With significant variations across countries and climatic zones, Reardon et al. (2007, in Bezu and Holden, 2014) estimated the share of rural non-farm income to household total income to be approximately 35 per cent in Africa. Productivity and stability of these enterprises remains low, and, for the reasons alluded to above, young men, and especially young women, find it difficult to be enterprise owners (Fox and Sohnesen, 2012).

Nonetheless, most young Africans are economically active, contributing to household income, primarily through work in the informal sector (USAID, 2008). School-to-work transition surveys from eight sub-Saharan African countries suggest that between 83 per cent and 96 per cent of the jobs held by youth aged 15–29 are either informal employment in the informal sector, or informal jobs in the formal sector (INSTAT, 2014; Shehu and Nilsson, 2014). Elder and Koné (2014) found that in six of the eight countries, involuntary reasons for taking up self-employment among young workers, such as an inability to find paid employment or as a family requirement, exceeded voluntary reasons, such as gaining a higher income or greater independence.

Despite high rates of migration to urban areas, most sub-Saharan African youth continue to reside in rural areas and will continue to do so over the coming years; it is the only region where the rural population is continuing to grow in absolute terms (Brooks et al., 2012). Excluding South Africa and mineral-exporting countries, it has been estimated that two-thirds to three-quarters of the labour force is employed in agriculture in the region, but that this employment only contributes a quarter to a third of GDP (OECD 2009, in Brooks et al., 2012). But without sufficient opportunities in manufacturing or services to engage youth, agriculture will remain a significant sink of labour and source of economic opportunity. Many young Africans already work on family farms, but in the context of ageing farmers, engaging young people more productively in agribusiness and agricultural value chains is a developmental imperative. Not only can this offer sustainable opportunities for income generation, as the value of domestic food products rises, but it also will contribute to agricultural growth and food security for a growing and increasingly urban African population (Brooks et al., 2012; Koira, 2014).

Yet youth are often not interested in agriculture (Dalberg et al., 2013) – or, at least, not in the 'digging' they have seen their parents and grandparents endure. There is often a mismatch between growing youth aspirations and perceptions of farming as risky, dependent on hard manual labour rather than modern technology, and with few opportunities to earn a good, sustainable income (Noorani, 2015). More general 'push' and 'pull' factors behind rural-to-urban migration also play a role, including hierarchical social relations in rural areas (Leavy and Smith, 2010). A lack of perceived opportunity to make a broader contribution to one's community or country may also play a role in youth disinterest in farming.

Even where youth are interested in farming, in many (but not all) countries and regions, a lack of ownership of or access to land, or no expectation of inheriting land, is also a significant factor pushing youth away from choosing to work in agriculture (e.g. in Ethiopia: Bezu and Holden, 2014; Dalberg et al., 2013). This particularly affects young women (Jones et al., 2010). Lack of access to credit can also be an issue (Brooks et al., 2013), limiting capacity to invest in land and inputs, to purchase or rent equipment, and to hire labour.

Because there are a range of reasons why youth try to move away from farming, as well as many who remain committed to agriculture, engaging in mixed and multiple non-farm income-generating activities takes different forms. Sometimes these activities are undertaken instead of farming or to complement income from farming, particularly during lean seasons, but sometimes they are undertaken in order to raise income to invest in land or inputs to make farming possible (Berckmoes and White, 2014; Markel and Panetta, 2014).

An evolving comprehensive and holistic model

The experience of a participant in U-Learn, a programme undertaken by The MasterCard Foundation-partner Swisscontact in the Great Lakes region of Tanzania and Uganda, is illustrative of how mixed and informal livelihoods within and outside agriculture often manifest for rural and peri-urban African youth, and how youth can be supported to increase their economic opportunities and enhance their well-being:

> Twenty-one year old Petro lives in Mwanza, Tanzania. One of five children, he completed his education up to form 4 (comparable to GCSEs in some parts of the UK), and then did small-scale horticultural work on the family farm. After joining U-Learn, he gained electrical installation skills, and learned how to make a business plan, take care of customers, and save in an informal group. He received some tools from Swisscontact and bought others with his savings, and started undertaking electrical installation work locally. With the income generated and a loan from his savings group, he bought chickens. Initially many died, but with his income he was able to construct a coop and vaccinate them. While

the new activity is yet to generate an income, it provides eggs and meat for the family. Petro also breeds goats, rabbits, and pigeons. He is able to combine taking care of his animals, as well as supporting the family farm, with his electrical work. His income has meant that he has been able to start to construct a house for himself on his mother's land, as well as purchase a small piece of land to expand his poultry work. While he doesn't participate in his savings group any longer, he saves income with his mother and her savings group. As he is only reachable by mobile phone, Petro's goal is to have a shop where people can come to book electrical services and purchase materials.

Mixing livelihoods is neither restricted to rural areas and small towns, nor does it always include agriculture. Loveness, 21, was also trained via U-learn in Mwanza, focusing on cooking and decorating. She started working as a decorator for someone else, slowly saved up through her savings group to buy tools and chairs, and was able to start her own small business. Using the chairs as collateral, she was able to 'grow out of' her savings group and secure a small microfinance loan to establish a food stall at a local bar, adding to her port-folio of income-generating activities and supporting her goal of growing her main business in order to employ others. Maryann, 22, studied hospitality at a training centre established in Nairobi by CAP-Youth Empowerment Institute in partnership with The MasterCard Foundation. She works for an electronics retailer as a stock-taker, and also weaves mats to sell in a local market, because 'whatever you do you should do something else as well. You should not de-pend on one thing for money'. She is saving up to study marketing, and has become a mentor with a local organization to inspire other young women.

Early evidence suggests that in order to support young people to make informed choices and have the assets (knowledge, skills, confidence, networks, physical and financial resources) to successfully transition into sustainable work for themselves or others, a holistic approach is required that tackles both the 'supply' and 'demand' side of the challenge (USAID, 2013). Through its partnerships, the approach taken by The MasterCard Foundation is to foster the development of a broad skill set, access to resources, and connections to the market and social networks among youth, in part through engaging the private and public sector to better provide an enabling environment. This combination can help young people negotiate, cope with, and potentially thrive in challenging socio-economic contexts characterized by poverty, inequality, and limited and unstable markets for goods and services. Improving the quality and sustainability of necessity-driven entrepreneurship and self-employment (i.e. making vulnerable employment less vulnerable and increas-ingly 'decent') and, where possible, supporting the transition to formal sector work and opportunity-driven, job-creating business, arguably makes most sense in contexts where informality dominates.

As The MasterCard Foundation's economic opportunities for youth approach continues to evolve in partnership with NGOs, financial service providers, and other development stakeholders, key components of a holistic and comprehensive model that has the potential to reach and support marginalized young Africans have emerged. These include: market surveys and scans; support for engagement in agriculture; youth engagement; building skills; accessing the labour market; and financial inclusion.

Market surveys and scans

Conducting or reviewing existing market surveys, and periodically undertaking more localized market scans, is necessary to inform programming, particularly to ensure that skills training is tailored to market demand for labour, products, and services, and that youth are well-informed about the opportunities available. Engaging employers in the early design phase also improves the ability of training programmes to focus on skill sets required by the market (MasterCard Foundation, 2015b).

Supporting youth to engage productively and sustainably in agriculture

This relies in part on improving agriculture's image problem, and promoting 'farming as a business': helping youth identify opportunities with potential for sustainable income and technological innovation across the entire agricultural value chain – from production, and the goods and services required to support production, through storage, transport, processing, marketing, and sale (Koira, 2014). Many such opportunities do not require access to a significant amount of land, or any land at all. Supporting youth to organize into producer, processor, or service provision groups or cooperatives, in order to better access government and private resources and to learn from each other (Hartley, 2014), can play a role in helping youth overcome a lack of access to financial and technical services and social networks.

Youth engagement

Meaningfully engaging youth wherever possible improves the quality and outreach of programming and advocacy efforts, helps tailor interventions to youth interests and needs, and builds the confidence and communication and leadership skills of the young people involved. The Youth MicroFinance Project, a three-country initiative undertaken by The MasterCard Foundation partner Plan Canada in West Africa, engaged youth in advisory boards, as community volunteers and in evaluation, with positive effects on youth empowerment and on project management and implementation (Nayar, 2014). The MasterCard Foundation's Youth Think Tank, launched in 2012, engages young Africans to conduct research in their communities, make recommendations based on their findings and advise the Foundation; although new, the results of the initiative are influencing Foundation strategy.

Building skills

A wide range of knowledge and skills are required for a successful transition to working life: 1) foundation skills such as literacy and numeracy; 2) technical and vocational skills, which depend on market demand and youth interest; and 3) transferable skills.

Transferable skills can include the following:

- *Business and entrepreneurship skills* (including understanding the market and making business plans);
- *Financial literacy and capability* (money management knowledge, attitudes and skills) and *bank literacy* (how to use financial services, including digital financial services, and consumer rights awareness);
- *Employability and 'soft' skills* (e.g. job search and networking, comportment, teamwork, communication, customer relations, leadership);
- Related, *'life' skills*, defined by UNICEF (2003) as

  psychosocial abilities for adaptive and positive behaviour that enable individuals to deal effectively with the demands and challenges of everyday life [including:] cognitive skills for analysing and using information, personal skills for developing personal agency and managing oneself, and inter-personal skills for communicating and interacting effectively with others.

  These personal and interpersonal skills can include those around gender relations and sexual and reproductive health and rights – important for building self-confidence and especially useful for supporting young women to resist pressure for transactional sex while in education or at work (University of Minnesota, 2014b);
- *ICT skills;*
- *English or second-language skills.*

(Terms to describe skills are used differently and interchangeably across organizations; here the general approach is that suggested in UNESCO (2012).)

The exact combination needed depends on the level, quality, and content of education and skills already held by target youth, and market requirements. Second-chance opportunities to gain foundation and other skills are crucial for youth who have never attended school or have left early, and family responsibilities mean that opportunities to learn while earning is important for many. Each skill set can be adapted to the particular demands of farming, agricultural value chains, and agribusiness, but skill-building for the informal sector faces particular challenges, as identified in Box 1. Supporting training providers including technical and vocational education and training institutes to adapt training content and approaches to better meet the needs of youth within the informal sector, and supporting youth to access such training, can help them access the transferable skills most useful for negotiating multiple, sometimes unpredictable, livelihood options.

Box 1 Why skills development differs in the informal and formal sectors

Compared with the formal sector, small firms in the informal sector face:
- high opportunity cost to train;
- low cash flow to pay for training;
- greater needs for multiple skills;
- lack of capacity to identify training needs and design training programmes;
- lack of knowledge about benefits of training;
- absence of economies of scale for training, driving up cost;
- limited supply of trainer capacity serving the informal sector.

Source: Adams et al. (2014)

Accessing the labour market

Building young people's skills goes a long way in helping them to access economic opportunities. But in order for youth to ground and extend learning within real work or business contexts, it is often necessary to support their initial access to apprenticeships, internships, job placements, and mentorship from role models. Encouraging and supporting private sector employers to offer learning and earning opportunities to youth can be challenging, particularly when there is limited trust in youth's skills and attitudes. But engaging the private sector, from master craftspeople and small and medium enterprises, to large corporations where they exist, is crucial to further build the skills, networks, and capital necessary for youth to successfully move into more sustainable jobs or self-employment.

Financial inclusion

Youth require skills and access to opportunities to earn an income, and the knowledge of how to manage their money, as well as the financial products and services to do so sustainably. Livelihoods that are mixed over time and space, and agriculture in particular, provide inconsistent and often unpredictable incomes. Yet low-income Africans working in the informal sector, including young people, do have the capacity to save (MasterCard Foundation, 2015a). In this context, financial inclusion is a key tool – for consumption smoothing as income levels rise and fall, and for asset-building to improve resilience to shocks and for investment in businesses and in human capital. Financial behaviour tends to mirror diversified livelihoods, with individuals – including youth – combining the use of informal, semi-formal, and formal places to save and borrow (e.g. as described in the financial diaries collected from Plan youth savings groups members: Musa, 2014).

Starting with access to savings services – through savings groups, and through youth- and smallholder farmer-friendly products and services offered by formal financial service providers – is important for the development of a savings habit, to increase financial skills, and to build assets in a low risk manner. Saving and borrowing together in a group is a particularly useful entry point for youth (Dueck-Mbeba, 2015; Markel and Panetta, 2014; Ramirez and Fleischer-Proaño, 2013). Ensuring youth access to a fuller suite of appropriate formal financial services will require engagement with financial service providers and regulatory bodies, to support improvements in the enabling environment (MasterCard Foundation, 2015a).

While the merit of each model component is clear, The MasterCard Foundation's early experience suggests that it is in their effective integration that the real value emerges. For example, TechnoServe's STRYDE project, implemented in rural Kenya, Rwanda, and Uganda in partnership with the Foundation, combines three months of skill development and farming as business training with nine months of 'after-care' support, including mentorship, access to finance, and business plan competitions. According to internal project reports, this has resulted in an average increase in self-reported wages of 200 per cent 12 months after the project.

More broadly, the ability to influence decision-making and to be recognized as a contributor to the economic stability of households and communities is often emphasized by young people as a significant outcome of programming of this type (University of Minnesota, 2014a). Early evidence from several programmes in the Foundation's portfolio – such as those operated by Digital Opportunity Trust, TechnoServe, and the International Youth Foundation – suggests this type of empowerment is important for young women in particular (MasterCard Foundation, 2015b).

Conclusion

The experiences of The MasterCard Foundation and its partners, as well as others in the field, increasingly demonstrate how the barriers faced by young women and men in accessing sustainable livelihoods are many, so supporting their successful transition into employment and entrepreneurship requires a comprehensive and holistic approach. However, knowledge gaps remain, including a better understanding of the dynamics and composition of youth livelihoods in different rural African contexts, the longer-term outcomes of the holistic approach for youth, and, perhaps most importantly, how to reach scale with our combined efforts. The MasterCard Foundation has made an intentional commitment to build research, learning, and evaluation capacity across the Economic Opportunities for Youth portfolio to help close these knowledge gaps.

While a holistic, comprehensive approach is likely the most effective in terms of supporting successful transitions to employment or entrepreneurship among youth, it presents challenges to reaching scale – a key goal given the extent of unemployment and working poverty among youth. Tailored, wrap-around support to young people as they enter the labour market or try to start businesses is most likely to succeed for individual young people, but will be deemed too complex and costly for reaching tens of millions, particularly those who are most marginalized. Solving this problem will require different approaches.

In part, it will depend on a firmer understanding of which parts of the comprehensive approach can be successfully taken up by the public and private sectors. Indeed, focusing on the nexus of skill development, access to markets and jobs, financial inclusion, and engaging the private sector does not absolve governments of responsibility for investing in inclusive, equitable, quality, relevant basic education; social protection for informal workers; infrastructure (particularly electricity); and an enabling economic (including regulatory), social, and political environment that fosters high quality job creation. This requires strong, explicit, and joined up policy: 'government leadership and enabling environments to remove obstacles to youth employment and productivity' (MasterCard Foundation, 2015b) are required for a truly comprehensive approach.

For example, as public education systems commit to improving access, quality, and relevance – in line with the Education for All goals and the new sustainable development goals – a greater proportion of children and youth will build the foundation, transferable, and technical skills required to successfully take up existing economic opportunities and create new ones, and cope with changing, difficult economic contexts. The inclusion of financial and social education in national curricula, as advocated by Foundation partners Aflatoun and Child and Youth Finance International, will play an important part in scaling up this part of the approach, as will education systems that build stronger foundations in literacy, numeracy, ICT skills, and problem solving.

Building the business case for private sector investment also plays a role in bringing a comprehensive approach to scale. Businesses that recognize the value of adequately trained staff, in terms of the quality of products and services and reductions in staff turnover, are willing to invest in systems to support staff capacity development. Financial service providers that take a longer-term view on profitability increasingly recognize that child- and youth-friendly products and services offer opportunities for cross-selling and building a sustainable customer base.

Increased collaboration between governments, the private sector, civil society, and donors, such as via the recently established Solutions for Youth Employment coalition (http://s4ye.org/), needs to play a significant role in moving the field towards scale. And harnessing the power of new technologies – to extend access to education, information and financial services, and improve agricultural productivity, for example – will be crucial to the success of such coalitions.

And in part, it will require strong research and evaluation that not only identifies 'what works', but 'what is the minimum intervention that will work': what aspects of comprehensive support can we remove without harming effectiveness? It will also involve improving our understanding of when it is most effective to provide support. Interventions during early childhood may do much to support successful transitions to work in adulthood. And developing 'just in time' approaches that deliver skills training or behavioural nudges at the right moment can mean avoiding lengthy trainings or repeated processes that result in an extra time burden for young people and an extra resource burden for providers, but limited extra benefit.

References

Adams, A.V., de Silva, S.J. and Razmara, S. (2014) *Improving Skills Development in the Informal Sector: Strategies for Sub-Saharan Africa* [pdf], Washington, DC: World Bank <www.skillsforemployment.org/wcmstest4/groups/skills/documents/skpcontent/ddrf/mdy3/~edisp/wcmstest4_067645.pdf> [accessed 20 January 2015].

African Economic Outlook (AEO) (2012) 'Promoting youth employment in Africa' [webpage] <www.africaneconomicoutlook.org/en/theme/youth_employment/> [accessed 20 January 2015].

Banks, N. and Sulaiman, M. (2012) *Problem or Promise? Harnessing Youth Potential in Uganda* [pdf] BRAC Youth Watch Series <www.brac.net/sites/default/files/YW%202012.pdf> [accessed 20 January 2015].

Berckmoes, L. and White, B. (2014) 'Youth, farming and precarity in rural Burundi', *European Journal of Development Research* 26(2): 190–203 <http://dx.doi.org/10.1057/ejdr.2013.53>.

Bezu, S. and Holden, S. (2014) 'Are rural youth in Ethiopia abandoning agriculture?' *World Development* 64: 259–72 <http://dx.doi.org/10.1016/j.worlddev.2014.06.013>.

Brooks, K., Zorya, S. and Gautam, A. (2012) 'Employment in agriculture: jobs for Africa's youth' [online], *2012 Global Food Policy Report*, pp. 48–57, Washington, DC: IFPRI <www.ifpri.org/gfpr/2012/employment-agriculture> [accessed 20 January 2015].

Brooks, K., Zorya, S., Gautam, A. and Goyal, A. (2013) *Agriculture as a Sector of Opportunity for Young People in Africa* [pdf], Policy Research Working Paper 6473, Washington, DC: World Bank <http://elibrary.worldbank.org/doi/pdf/10.1596/1813-9450-6473> [accessed 20 January 2 015].

Dalberg Global Development Advisors, The MasterCard Foundation and Save The Children (2013) *Summary Report of Findings, Lessons Learned and Recommendations: Multi-Country Assessment of Youth Employment and Entrepreneurship Opportunities in Agriculture – Burkina Faso, Egypt, Ethiopia, Malawi, Uganda* [pdf] Save the Children/The MasterCard Foundation <http://youthinaction.savethechildren.ca/wp-content/uploads/2013/09/STC_Report_EN.pdf> [accessed 20 January 2015].

Demirgüç-Kunt, A. and Klapper, L. (2012) *Measuring Financial Inclusion: The Global Findex Database* [pdf], Policy Research Working Paper 6025, Washington, DC: World Bank <http://elibrary.worldbank.org/doi/pdf/10.1596/1813-9450-6025> [accessed 20 January 2015].

Demirgüç-Kunt, A., Klapper, L., Kumar, A. and Randall, D. (2013) 'The Global Findex database: financial inclusion of youth' [webpage], Findex notes no. 10, Washington, DC: World Bank <http://documents.worldbank.org/curated/en/2013/10/18477405/global-findex-database-financial-inclusion-youth> [accessed 20 January 2015].

Dueck-Mbeba, R. (2015) 'What happens when youth save together?' [blog], Toronto: The MasterCard Foundation <www.mastercardfdn.org/what-happens-when-youth-save-together> [accessed 11 March 2015].

Elder, S. and Koné, K.S. (2014) *Labour Market Transitions of Young Women and Men in Sub-Saharan Africa* [pdf], Work4Youth Publication Series No. 9, Geneva: ILO <www.ilo.org/wcmsp5/groups/public/---ed_emp/documents/publication/wcms_235754.pdf> [accessed 20 January 2015].

FAO, CTA and IFAD (2014) *Youth and Agriculture: Key Challenges and Concrete Solutions* [pdf] Rome: FAO <www.fao.org/3/a-i3947e.pdf> [accessed 20 January 2015].

Fox, L. and Sohnesen, T.P. (2012) *Household Enterprises in Sub-Saharan Africa: Why They Matter for Growth, Jobs, and Livelihoods* [pdf], Policy Research Working Paper 6184, Washington, DC: World Bank <http://elibrary.worldbank.org/doi/pdf/10.1596/1813-9450-6184> [accessed 20 January 2015].

Guarcello, L., Manacorda, M., Rosati, F., Fares, J., Lyon, S. and Valdivia, C. (2007) 'School-to-work transitions in sub-Saharan Africa: an overview', in M. Garcia and J. Fares (eds), *Youth in Africa's Labor Market, Directions in Development*, Washington, DC: World Bank.

Hartley, S. (2014) 'Collective learning in youth-focused co-operatives in Lesotho and Uganda', *Journal of International Development* 26(5): 713–30 <http://dx.doi.org/10.1002/jid.3000>.

International Labour Organization (ILO) (2013) *Global Employment Trends for Youth 2013: A Generation at Risk* [online], Geneva: ILO <www.ilo.org/global/research/global-reports/global-employment-trends/youth/2013/lang--en/index.htm> [accessed 20 January 2015].

ILO (2014) 'Global employment trends 2014: the risk of a jobless recovery' [online], Geneva: ILO <www.ilo.org/global/research/global-reports/global-employment-trends/2014/WCMS_233953/lang--en/index.htm> [accessed 20 January 2015].

INSTAT (2014) *Enquête sur la transition des jeunes vers la vie active – ETVA Madagascar 2013* [pdf], INSTAT/ILO: Antananarivo <www.ilo.org/wcmsp5/groups/public/---dgreports/---dcomm/documents/publication/wcms_244496.pdf> [accessed 20 January 2015].

Jones, N., Harper, C., Watson, C., Espey, J., Wadugodapitiya, D., Page, E., Stavropoulou, M., Presler-Marshall, E. and Clench, B. (2010) *Stemming Girls' Chronic Poverty: Catalysing Development Change by Building Just Social Institutions* [pdf], London: Chronic Poverty Research Centre <www.chron-icpoverty.org/uploads/assets/files/reports/Full_report.pdf> [accessed 20 January 2015].

Koira, A.K. (2014) *Agribusiness in Sub-Saharan Africa: Pathways for Developing Innovative Programs for Youth and the Rural Poor* [pdf] The MasterCard Foundation <www.mastercardfdn.org/download/agribusiness-in-sub-saharan-africa> [accessed 11 March 2015].

Leavy, J. and Smith, S. (2010) *Future Farmers? Exploring Youth Aspirations for African Agriculture* [online], Future Agricultures Consortium Policy Brief 037, <www.future-agricultures.org/publications/research-and-analysis/ 945-future-farmers-exploring-youth-aspirations-for-african-agriculture/ file> [accessed 20 January 2015].

Markel, E. and Panetta, D. (2014) *Youth Savings Groups, Entrepreneurship and Employment* [online], Plan UK: London <www.plan-uk.org/resources/ documents/494816/> [accessed 20 January 2015].

MasterCard Foundation (2013) *2013–2014 Youth Think Tank Initiative – Final Report: March 2013* [pdf], Toronto: The MasterCard Foundation <www.mastercardfdn.org/wp-content/uploads/Youth-Think-Tank-Final-Report-June-2013.pdf> [accessed 20 January 2015].

MasterCard Foundation (2014) *2013–2014 Youth Think Tank Report: Engaging Young People* [pdf], Toronto: The MasterCard Foundation <www.master-cardfdn.org/ytt2014> [accessed 20 January 2015].

MasterCard Foundation (2015a) *Financial Services for Young People: Prospects and Challenges*, Toronto: The MasterCard Foundation.

MasterCard Foundation (2015b) *Youth at Work: Building Economic Opportunities for Young People in Africa. Thematic Review*, Toronto: The MasterCard Foundation.

Moore, K. (2005) 'Chronic, life-course and intergenerational poverty', in *World Youth Report 2005: Young People Today and in 2015* [pdf], New York: United Nations Program on Youth, pp. 42–65 <www.un.org/esa/socdev/unyin/ documents/wyr05book.pdf> [accessed 20 January 2015].

Murray, C. (2001) *Livelihoods Research: Some Conceptual and Methodological Issues* [pdf], Background Paper 5, Manchester: Chronic Poverty Research Centre <www.chronicpoverty.org/uploads/publication_files/WP05_Murray.pdf> [accessed 20 January 2015].

Musa, A.S.M. with Hasan, E. and Lam, B. (2014) *Counting Change: How Youth Manage their Money* [pdf], Toronto: Plan Canada <http://plancanada.ca/ downloads/mcf/CountingChange_PlanCanada2014.pdf> [accessed 20 January 2015].

Nayar, N. (2014) *An Integrated Approach to Empower Youth in Niger, Senegal and Sierra Leone: Findings and Lessons from the Youth Microfinance Project* [pdf], Toronto: Plan Canada <http://plancanada.ca/downloads/mcf/Plan%20 Canada_EmpoweringYouth_FINAL.pdf> [accessed 20 January 2015].

Noorani, M. (2015) *To Farm or Not to Farm? Rural Youth Perceptions of Farming and their Decision of Whether or Not to Work as a Farmer: A Case Study of Rural Youth in Kiambu County, Kenya* [pdf], MA thesis, University of Ottawa, Canada <https://www.ruor.uottawa.ca/bitstream/10393/31960/1/Noorani_ Mohamed_2015_thesis.pdf> [accessed 11 March 2015].

Ramirez, R. and Fleischer-Proaño, L. (2013) *Saving Together: Group-Based Approaches to Promote Youth Savings* [pdf], Davis, CA: Freedom from Hunger <https://www.freedomfromhunger.org/sites/default/files/SavingTogether_ Eng_Web.pdf> [accessed 20 January 2015].

Shehu, E. and Nilsson, B. (2014) *Informal Employment Among Youth: Evidence from 20 School-to-Work Transition Surveys* [pdf], Work4Youth Publication Series No. 8, Geneva: ILO <www.ilo.org/wcmsp5/groups/

public/---dgreports/---dcomm/documents/publication/wcms_234911.pdf> [accessed 20 January 2015].

Shepherd, A. with Scott, L. and CPRC (2011) *Tackling Chronic Poverty: The Policy Implications of Research on Chronic Poverty and Poverty Dynamics* [online], London: Chronic Poverty Research Centre <www.chronicpoverty. org/publications/details/tackling-chronic-poverty1> [accessed 20 January 2015].

Sparreboom, T. and Staneva, A. (2014) *Is Education the Solution to Decent Work for Youth in Developing Economies? Identifying Qualifications Mismatch from 28 School-to-Work Transition Surveys* [pdf], Work4Youth Publication Series No. 23, Geneva: ILO <www.ilo.org/wcmsp5/groups/public/---dgreports/---dcomm/documents/publication/wcms_326260.pdf> [accessed 20 January 2015].

Sumberg, J. and Okali, C. (2013) 'Young people, agriculture, and transformation in rural Africa: an "opportunity space" approach', *Innovations: Technology, Governance, Globalization* 8(1–2): 259–69 <http://dx.doi. org/10.1162/INOV_a_00178>.

UNESCO (2012) *Education for All Global Monitoring Report 2012 – Youth and Skills: Putting Education to Work* [pdf], Paris: UNESCO <http://unesdoc. unesco.org/images/0021/002180/218003e.pdf> [accessed 20 January 2015].

UNESCO (2013) *Education for All Global Monitoring Report 2013/4 – Teaching and Learning: Achieving Quality for All* [pdf], Paris: UNESCO <http://unesdoc. unesco.org/images/0022/002256/225660e.pdf> [accessed 20 January 2015].

UNICEF (2003) 'Life skills: definition of terms' [webpage], UNICEF <www. unicef.org/lifeskills/index_7308.html> [accessed 20 January 2015].

University of Minnesota (2014a) 'The MasterCard Foundation Learn Earn and Save Initiative – longitudinal evaluation of year 3: cross-program report', Toronto: The MasterCard Foundation (unpublished).

University of Minnesota (2014b) 'The MasterCard Foundation Learn Earn and Save Initiative – year 3 synthesis report for Fundación Paraguaya', Toronto: The MasterCard Foundation (unpublished).

UNPD (Population Division of the Department of Economic and Social Affairs of the United Nations Secretariat) (2012) *World Population Prospects: The 2012 Revision* [webpage], <http://esa.un.org/unpd/wpp/ index.htm> [accessed 20 January 2015].

USAID (2008) *Youth Livelihoods Development Program Guide* [pdf], Washington, DC: USAID <www.equip123.net/docs/e3-LivelihoodsGuide.pdf> [accessed 20 January 2015].

USAID (2013) *State of the Field Report: Examining the Evidence in Youth Workforce Development – USAID Youth Research, Evaluation, and Learning Project* [pdf], Washington, DC: USAID <www.usaid.gov/sites/default/files/ documents/1865/USAID%20state%20of%20the%20field%20youth%20 workforce%20development%20final%202_11.pdf> [accessed 20 January 2015].

World Bank (2013) *World Development Report 2013: Jobs* [online], Washington, DC: World Bank <http://econ.worldbank.org/external/default/main?conten tMDK=23044836&theSitePK=8258025&piPK=8258412&pagePK=8258258> [accessed 20 January 2015].

About the author

Karen Moore (kmoore@mastercardfdn.org) is Programme Manager at Economic Opportunities for Youth, The MasterCard Foundation (Toronto, Canada). The author acknowledges helpful comments from two anonymous reviewers, and from colleagues across the Foundation. This article is not intended as a comprehensive statement of the Foundation's agreed policies or strategies. The views and opinions expressed are those of the author.

CHAPTER 11

Do youth need savings? The experience of YouthSave in Colombia, Ghana, Kenya, and Nepal

Rani Deshpande

Abstract

YouthSave was a multi-country project that designed and tested the outcomes and impact of safe, accessible savings accounts for youth aged 12–18 in Colombia, Ghana, Kenya, and Nepal, in order to gauge the potential of youth savings accounts as tools for youth development and financial inclusion. Over three years of product rollout, over 133,000 youth opened accounts and collectively saved over US$1 m. The project included rigorous research components, including a randomized experimental impact evaluation, and has produced numerous publications on both operational and research findings. This paper provides a high-level summary of those findings and ends with five lessons of particular relevance to practitioners, donors, and policymakers looking to maximize the potential of youth savings.

Keywords: youth, savings, youth financial inclusion, youth development, youth livelihoods, financial capability

> *My son got sick a couple of years ago. I used all the money I had then to look after him, going to hospitals and buying all the medications for him. It got to a point that I was totally out of money to do anything more. Now, my sick son called me up and directed me to where he was keeping his money in a susu box. To be honest with you all, I had no idea that he had a box like that in the house. He told me ... that it is his contribution to me for all the bills I have to shoulder and that he has been saving for the past two years. I was touched and now he is well and waiting to get back into school again (parent, participant in YouthSave market research, Accra).*

THE IMPORTANCE OF YOUTH SAVINGS has not always been well understood; in fact, there is a widespread perception that young people – especially poor or low-income young people – do not or cannot save. However, testimonials like the one above illustrate not only that young people in developing countries are saving, but also the critical role those resources can play in ensuring well-being for themselves and their households: both their families of origin and the ones they will create.

http://dx.doi.org/10.3362/9781780448879.011

Understanding the potential of mechanisms to help youth transition successfully to adulthood has taken on particular urgency in light of demographic trends. The bulging proportion of young people in the world today has been extensively documented and need not be reiterated here. Young people also tend to suffer greater financial exclusion and un- and underemployment than their adult counterparts (World Bank, 2015; Moore, 2015). The numbers and needs of young people in the world today have in turn prompted a growing number of governments, NGOs, and donors to explore policy and programmatic approaches to help them become healthy, productive citizens. Previous research indicated that savings could be one of these mechanisms, having shown an association with improved psychosocial, educational, and health-related outcomes (Bruce and Hallman, 2008; Deshpande and Zimmerman, 2010).

YouthSave was launched in 2010 to deepen the understanding of whether young people could be effectively reached through tailored youth savings accounts offered at scale through commercial financial institutions; if so, what types of youth would save in them, and how; and what would be the impact of these savings accounts on young people's lives. In addition, YouthSave sought to evaluate the business case for such accounts, i.e. the impetus for the private sector to offer them on a sustainable basis, reducing the burden on public resources.

Created in partnership with the MasterCard Foundation, YouthSave investigated the potential of savings accounts as a tool for youth development and financial inclusion in developing countries, by co-designing tailored, sustainable savings products with local financial institutions and assessing their performance and development outcomes with local researchers. The project was an initiative of the YouthSave Consortium, led by Save the Children in partnership with the Center for Social Development at Washington University in St Louis, New America, and the Consultative Group to Assist the Poor (CGAP).

Over the last five years YouthSave has produced numerous publications detailing our investigations into each of these questions. This paper provides a high-level summary of the answers, with a focus on beneficiary-level outcomes and impact, and gives references to additional research and reports for readers seeking greater understanding of the YouthSave project and research. For guidance on how commercial financial service providers might analyse whether and how to enter the market for youth savings, see CGAP's 2014 paper (Kilara et al., 2014); and for more information on the project see the New America website.

Project overview

The YouthSave Consortium worked with commercial banks in Colombia, Ghana, Kenya, and Nepal to co-design, pilot, and roll out savings accounts tailored to the needs, preferences, and constraints of low-income youth aged

12–18. YouthSave implementation countries were chosen on the basis of multiple factors including political and economic stability, legal and regulatory environment, existence of appropriate bank and research partners locally, and geographic diversity. YouthSave's bank partners were BCS in Colombia, HFC Bank in Ghana, Kenya Post Office Savings Bank, and Bank of Kathmandu in Nepal (for more information, see Dueck-Mbeba and Maftei, 2015).

In Ghana, Kenya, and Nepal, these accounts were regular savings accounts, generally with low or no minimum balances and no maintenance fees; some also featured various types of restrictions on or disincentives to withdrawing. In Colombia, where the partner bank already had a well-established basic youth savings account, it rolled out a programmed savings account that asked youth to set a savings goal and contribute to it monthly. A complete description of the account features in each country is available in YouthSave (2015: Appendix 2). As of May 2015, after three years of account rollout, over 133,000 youth had opened accounts across the four countries and had used them to collectively save over US$1 m.

In Colombia, Kenya, and Nepal, the project also provided marginalized youth with financial education (FE) meant to link them to, and help them understand how to make the best use of, these accounts. The FE took various forms in various countries depending on market research results, always including some form of face-to-face education but also encompassing community events, mass media, and text messaging. A complete description of YouthSave's FE programming is available in YouthSave (2015: Appendix 3). Across the three countries, over 44,000 youth received face-to-face FE and 48,000 individuals were reached through community-level events, while in Nepal, a radio drama on savings reached an estimated listenership of 660,000.

While routine monitoring tracked basic project performance, three rigorous research methodologies were implemented to assess the project's beneficiary-level outcomes and impact. First, the Savings Demand Assessment (SDA) collected and analysed demographic and transactional data on 66,000 account holders to understand which youth were opening accounts and how they were using them. Second, the project conducted in-depth qualitative research on a select number of youth to understand their subjective experiences of saving in the account.

Third, in Ghana, a randomized experimental study investigated the impact of the opportunity to open an account on youths' lives in terms of financial capability (see Box 1), cognitive functioning, educational outcomes, and health-related attitudes and behaviours. The experiment involved over 6,000 youth and 4,500 of their caregivers at baseline. Youth were distributed over 50 control and 50 treatment schools, in two arms. In the first treatment

---

Box 1 YouthSave's definition of financial capability

Based on the work of Johnson and Sherraden, YouthSave considered financial capability to result 'when individuals develop financial knowledge and skills, but also gain access to financial instruments and institutions' (Johnson and Sherraden, 2007).

arm, YouthSave's partner bank conducted only marketing outreach for the savings account. In the second, students were actually able to transact in their accounts through the schools. The endline survey was conducted three years after the baseline; however due to the way that students aged into middle school, not all of them received an equal duration of treatment (Chowa et al., 2015a). FE was not conducted in Ghana to avoid contaminating this study.

Encouraging results

Uptake

Youth self-reporting indicated that after FE interventions between 15 per cent and 42 per cent opened a savings account at either the YouthSave partner bank or another financial services provider, depending on the country (Kosmynina, 2015). In Ghana, the experimental study demonstrated uptake rates for the YouthSave account of 11 per cent when youth were exposed to school-based account marketing and 21 per cent when they were able to transact in the account through their schools, compared with 0.3 per cent in control schools which were not exposed to the account at all (Chowa et al., 2015b). These results illustrate the demand that exists among youth for attractive savings products and the role of sustained engagement with schools providing convenient transaction services in activating that demand.

What types of youth opened YouthSave accounts? The SDA revealed that, as of May 2015, 48 per cent were from households living on less than $2.50/day per capita. Almost 90 per cent indicated they had earned no income within the past six months, and a similar proportion indicated their source of funds saved would be parents or family, while 7 per cent indicated they would earn funds from work. This pattern is consistent with their school status and age; 98.1 per cent were in school and almost 80 per cent were between 13 and 18 years old. Overall, 43.5 per cent were girls, but this proportion varied substantially by country, from a high of 54.3 per cent in Ghana to a low of 41.1 per cent in Kenya. Finally, using conservative estimates, 17 per cent were from households where no one had previously owned a bank account; a comparison with national rates of banked adults and youth is shown by country in Figure 1 (Johnson et al., 2015; World Bank, 2015).

Other dimensions of financial capability

The Ghana experiment also indicated robust positive effects on measures of financial capability aside from account uptake. While students at control schools made virtually no deposits in their accounts, students at treatment schools made the equivalent of three deposits per year, on average. Within the treatment group, twice as many students made deposits if in-school banking allowed them to transact in their accounts at school, compared with students who only received marketing outreach through their schools.

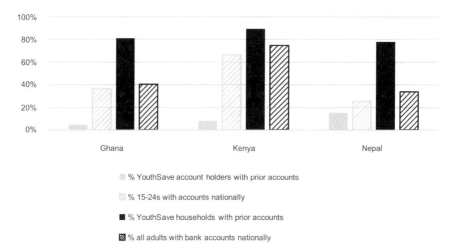

Figure 1 Rates of youth and adults with bank accounts, by country

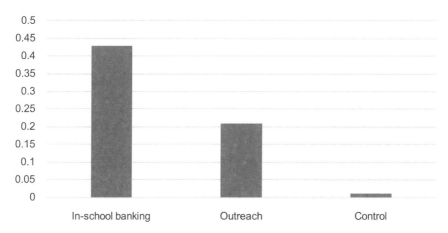

Figure 2 Average monthly net savings by treatment condition (PPP-adjusted US$)
Source: Lee et al. (2015)

Figure 2 shows a similar pattern in the Ghana experiment participants' average monthly net savings (AMNS, defined as deposits and interest credited to the account minus withdrawals and taxes/fees taken out of the account, divided by the number of months the account has been open), with students who received in-school banking saving significantly more. At these rates, students who opened accounts at treatment schools would save on average the equivalent of about $25 on an annualized basis – a meaningful start on annual educational expenses. And indeed, between baseline and endline there was a statistically significant difference in the proportion of students who said they were saving for either college or a business across treatment and control schools (Chowa et al., 2015b). As illustrated in Figure 3, the largest proportion of account holders across the project were saving for their own education.

Total numbers of accounts also increased steadily between rollout and project end, as did total balances in most countries – although often not as fast as accounts (see Figure 4). In countries with the fastest rates of account growth, this often meant that average balances per account were flat. Still, as discussed further below, average balances per account tended to increase the longer *an individual account* stayed open – a positive sign.

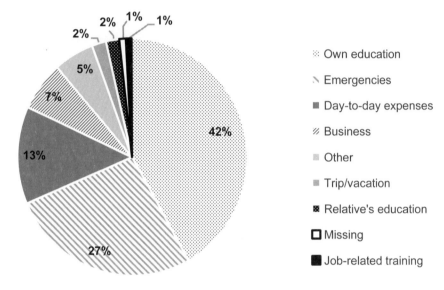

Figure 3 What were YouthSave participants saving for?
Source: Johnson et al. (2015)

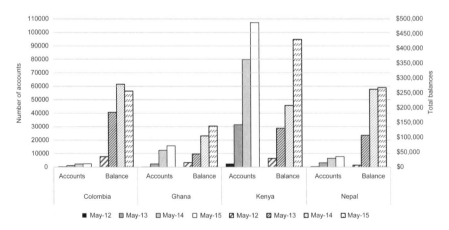

Figure 4 Cumulative accounts and total balances (nominal US$) by year and country
Source: Save the Children monitoring data, unpublished

Financial education

Finally, although YouthSave's performance monitoring of financial education activities lacked a counterfactual, the analysis of results also showed statistically significant changes in knowledge, attitudes, and behaviour up to 18 months after the interventions in Colombia, Kenya, and Nepal. The most dramatic knowledge/attitude changes were seen in values-related questions on topics such as appropriate and healthy ways to save and more technical knowledge related to bank accounts (e.g. minimum age to open), as opposed to more common-sense issues such as the importance of saving, where scores tended to start out high. In addition, after FE, a greater number of youth reported saving, and saving more (Kosmynina, 2015).

Study time

Another positive result of the project was no result at all: 'in terms of the amount of time that youth reported spending on their schoolwork outside normal school hours, neither the treatment nor control group reported significant changes in how long they study' (Chowa et al., 2015b: 31). This addressed a key concern that market research had revealed among many adult stakeholders in YouthSave communities, who feared that encouraging saving among young people might lead them to deprioritize education. The lack of such an effect is consistent with the results of other studies in Ghana and elsewhere (Berry et al., 2015; Sulaiman, 2016).

Areas for further work

Gender

While the percentage of female account holders was equal or greater to that of males in Ghana (54 per cent) and Colombia (49.9 per cent), girls made up only 41 per cent of account holders in Kenya and Nepal. Interestingly, however, the only statistically significant difference in girls' and boys' AMNS across the four countries was in Nepal, where girls saved slightly more. In other words, when girls succeeded in opening accounts, they saved as much as or more than boys – suggesting that girls in some countries may be experiencing different barriers or incentives for access, which only a certain proportion can overcome (Johnson et al., 2015). Data from the financial education monitoring provides some clues: as seen in Figure 5, while both boys and girls cited lack of official IDs as the key impediment to opening accounts in Nepal and Kenya, girls appeared disproportionately affected. In Kenya, girls also cited lack of parental approval more frequently than boys, and in Nepal slightly more girls said they could not get an adult to open the account with them (Kosmynina, 2015).

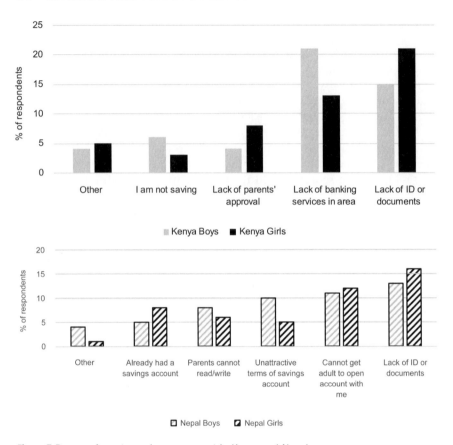

Figure 5 Reasons for not opening an account in Kenya and Nepal

Focus groups and interviews conducted in Kenya subsequent to the project implementation period corroborated the importance of parental support for girls in opening accounts, especially from their fathers. Families were also less likely to allow girls the physical mobility needed to earn money through odd jobs after school. Perhaps for these reasons, this qualitative work also pointed to a 'confidence gap' between boys and girls such that, even after financial education, girls were less likely to believe they could successfully open an account and accumulate savings (Williams, n.d.). In addition, school-based strategies may have more difficulty reaching older girls as their enrolment numbers drop off after primary school in many countries.

Outreach to very poor youth

Uptake by those living on less than $1.25/day was also considerably less, proportionally, than the four country averages, totalling only 1.6 per cent of all account holders (Johnson et al., 2015). The commercial strategy for scale chosen by YouthSave may have been a driver of this disparity, with all four partner banks choosing to focus their outreach almost exclusively on schools (though mainly low-incomes schools), where young people could be accessed most cost-effectively. In Ghana and Nepal, YouthSave also partnered with local NGOs serving out-of-school youth in order to increase outreach to this segment; however, these efforts turned out to be far more time- and cost-intensive per account opened than school-based outreach due to the physical dispersion, inconsistent schedules, and greater need for social intermediation of out-of-school youth.

Account inactivity

As the project came to a close, dormancy rates (variously defined by the partner banks as no transactions in an account over the previous 6 or 12 months) were ticking upward, often in tandem with concerted efforts to open more accounts. Also, AMNS was decreasing the longer any individual account was open (see Figure 6) (Johnson et al., 2015). While, as mentioned above, this decrease did not affect the total balance in individual accounts over time – AMNS was still positive, so average total net savings was still rising the longer an individual account was open – it is not certain how long this trend might last. If AMNS in enough accounts became negative, total balances – in individual accounts and for the product as a whole – would drop, as happened in Colombia in 2015 (illustrated in Figure 4 above).

Youth development impact

Finally, impacts on cognitive functioning, educational outcomes, and health-related attitudes and behaviours were modest and mixed over the relatively short time between baseline and endline surveys in the Ghana experiment. While many results were positive, few were statistically significant at the p=.05 level. A number of counter-intuitive outcomes were also observed; for example, in-school banking youth experienced the largest increase in orientation towards success from baseline to endline – but also the largest increase in uncertainty towards the future. Study time increased with greater exposure to the intervention; however commitment to school decreased. And compared with control youth, 'treatment youth performed better on parental connection, perceived barriers to condom use, perceived susceptibility to HIV, and perceived severity of HIV'. However,

> treatment youth performed worse on attitudes toward sex, motivations to engage in sex, and sense of belonging with peers. In addition, the impacts of YouthSave on health appeared to differ based on type of health outcomes. While effects on health-related attitudes were mixed, effects on health behaviours (e.g., actual condom use, engagement in paid or unwilling sex) were consistently positive (Chowa et al., 2015a: 88).

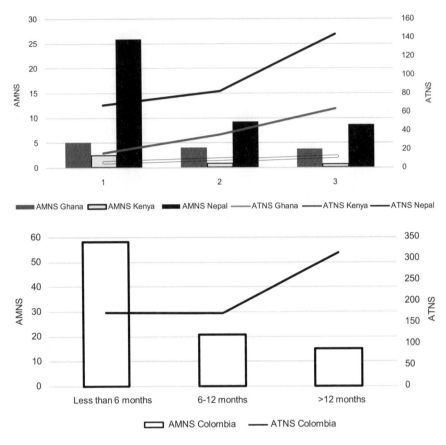

Figure 6 Average monthly net savings (AMNS) per account and average total net savings (ATNS) per account, (a) by country and (b) by length of time accounts have been open (US$, PPP-adjusted)

Note: The significantly higher account balances in Colombia compared with other countries may have been driven by the programmed savings design of the Colombian product or by the relatively lower proportion of account holders living on less than $2.50/day. However, the product design may also have contributed to a higher account closure rate: 21 per cent in Colombia vs. negligible in the other countries, triggering a drop in balances for the product as a whole as more youth achieved their goals, withdrew their funds, and closed their account (Johnson et al., 2015).

Lessons

So in sum, do youth need savings? It is clear that for youth, as for adults, savings can provide a valuable cushion for emergencies and resource for investment. What is less clear is whether savings during adolescence can single-handedly produce improvements in non-financial youth development domains in the short term. But indeed, this does not appear to be where youth themselves are focused – their demand for safe and attractive savings vehicles is clear from the response to YouthSave accounts. Many insights on how to fulfil that demand have emerged from YouthSave's operational experimentation and research; five of the most important for practitioners, donors, and policymakers are highlighted here:

Complement good product design with accessibility and motivation

YouthSave's account uptake was underpinned by products designed using a youth-inclusive market research methodology that ensured they would be attractive to low-income young people (Deshpande, 2012). But to maximize uptake and usage across youth sub-segments, *good product design must be complemented by effective delivery and motivational mechanisms.* For example, uptake increased whenever YouthSave's partner banks undertook concerted school-based marketing and/or delivery campaigns (Johnson et al., 2015); data from the Ghana experiment demonstrated that the number of bank visits to schools was one driver of account opening, as well as depositing (Chowa et al., 2015b). Staff incentives had a similar effect on opening, while incentives to account holders were associated with both higher uptake and savings, as was the use of ICT-enabled delivery channels such as mobile phone banking (Johnson et al., 2015). Finally, a randomized controlled trial in Colombia proved that SMS reminders to deposit were effective in increasing savings balances (Rodriguez and Saavedra, 2015).

Optimize the role of adults in youth savings

A key challenge in youth savings account design is structuring the role of adults, who must usually be co-signatories on accounts for legal minors. YouthSave's account analysis indicated that when a parent was the co-signatory, as opposed to another adult, youth tended to save more. Joint parent–child ownership of an account can therefore be a driver of positive savings performance. Paradoxically, however, YouthSave's market research revealed a strong preference for privacy – especially from parents – in matters related to savings among target youth. Some even said they did not know a single adult whom they trusted enough to open an account with, which may be especially plausible for marginalized youth with difficult living situations.

Adult involvement in youth savings can therefore be a protective or a risk factor, and *programme/product design must attempt to maximize the benefits while minimizing the risks.* One way in which YouthSave banks have attempted to do this is by requiring the youth's presence/signature for withdrawals, even though minor youth are required to open accounts in conjunction with a trusted adult, who is the owner of the account in the eyes of the law. In addition to reducing the risk of adult expropriation of the funds in these situations, this measure signals the youth's affective and effective ownership over the funds – fulfilling another key youth concern that emerged during market research (Deshpande, 2012).

Provide financial education to ensure youth understand how to safely use savings accounts

The value of FE has been questioned as some research has indicated a lack of impact on actual financial behaviours (Mandell and Schmid Klein, 2009). Some of the evidence from YouthSave supports that conclusion; for example, in the Colombian RCT mentioned above, reminders to deposit increased savings while FE messages sent via SMS had no effect on savings levels. However, results from YouthSave's face-to-face financial education activities indicate that, *properly implemented, FE can affect knowledge, attitudes, and even behaviours* – a conclusion consistent with recent rigorous research from other youth financial capability initiatives (O'Prey and Shephard, 2014; Innovations for Poverty Action, 2014).

Moreover, YouthSave experience indicates that the knowledge and attitude changes engendered by financial education are important in and of themselves – beyond their role in spurring behaviour change – as they can play a role in protecting young people from some of the risks that may attach to saving. For example, we found that one of the most common actions youth tend to take in an attempt to save is cutting back on food or snack purchases outside the home. This might be a valid strategy if the food/snacks are truly superfluous, but not if it means skipping meals; by covering healthy and appropriate ways to save, FE can help ensure youth know the difference. Similarly, FE can help teach youth how to be safe while conducting bank transactions, and what questions to ask to choose the right financial services provider and products.

Deploy tailored strategies and dedicated resources to reach the most deprived youth

What is true for average youth in low-income countries is doubly true for the most deprived – appropriate design is critical, but it must be buttressed by social intermediation mechanisms capable of ensuring effective access to and usage of the accounts. For example, there is some reason to think that YouthSave partner banks' outreach to low-income middle schools attracted more low-income and female youth than other marketing strategies, such as mass media; however, it could not reach those youth who had already dropped out. Nor could it address the obstacles related to identification documents, parental approval, and confidence that girls seem to face disproportionately to boys. *Lifting these roadblocks would require other programmatic components that are not likely to be supported by the private sector as part of a purely commercial strategy* – highlighting the need for continued public/private/donor partnerships in this space.

To impact non-financial outcomes, consider resource transfers and integrated programming

For the reasons mentioned at the outset, there has been intense interest over the last decade in finding ways to impact multiple youth development outcomes as cost-effectively as possible. Financial inclusion efforts have been attractive from this point of view for their potential to achieve resource-efficient scale and sustainability through the private sector. YouthSave and similar youth financial inclusion initiatives are testament to the expertise that the financial inclusion field has achieved in designing appropriate products for massive uptake and increasingly – though not yet perfectly – consistent usage. However, the preponderance of evidence from YouthSave and other research suggests that *while economic strengthening programming including financial capability initiatives may be successful in producing financial/economic results, its ability to independently spur changes in other youth development domains is limited*, at least in the short term, in developing countries (see Ellis and Chaffin, 2015; Parr and Bachay, 2015; Sulaiman, 2016). While there have been a few exceptions, generally speaking programmes combining economic strengthening with psychosocial, health-related, or educational support have more reliably affected non-financial youth outcomes in the short time frames covered by most impact evaluations (see, for example, the studies on the SUUBI-Maka, and BRIDGES projects in Uganda, including Ssewamala et al., 2015; Jennings et al., 2015; Karimli and Ssewamala, 2015; also Scales et al., 2013; Edmeades et al., 2014; and the Population Council's body of work on adolescent girls' empowerment).

This is not to underplay the importance of economic well-being in driving youth outcomes – across the world better indicators of health and education are associated with greater wealth levels both across and between countries. In YouthSave itself, an analysis of treatment youth in the Ghana experiment indicates that household living conditions and the amount of money in a youth's possession at baseline were the two factors most highly correlated with both financial and non-financial outcomes (Chowa and Masa, 2016). But the path by which financial well-being translates into other realms may be through the acquisition of intermediary assets that support improved non-economic outcomes over time, possibly over generations. To significantly shortcut this intergenerational lag for vulnerable youth, it is plausible that they must have access to those non-economic assets in real-time, alongside mechanisms that increase their financial ability to then sustain those improvements.

References

Berry, J., Karlan, D. and Pradhan, M. (2015) *The Impact of Financial Education for Youth in Ghana*, New Haven, CT: IPA.

Bruce, J. and Hallman, K. (2008) 'Reaching the girls left behind', *Gender and Development* 16(2): 227–45 <http://dx.doi.org/10.1080/13552070802118149>.

Chowa, G. and Masa, R. (2016) *Facilitators and Barriers of Youth Savings in Ghana YouthSave Experiment: A Segmentation Analysis of Youth in the Intervention Schools*, Chapel Hill, NC: University of North Carolina.

Chowa, G., Masa, R., Ansong, D., Despard, M., Wu, S., Hughes, D., Osei-Akoto, I., Afranie, S., Mark-Sowah, N.A., Ofori-Acquah, C., Lee, Y., Johnson, L. and Sherraden, M. (2015a) *Impacts of Financial Inclusion on Youth Development:*

Findings from the Ghana YouthSave Experiment, CSD Research Paper No. 15-35, St Louis, MO: Center for Social Development at Washington University in St Louis.

Chowa, G., Osei-Akoto, I., Ansong, D., Masa, R., Lee, Y., Johnson, L., and Sherraden, M. (2015b) 'The Ghana experiment: an overview of findings', in YouthSave Initiative, *YouthSave 2010–2015: Findings from a Global Financial Inclusion Partnership*, pp. 27–30, Washington, DC: YouthSave Initiative.

Deshpande, R. (2012) *What Do Youth Savers Want?*, Washington, DC: Save the Children.

Deshpande, R. and Zimmerman, J. (eds.) (2010) *Youth Savings in Developing Countries*, Washington, DC: YouthSave Initiative.

Dueck-Mbeba, R. and Maftei, A. (2015) 'YouthSave implementation context', in YouthSave Initiative, *YouthSave 2010–2015: Findings from a Global Financial Inclusion Partnership*, pp. 13–19, Washington, DC: YouthSave Initiative.

Edmeades, J. and Hayes, R. with Gaynair, G. (2014) *Improving the Lives of Married Adolescent Girls in Amhara, Ethiopia: A Summary of the Evidence*, Washington, DC: International Center for Research on Women.

Ellis, C.M. and Chaffin, J. (2015) *Outcomes for Children and Youth from NGO-Supported Microeconomic Interventions: A Research Synthesis*, London: Save the Children UK.

Innovations for Poverty Action (2014) *Evidence on Child and Youth Savings*, New Haven, CT: Innovations for Poverty Action.

Jennings, L., Ssewamala, F.M. and Nabunya, P. (2015) 'Effect of savings-led economic empowerment on HIV preventive practices among orphaned adolescents in rural Uganda: results from the Suubi-Maka randomized experiment', *AIDS Care* 28(3): 273–82 <http://dx.doi.org/10.1080/095401 21.2015.1109585>.

Johnson, E. and Sherraden, M.S. (2007) 'From financial literacy to financial capability among youth', *Journal of Sociology and Social Welfare* 34(3): 119–45.

Johnson, L., Lee, Y., Ansong, D., Sherraden, M., Chowa, G., Ssewamala, F., Zou, L., Sherraden, M., Njenga, M., Kieyah, J., Osei-Akoto, I., Sharma, S., Manandhar, J., Rodriguez, C., Merchán, F., and Saavedra, J. (2015) *Youth Savings Patterns and Performance in Colombia, Ghana, Kenya, and Nepal*, YouthSave Research Report, CSD Publication No. 15-01, St Louis, MO: Center for Social Development at Washington University in St Louis.

Karimli, L. and Ssewamala, F. (2015) 'Do savings mediate changes in adolescents' future orientation and health-related outcomes? Findings from randomized experiment in Uganda', *Journal of Adolescent Health* 57: 425–32.

Kilara, T., Magnoni, B. and Zimmerman, E. (2014) *The Business Case for Youth Savings: a Framework*, CGAP Focus Note No. 96, Washington, DC: World Bank.

Kosmynina, D. (2015) *Towards Financially Capable Youth: Insights from YouthSave's Financial Education*, Washington, DC: Save the Children.

Lee, Y., Johnson, L., Sherraden, M., Ansong, D., Chowa, G., and Osei-Akoto, I. (2015) *'Taking the Bank to the Youth': Impacts on Saving and Asset Building from the Ghana YouthSave Experiment*, CSD Working Paper No. 15-43, St Louis, MO: Center for Social Development at Washington University in St Louis.

Mandell, L. and Schmid Klein, L. (2009) 'The impact of financial literacy education on subsequent financial behavior', *Journal of Financial Counseling and Planning* 20(1): 15–24.

Moore, K. (2015) 'Fostering economic opportunities for youth in Africa: a comprehensive approach', *Enterprise Development and Microfinance* 26(2): 195–209 <http://dx.doi.org/ 10.3362/1755-1986.2015.017>.

New America (n.d.) 'YouthSave' [online], Washington, DC: New America <www.newamerica.org/asset-building/youthsave/> [accessed 13 June 2016].

O'Prey, L. and Shephard, D. (2014) *Financial Education for Children and Youth: A Systematic Review and Meta-analysis*, Aflatoun Working Paper 2014.1C, Netherlands: Aflatoun.

Parr, L. and Bachay, J. (2015) *The Impact of Savings Groups on Children's Well-Being: A Review of the Literature*, Washington, DC: USAID.

Population Council, 'Adolescent girls' empowerment' [online], New York: Population Council <www.popcouncil.org/research/adolescent-girls-empowerment> [accessed 2 June 2016].

Rodriguez, C. and Saavedra, J.E. (2015) *Nudging Youth to Develop Savings Habits*, CESR-Schaeffer Working Paper Series No. 2015-018, Los Angeles, CA: University of Southern California.

Scales, P.C., Benson, P.L., Dershem, L., Fraher, K., Makonnen, R., Nazneen, S., Syvertsen, A.K. and Titus, S. (2013) 'Building developmental assets to empower adolescent girls in rural Bangladesh: Evaluation of project Kishoree Kontha', *Journal of Research on Adolescence* 23: 171–84 <http://dx.doi.org/ 10.1111/j.1532-7795.2012.00805.x>.

Ssewamala, F.M., Karimli, L., Torsten, N., Wang, J.S., Han, C.K., Ilic, V., and Nabunya, P. (2015) 'Applying a family-level economic strengthening intervention to improve education and health-related outcomes of school-going aids-orphaned children: lessons from a randomized experiment in southern Uganda', *Prevention Science* 17: 134–43 <http://dx.doi.org/10.1007/s11121-015-0580-9>.

Sulaiman, M. (2016) 'Does wealth increase affect school enrolment in ultra-poor households: evidence from an experiment in Bangladesh', in R. Morgan (ed.), *The Global Child Poverty Challenge: In Search of Solutions*, Rugby, UK: Practical Action Publishing.

Williams, C. (n.d.) 'The gendered dimensions of effective financial inclusion: an investigation into girls saving as part of the YouthSave Project', unpublished draft.

World Bank (2015) *The Little Data Book on Financial Inclusion 2015*, Washington, DC: World Bank.

YouthSave Initiative (2015) *YouthSave 2010–2015: Findings from a Global Financial Inclusion Partnership*, Washington, DC: YouthSave Initiative.

About the author

Rani Deshpande is Director of Financial Services and Employment at Save the Children, where she leads global work designed to provide households and youth with the opportunities, skills, and tools they need to earn and manage income.

CHAPTER 12

Conclusion: towards effective action in addressing child poverty through public policy

Richard Morgan

Abstract

Leading international child-oriented agencies have come together to form a new global Coalition to End Child Poverty. This chapter outlines some of the policy recommendations of the Coalition, policies that governments and agencies can readily take up to diminish child poverty and reduce the damage it causes.

Keywords: child poverty; Coalition to End Child Poverty; child protection; child-sensitive approach

> 'The natural distribution is neither just nor unjust; nor is it unjust that persons are born into society at some particular position. These are simply natural facts. What is just and unjust is the way that institutions deal with these facts.' John Rawls, *A Theory of Justice*

Research, analysis, and voice contained in this book and in evolution elsewhere provide a basis for action by governments, NGOs, donor partners and the private sector to address childhood poverty as a specific and discrete challenge to human development and civilization. It is clear that the problem of poverty among children remains widespread, even in some of the wealthiest societies, and is inevitably serious in the damage it causes.

The knowledge we have to help address this challenge is a substantial asset, growing but far from complete. With careful testing and adaptation, responsive to the objective needs of children and to their own experience, we can expect to make a decisive impact in both the economic and social development spheres, if the will and intent are there. The questions we face are now much less around 'why' and even 'how', and centre much more on 'why not'? The elimination of childhood poverty and its associated deprivations, at least in their more severe forms, is not only a new international commitment within the Sustainable Development Goals; it is very much 'within human reach'.

Save the Children and the United Nations Children's Fund (UNICEF), together with a further twenty concerned, child-oriented agencies, have launched a new global Coalition to End Child Poverty. This group aims to highlight evidence of the harms done to children, families and societies by the

http://dx.doi.org/10.3362/9781780448879.012

failure to act on child poverty and to present potential solutions to national and international decision-makers which they can readily and affordably take up. The findings, analysis and arguments provided by the researchers and analysts who contributed to this collection will continue to inform the work of the Coalition and other policy advocates who work to suggest answers and promote serious, sustained action from all levels of human society. Among the policy-level responses being developed by the Coalition are the following:

A call for every country, and sub-national authorities within countries, to ensure that reducing child poverty is an explicit priority on their agenda, and included as appropriate in national plans, policies and budgets. This involves the better measurement of multidimensional and monetary poverty, disaggregated by age, gender and household characteristics; as well dedicated methods to promote the participation and obtain the views of children living in poverty. If child poverty is not expressly considered in public policy, experience shows that it is unlikely to be effectively addressed, even where overall poverty reduction efforts are in place.

Expand child-sensitive social protection systems and programmes, using the best available information on impacts and effectiveness. Child-sensitive social protection can reduce the depth of poverty and improve child wellbeing. While this can include child and family grants, it also goes well beyond this to effective social protection systems, including child care, parenting support and responses to the impact of shocks and humanitarian crises on families in poverty and their children.

Ensure essential basic services reach, include and benefit the poorest children and their families or caregivers. Major inequalities are evident in access to public service provision, with the poorest children – also often in neglected geographic areas or among disadvantaged minority groups — often lacking effective access to quality health care, pre-school and basic education, clean water, safe sanitation and electricity. They and their families, meanwhile, face both overt and hidden barriers of affordability to using these services and are widely excluded from financial systems and employment opportunities. More needs to be done to improve and ensure access of children and caregivers in the poorest families to quality services, reducing barriers that may be rooted in both monetary poverty and deeper discriminations and exclusion. This will involve an overall strategy and political commitment to include the poorest and most excluded people in society in the aims of public policy, backed by explicit standards for service provision and dedicated budgets for programme delivery.

Aim to craft policies that shape economic growth and employment patterns that are increasingly effective in including those groups in society who are poorest and most deprived. It is widely accepted that 'shared prosperity' is crucial to eradicate extreme poverty. The poorest children often live in economically marginalized families without adequate and decent work. The ability of their parents and other caregivers to earn good livelihoods, and the opportunities which they themselves have to obtain skills, knowledge and competencies for work and parenthood, will be essential in lifting the children and young people of this and coming generations out of poverty.

In addition to these more generic propositions for decision-makers, I believe that the work presented in these pages points to a further imperative for the design, funding, implementation and assessment of interventions which aim to improve (or transform) the lives of children growing up in poverty. That is, the need for a care and specificity which recognizes the uniqueness of children as individuals. Interventions in children's lives – whether through cash transfers, skills training, finance options or assets provided to their families – are inevitably blunt instruments. Children are unalike in their biology, age and vulnerabilities; in their roles within immediate and wider families; in how they are cared for, nourished and treated; in how poverty affects and has affected them; in what they are capable of (now and later); in their motivations, hopes and aspirations.

It is difficult for policies and programmes to recognize and account for all these factors and more. However, at least a basic level of child sensitivity is called for among (adult) decision-makers – both to increase the chances of effectiveness and success and to ensure due diligence and responsibility among those who intervene with the best of intentions. Child sensitivity involves a duty of care, to make best efforts to 'do no harm' through unintended consequences, using techniques such as prior child-level risk assessment, routine monitoring and discussions on programme impacts directly with children and their caregivers. Local groups and culturally attuned, child-oriented intermediaries are often central to making this happen.

A child-sensitive approach also suggests programme designs which recognize children as both *highly vulnerable* individuals, in multiple and varied ways; and also as *active agents* who, increasingly as they grow, are able to take their own decisions and develop informed judgments on opportunities to save, spend, learn, gain skills, migrate, benefit from decent work, and prepare to better their lives. It is hoped that this book has helped to illustrate some of the ways, in diverse situations, in which children's vulnerabilities and choices can be taken as central in the search for solutions to childhood poverty.

About the author

Richard Morgan is Director of the Child Poverty Global Initiative, Save the Children